USING
wordpress®

Tris Hussey

800 East 96th Street, Indianapolis, Indiana 46240 USA

Using WordPress®

Copyright © 2011 by Pearson Education, Inc.

Library of Congress Cataloging-in-Publication Data:
Hussey, Tris.
  Using WordPress / Tris Hussey.
    p. cm.
  ISBN 978-0-7897-4634-4
  1. WordPress (Electronic resource) 2. Blogs—Computer programs. 3. Web sites—Authoring programs. I. Title.
TK5105.8885.W66H97 2011
006.7—dc22
                    2010024810

Printed in the United States of America

First Printing: August 2010

Trademarks

All terms mentioned in this book that are known to be trademarks or service marks have been appropriately capitalized. Que Publishing cannot attest to the accuracy of this information. Use of a term in this book should not be regarded as affecting the validity of any trademark or service mark.

Mac OS and Snow Leopard are registered trademarks of Apple Inc.

Warning and Disclaimer

Every effort has been made to make this book as complete and as accurate as possible, but no warranty or fitness is implied. The information provided is on an "as is" basis. The author and the publisher shall have neither liability nor responsibility to any person or entity with respect to any loss or damages arising from the information contained in this book.

Bulk Sales

Que Publishing offers excellent discounts on this book when ordered in quantity for bulk purchases or special sales. For more information, please contact

U.S. Corporate and Government Sales
1-800-382-3419
corpsales@pearsontechgroup.com
For sales outside of the U.S., please contact
International Sales
international@pearson.com

ISBN-13: 978-0-7897-4634-4
ISBN-10: 0-7897-4634-4

Associate Publisher
Greg Wiegand

Acquisitions Editor
Michelle Newcomb

Development Editor
The Wordsmithery LLC

Managing Editor
Kristy Hart

Project Editor
Anne Goebel

Copy Editor
Water Crest Publishing

Senior Indexer
Cheryl Lenser

Proofreader
Apostrophe Editing Services

Technical Editors
Duke Hillard
Todd Meiste

Publishing Coordinator
Cindy Teeters

Interior Designer
Anne Jones

Cover Designer
Anna Stingley

Multimedia Developer
John Herrin

Compositor
Nonie Ratcliff

Contents at a Glance

The following chapters can be accessed online at quepublishing.com/using or usingwordpressbook.com:

Media Table of Contents

To register this product and gain access to the Free Web Edition and the audio and video files, go to quepublishing.com/using.

Table of Contents

About the Author

This is the second book from **Tris Hussey**, a long-time technologist, blogger, and writer, who started off as an academic and found tech support much more to his liking. After picking up blogging on a whim in 2004, he quickly became Canada's first professional blogger and a leading expert in business blogging. He has been a part of several Web 2.0 startups, from blogging software to blogging agencies.

In addition to writing and consulting, Tris gives workshops and teaches classes on social media, blogging, podcasting, and WordPress at the University of British Columbia and The British Columbia Institute of Technology.

Tris lives and works in beautiful Vancouver, British Columbia.

Dedication

For Sheila, who encouraged and supported me throughout writing this book, before the first one was done!

Acknowledgments

This book couldn't have happened without the help, direction, and prodding of many, many people. Thanks to the whole editorial team at Pearson, especially my editor Michelle, whose patience is amazing when working with scatter-brained authors. Thanks to Catherine Winters, who patiently sat recording audio segments not just once, but twice! The entire WordPress community has been invaluable in checking, testing, and answering myriad questions for this book. (Yes, Andrew Nacin, I'm talking about you.) This book is a community effort! Thanks to my friends and family for inspiring and supporting me while I've been writing this book. Most importantly, thanks to my beloved Sheila for supporting me and believing in me through this whole process.

We Want to Hear from You!

As the reader of this book, *you* are our most important critic and commentator. We value your opinion and want to know what we're doing right, what we could do better, what areas you'd like to see us publish in, and any other words of wisdom you're willing to pass our way.

As an associate publisher for Que Publishing, I welcome your comments. You can email or write me directly to let me know what you did or didn't like about this book—as well as what we can do to make our books better.

Please note that I cannot help you with technical problems related to the topic of this book. We do have a User Services group, however, where I will forward specific technical questions related to the book.

When you write, please be sure to include this book's title and author as well as your name, email address, and phone number. I will carefully review your comments and share them with the author and editors who worked on the book.

Email: feedback@quepublishing.com

Mail: Greg Wiegand
         Associate Publisher
         Que Publishing
         800 East 96th Street
         Indianapolis, IN 46240 USA

Reader Services

Visit our website and register this book at quepublishing.com/using for convenient access to any updates, downloads, or errata that might be available for this book.

Introduction

In the beginning, there was b2 (also known as cafelog), and an 18-year-old programmer by the name of Matt Mullenweg used this blog platform to document his trip to Washington DC. Then in late 2002, b2's development stopped. In January 2003, Matt teamed up with Mike Little to announce that they were going to continue development of b2 with a fork from the original source code. In May 2003, WordPress 0.70 was launched, and the rest is now part of Internet lore. Matt, it is worth noting, was a freshman at the University of Houston when he started working on WordPress. As of September 2009, there were roughly 202 million websites using WordPress, and WordPress (or WP, as most people call it) is now considered the leading open-source blog platform in use.

I don't remember when I first met Matt in person, but I'm happy to count him as a friend. Matt is one of those scary brilliant people who just *knows* things, and he is also one of the nicest people I know.

I didn't use WordPress as my primary (and essentially exclusive) blog engine right away. Like many bloggers, when I started my first blog in the spring 2004, I set it up on Blogger (owned by Google). Within a few months, I outgrew Blogger and moved on to what seemed to be the powerhouse blog engine of the time: Blogware. It had features that WordPress wouldn't have for another year, and I remember talking with Matt in the summer 2005, and telling him I wouldn't switch to WordPress because it lacked the features I needed. I remember showing him some of the tools I used to tweak my blog's layout in Blogware—features that later became part of WordPress. (I don't claim that I inspired Matt to put those in; I just find this to be interesting.) Some four years later, I wouldn't use anything *except* WordPress as a blog engine, and I now teach people how to use WordPress to build "regular" websites.

This book is intended to be a step-by-step guide to using WordPress (hence the title), with enough detail to have you well on your way to manage most WordPress blogs. I'm not going to claim that it is an *exhaustive* tome on all things WordPress;

I'm leaving that task to my geekier friends (many of whom I will be citing and interviewing for this book). The book includes screenshots of how you do everything, from installing WordPress to fixing it when it's broken, and also includes podcast interviews on other topics related to WordPress and the larger WordPress community.

Beyond its flexibility and ease of use, one of the biggest reasons I use WordPress is the worldwide community of users who contribute to the platform through plugins, themes, and help, and even how WordPress works. This community is one of the strengths of WordPress because the wealth of talent and imagination of its users keeps pushing the core developers to constantly improve WordPress.

For the last several versions of WordPress since version 2.1, the user community has recommended what new features should be added to WordPress. It's the developers who put things in place, but the community helps set the priorities.

Before I continue into an overview of WordPress and this book, I should mention that this book is written using the latest version of WordPress available (3.0). By the time this book is in your hands, more updates will undoubtedly have been made to WordPress. Working with some of the key WordPress developers, I have written this book as "future proof" as possible, but that said, I will post updates on www.usingwordpressbook.com so that you can always have access to the latest information and changes to WordPress.

What Is WordPress?

So, you ask, what *exactly* is a blog engine, and what makes WordPress a blog engine? First, a blog simply is a website made up of individual articles or *posts*, where the posts are listed on the home page with the newest article at the top of the page (in reverse chronological order). A blog engine is the software that runs on a web server, not your machine at home, which makes a blog work.

Most blog engines work by combining scripts and code to display the pages and a database to store the articles and other settings. Blog engines also tend to use *templates or themes* to style how the web pages look to visitors. Altogether, that's the blog engine, and WordPress does all of that (and a few other tricks as well). This is a complicated way of saying that WordPress is a *content management system* (or CMS).

Not long ago, CMS-based websites were "the next big thing" online. Many large companies used them for their websites because they could enable people to author content, without having to learn HTML (the coding that makes the Web what it is) or worry that someone would "break" the website accidentally. A CMS with the features, power, and flexibility of WordPress would cost tens, if not hundreds, of thousands of dollars. Now, WordPress is available as free, open-source software that you can download and install in minutes. Everything starts at WordPress.org (Figure IN.1) where you can download WordPress to install it (we'll get there, don't worry), download plugins and themes to extend WordPress' built-in capabilities, and start to learn all things WordPress. This is the hub for the WordPress community.

Figure IN.1   *The WordPress.org home page, where you can download WordPress to install it and learn all things WordPress.*

WordPress is open source, which means that users can look at the inner workings of WordPress and even modify how things work to their own liking. If your customizations or fixes are good enough or add a new (and needed) feature to WordPress, you can submit your changes to the community for review and inclusion as part of the WordPress *core*. To maintain order, continuity, and security in WordPress, five core developers are allowed to commit new code into the WordPress core. Even if your code might not be something that can be added to the WordPress core, you can release it as a *plugin*. A plugin is an extension to WordPress that adds a feature or functionality to WordPress that it doesn't have out-of-the-box—it's like putting a sunroof in your car if your car didn't come with it in the first place. I cover plugins in great detail in Chapter 6, "Finding and Using Plugins."

WordPress.org Versus WordPress.com

WordPress comes in two main "flavors": WordPress.org and WordPress.com. WordPress.*org* is where you go to download WordPress and where you find plugins and themes to add onto your install. WordPress.*com* is a service run by the company Automattic that Matt Mullenweg and others founded to provide a free, hosted version of WordPress. WordPress.com was built on a fork from the WordPress tree called WordPress MU (multiuser), which enables you to have one install of WordPress that controls and manages many blogs at once. WordPress and WordPress MU have now been combined into WordPress as a whole. If you're confused, don't worry—most people are at first. It will start to make sense. For now, just remember that WordPress.org and WordPress.com are different, but related, versions of WordPress.

WordPress.com is run and owned by Automattic, which also curates and provides resources to WordPress.org. Matt Mullenweg and his associates founded Automattic to provide resources to the WordPress community and provide high-end hosting services to companies. Automattic provides the infrastructure to curate and support WordPress.org (and the new nonprofit WordPress Foundation) and employs many of the core WordPress developers. Automattic also acquires companies that have built WordPress plugins or extensions that would be better if the developers had more support (that is, a job and salary). Don't think of Automattic as the overlord of WordPress, though; the people there care *passionately* about open source and ensuring that WordPress will continue to grow and be developed long into the future.

 SHOW ME   Media IN.1—Important WordPress-Related Websites
Access this video file through your registered Web Edition at
my.safaribooksonline.com/9780132182836/media

WordPress Conventions

You need to be aware of a few conventions used in this book. The proper way to spell WordPress is with a capital "W" and capital "P," and we often abbreviate it "WP" (and use variations such as WP.org, WP.com, and WPMU). Plugins are spelled as such and not "plug ins" or "plug-ins." (Don't laugh—there was a debate about the proper spelling that was only just settled in January 2009.) *Themes* are the files that make a blog look the way it does (also known as *templates*).

At WordPress.org, the documentation is called The Codex (yes, WP folks tend to have a flair for the dramatic), and the bit of code that does a lot of the legwork for all WP blogs is The Loop, which is the bit of code that looks like this:

```
if (have_posts()) :
    while (have_posts()) :
        the_post();
```

```
    the_content();
  endwhile;
endif;
```

All this does is go through the database and pull out all the posts written in the blog. It's so simple that you can understand why in the footer of WordPress.org, it says: Code is Poetry.

This book walks you through, step by step, how to make a great blog (or website) using WordPress. I start with buying a domain, picking a webhost, and getting your domain to work with your host. Then I move onto all the parts of WordPress, from installing to configuring to customizing to writing content. In each chapter, I note how WordPress.com differs from the self-installed version, and in Chapter 5, "How WordPress.com Is Different Than WordPress.org," I cover the topic in greater detail. By the end of the book, you will be well on your way to being a WordPress ninja.

 TELL ME MORE   Media IN.2—WordPress and the WordPress Community

Access this audio recording through your registered Web Edition at
my.safaribooksonline.com/9780132182836/media

Using This Book

This book enables you to customize your own learning experience. Step-by-step instructions give you a solid foundation in using WordPress, while rich and varied online content, including video tutorials and audio sidebars, provides the following:

- Demonstrations of step-by-step tasks covered in the book
- Additional tips or information on a topic
- Practical advice and suggestions
- Direction for more advanced tasks not covered in the book

Here's a quick look at a few structural features designed to help you get the most out of this book:

- **Chapter objective:** At the beginning of each chapter is a brief summary of topics addressed in that chapter. This objective enables you to quickly see what the chapter covers.

- **Notes:** Notes provide additional commentary or explanation that doesn't fit neatly into the surrounding text. Notes give detailed explanations of how something works, alternative ways of performing a task, and other tidbits to get you on your way.

 LET ME TRY IT tasks are presented in a step-by-step sequence so you that can easily follow along.

 SHOW ME video walks through tasks you've just got to see—including bonus advanced techniques.

 TELL ME MORE audio delivers practical insights straight from the experts.

Special Features

More than just a book, your USING product integrates step-by-step video tutorials and valuable audio sidebars delivered through the Free Web Edition that comes with every USING book. For the price of the book, you get online access anywhere with a web connection—no books to carry, content is updated as the technology changes, and the benefit of video and audio learning.

About the USING Web Edition

The Web Edition of every USING book is powered by Safari Books Online, enabling you to access the video tutorials and valuable audio sidebars. Plus, you can search the contents of the book, highlight text and attach a note to that text, print your notes and highlights in a custom summary, and cut and paste directly from Safari Books Online.

To register this product and gain access to the Free Web Edition and the audio and video files, go to quepublishing.com/using.

This chapter gives you everything you need to know about buying domains, choosing a web host, and other aspects of laying the foundation for your new site.

1

Domains and Hosts: Getting the Foundation in Place

For you to have a website like usingwordpressbook.com (the site for this book), you first need to register (buy) a domain name, find a webhost where your blog will live, and get your domain associated with that host. Only then can you get down to business of setting up WordPress and getting things going. This all sounds like a complicated process, but trust me, it isn't. Far from it,—this is probably one of the easiest parts of starting a website!

In this chapter, I first explain a few basics about domain names and DNS; then I discuss how to choose a good domain name and how to register it. Finally, I review everything you need to know to work with a webhost.

Understanding DNS Basics

What's in a name? Well, a rose by any other name would still smell as sweet, but websites without (domain) names are rather hard to find. The Internet is based on connectivity—and I don't mean just connecting you to your favorite site; I mean connecting all the computers on the Internet to each other. If you imagine how many computers might be online at any given *moment*, how do we manage to keep things sorted out and all the various computers and people going to the right places? The answer is three little letters: DNS.

DNS stands for the *Domain Name System*, which is very much like a phone directory because it matches words and names (for example, Google.com) to numbers (IP addresses), such as 74.125.45.100. (This particular IP address matches, or resolves to, Google.com.) Not all devices require domain names, but every computer or device on the Internet must have an IP address. If you want to do a search at Google.com, remembering the name is *a lot* easier than remembering 74.125.45.100. The Domain Name System was built and designed so we could assign easy-to-remember names to the IP addresses of servers and other computers on the Internet.

For every domain, there is a DNS server that holds a master record with the IP address that maps to it. One thing that makes DNS interesting is that there isn't one DNS server on the Internet, but *thousands,* and each server holds the records for not only the domains it is responsible for, but many other domains in the world. Why this redundancy? Time. It saves a vast amount of time. When you go to your browser and type www.google.com into your address bar, your computer queries a DNS server to know where it should go. If that DNS server doesn't know, it has to ask another one and so on until an answer is found. The whole process is sped up if you just get the answer from the first server, so the data is replicated around the Internet to speed things up for everyone.

The Internet, along with the computer mouse, Woodstock, the first Apollo Moon landing, and the author of this book, celebrated its 40th birthday in 2009. It was developed initially as a project for the U.S. Defense Department and was known as DARPA or ARPANET for the first years of its existence.

Choosing a Good Domain Name

How do you pick a good domain name? Is there some kind of magic tool or formula that can give you insight? Maybe the Internet equivalent of a crystal ball? I'm sorry to say that there is no magic or special trick involved—choosing a domain name is often a process of trial and error combined with just a little bit of luck.

If you've been using the Internet for any amount of time, you've likely come across hundreds, if not thousands, of domain names. Some, like Apple.com or Microsoft.com, are easy to remember and are obvious as to who is the likely owner. Other domain names aren't as well chosen or obvious.

Top 10 Worst Domain Names Found by Independent Sources

www.whorepresents.com—Who Represents

www.expertsexchange.com—Experts Exchange

www.penisland.net—Pen Island

www.therapistfinder.com—Therapist Finder

www.powergenitalia.com—Italian Power Generator

www.molestationnursery.com—Mole Station Native Nursery

www.speedofart.com

www.gotahoe.com—Lake Tahoe

Granted, the domain names in the Note are extreme examples, but they are *real* examples. As you're going through the process of finding the right domain name, keep these in mind and try to analyze your domain name ideas to make sure they don't have a secondary meaning.

What, then, *does* make for a good domain name? Good domain names have all or most of these characteristics:

- Easy to remember.

- Easy to spell.

- When you read the domain name, it's easy to associate with the website it matches with.

- Has search engine-friendly keywords (for example, your company's name, product, or service).

When you have a new site to build, or just need to register a new domain, the first thing to do is to start building (brainstorming, really) a list of potential domain names. As you're thinking and coming up with potential names, head over to your friendly neighborhood domain registrar like NameCheap.com, GoDaddy.com, or NetworkSolutions.com (there are many others, but these are ones that I would use) and use their handy search tool to check if a domain is available. See Figure 1.1 for the Namecheap.com homepage and Figure 1.2 for search results.

I used the search tool to search for wordpressbook.com and Namecheap gave me the result shown in Figure 1.2.

As you can see, someone has already registered that domain name, but there are domains that don't end in .com that *are* available. Should I choose any of these? What about the variations that are suggested to the right? Some of those look pretty good, don't they? The choice is going to be up to you. However, I do caution *against* .info domains at this time (and this will change in the future, I hope), because initially spammers purchased .info names in bulk, and Google looks at any site with a .info with suspicion. Right now using a .info domain name could mean that it will take longer for your website to appear in Google search results. What about the other options?

Figure 1.1   *Namecheap.com home page with the domain search area highlighted*

Figure 1.2   *Namecheap results page for a domain search (for wordpressbook.com)*

 **LET ME TRY IT**

Search for a Good Domain Name

Here's what you need to do to search for a good domain name:

1. Go to NameCheap.com in your web browser (IE, Firefox, Safari, Chrome, and so on).

2. Using the search box on any of the sites, enter a word or words in the box and click Search or Go to start the search.

3. Review the results.

4. Keep searching and refining, until you find a domain name you like.

TLD is short for Top-Level Domain. The TLD is the last part of a domain name like .com, .ca, .org, or .net. ICANN (Internet Corporation for Assigned Names and Numbers) sets the rules for what TLDs are allowed and recognized. (It also divvies up IP addresses.) You can visit www.icann.org for the entire list of TLDs in the world, such as .tv, which is the official TLD for the country of Tuvalu.

Before you settle for a domain that you aren't happy with, try variations of the original search with a hyphen (for example, Wordpress-book.com) or adding more or different words (such as writingwordpressbooks.com, usingwordpress.com, or usingwordpressbook.com). If you're wondering, yes, this is exactly the process I went through to find the domain for this book's website (usingwordpressbook.com). Personally, I don't like using hyphens in domain names; I've found that people have a hard time remembering them, and I try to stick to a .com domain. People are so used to domains without hyphens that end in .com, it can be a challenge to keep your *correct* domain in their head if you use hyphens or a TLD other than .com. Also, try to avoid strange spellings and ambiguous characters (the letter O versus zero is a common one) that could confuse people.

Do you have a great domain yet? Still stuck? You can try sites like NameTumbler.com or NameBoy.com to get suggestions for domain names based on keywords you enter. (Don't feel obligated to use their domain registration services.) You might not find the perfect domain name through either site, but you might be inspired and think of a new domain name.

Keep at it—sometimes it takes one of those "bolts from the blue" to have the perfect name drop into your lap. When you have the name, it's time to register it.

Registering Your Domain

I've already mentioned three reputable domain registrars (there are many other great ones, too), but registering a domain name is a lot more than just finding a good name and picking a registrar. When you register a domain name, it's really like a lease—you have the domain name for a year. (You can register for longer periods, but never forever.) At the end of the period, you have to renew the domain name. If you don't renew it, the domain becomes available to other people to register. It is still pretty common for someone to accidentally let a domain lapse (you're given a 30-day grace period after the registration expires); it's even happened to me.

The actual mechanics of registering a domain are easy. When you find the perfect domain, the registrar walks you through the rest of the steps (and happily takes your money in a variety of forms at the end of the process). After you complete the registration, you should receive emails confirming your domain registration. If you register a domain for your company, I suggest printing out all the information, including usernames and passwords, and putting it in a binder with a clear label like Company-Owned Domains. As an individual, I make sure I mark the emails in Gmail (the email service I use) and print out the receipt. I also suggest that if you start using one registrar, keep using that company for all your domains, and that you also use the same login for all domains you register. Doing this helps to make sure important domains aren't forgotten and lost. I manage 20 domains, and all but one or two are with the same registrar. At a glance, I can see what domains are coming up for renewal and update my contact information for all my domains at one time.

Here is the key part of registering a domain name: Enter your contact information correctly and keep it up to date. About a month before your domain expires, the domain registrar will send you a nice little email to remind you that your domain is coming up for renewal. My registrar then sends emails with increasing velocity up to the expiration date until I either re-register or the domain expires. Why so many emails? Beyond the registrar's desire to keep your business, they also don't want to be on the hook if a domain expires and a customer complains, "I had no idea that my domain was expiring...." Now here's the thing: If your email address that you gave when you registered your domain isn't valid anymore, what happens? Well, you might not find out that your domain is expiring (or has expired) until it is too late.

Why Do I Use Gmail?

When Google launched its email service in April 2004, not only was it invite-only, but it offered something that no other email provider could give: 1 gigabyte of email storage. Yahoo! Mail and Microsoft's Hotmail scrambled to keep up with Gmail. The ever-increasing storage space (more than 7GBs now) is nice, but what I rely on it for is to have an email address that doesn't change. Instead of using the email address provided by my ISP or an employer, I use Gmail so I know that my email address will always be the same. I use Gmail to register all my domains and other services so that I know that if one of my domains expires (like larixconsulting.com, trishussey.com, or usingwordpressbook.com), my important emails won't be disrupted.

What if Google stops offering Gmail? Well, about 150 million other users and I are going to be miffed!

When I started working with websites and domains almost 15 years ago, it was pretty common for companies to have a lot of trouble re-registering and updating their domain names. Back then, not only were the updates sent only to the email address provided, but any updates had to *come from* that email address as well. Even worse, the "your domain is expiring" notices were sent by mail to the person who registered the domain. Imagine this situation: Someone registers yourcompany.com and uses her company email address for the contact info, but then that person leaves the company. All emails to that person bounce back to the registrar, and paper mail notices just get left in the mailroom, so one day you get a call that no one can send your company email and your website looks strange. Yeah, your domain expired, and you never knew. Fifteen years ago, to change the contact information tied to a domain of the person who was no longer at the company required faxes sent to the registrar that had been signed by a vice-president or higher person in your company. Today, the updating process is a lot easier, especially because most domain registrars use a username/password system to gain access to domain-updating areas.

The moral of this story is twofold. First, if you register a domain for your company, make sure the email address used goes to a generic, catch-all email account *and not one using the domain name you register*. Second, if you register domains just for yourself, use an email address from Google, Yahoo, and so on that you can always access and be tied to you. Using your work email address or the address you got from your Internet service provider aren't good choices; either of those could change, and you'd miss getting updates. Yes, you can update your contact info for your domain, and you should always keep this info up to date, but let's be realistic here—it's easy to forget to update the contact information for your domain.

Now that you have a great domain name and you've registered it, there's only one thing between you and a WordPress-powered site: a webhost.

All About Webhosts and Hosting Websites

Without a webhost, you can't have a website. A *webhost* is, simply, a server on the Internet that is set up for you to store and create websites. If you're thinking of using WordPress.com for your site, that is your host. Webhosts are a strange service, and I've found over the years that all webhosts are terrible and all webhosts are great—it just depends on who you ask. That said, there are some general things to look for when choosing a webhost that should make the process easier.

Choosing a Webhost

The first step in picking a good webhost is hitting the balance between cost and features. It's pretty logical that, in general, the more you pay, the more features you get in return. To a certain point, most of the extra money you will pay is for more storage space and more bandwidth that you are allotted to use in a given month. When you reach a certain level of hosting, you begin paying for stability, redundancy, and backup servers. That's the scale used by companies whose bread and butter is made on the Web. Me, I'm not to the level of needing redundant backups of my site, so I stick with what most folks have: shared hosting. Shared hosting is just lots of users and websites sharing space on one physical server. This doesn't mean that other people can get in and mess around with your site; it just means it's like living in an apartment building. You're all given a certain amount of space and amenities for a certain amount of money per month. And, just like living in an apartment building, there are going to be some rules and restrictions that you'll have to abide by so you don't disrupt the neighbors. Don't worry; the restrictions don't really affect 99% of users. If you're in the 1% of people who are power users, however, you might consider signing up for a dedicated server.

Bandwidth is a measure of how much data is sent to and from one computer to another. When you talk about websites and webhosts, most of your bandwidth, sometimes called *transfer*, is taken up by people visiting your site. Every page viewed sends data from the server to your visitor. That data is composed of the pages, images, and other information you put up on your site. A site with only text uses far less bandwidth than a site full of high-resolution pictures and videos.

As you can guess, a dedicated server is when you have a whole server to yourself. It's like renting a house. You don't own it, but you're allowed to do a lot there, short of burning it to the ground. (If you do that, you might have to cough up for the replacement cost.) When you have a dedicated server, the hosting company will keep tabs on the server, make sure it stays running, and reboot it if needed, but the rest is up to you. You have the keys to the kingdom, which can be both a blessing and a curse. You can install almost anything you want on the server, but if what you install makes the server crash, you might have to do a lot of the fixing yourself.

I think you can understand, then, why most of us use shared hosting. Yeah, we like to have powerful servers, but we accept the limitations of being in a shared situation in exchange for the security and stability. The jump to a dedicated server means going to a monthly cost of around $80 to $100 for a basic setup (compared to $10 or $12 per month for shared hosting). Unless you're running lots and lots of sites or need to run specialized or custom software, chances are a dedicated server is overkill (and overspending).

What makes for a good shared hosting account? Although some things will vary, for a starter/entry level package, I look for the following:

- 2 to 5 gigabytes (GB) of storage
- 30 to 50GB of transfer
- CPanel with Fantastico installs (CPanel and Fantastico are brand names for web-based tools to manage your hosting account and install software, such as WordPress, on your account. Web-based control panel and one-click installs are the same thing, and you're good to go.)
- Unlimited domains and subdomains
- Unlimited databases
- Support for WordPress

Details on the server requirements to install WordPress are covered in Chapter 2, "Installing WordPress on Your Own Server." If hosts provide details on their core server package, look for PHP version 4 or higher and MySQL version 4 or higher to ensure that you can install WordPress. If in doubt, ask before you sign up for a package. I talk more about PHP and MySQL in Chapter 2.

Those are just a few of the key features that I find most people need and want. Yes, most hosts also offer tons of email addresses and FTP accounts, but my experience is that few people use a fraction of those allotments, if they use them at all. A starter plan like the preceding one should be roughly $10 to $12 per month. For most shared hosting plans, the more you pay, the more disk space and transfer allotment you're given. How do you pick where to start? I find that one step above basic is right for small businesses, and a basic shared hosting account is good for individuals.

WordPress.org Recommended Hosts

Because the WordPress community and Automattic have worked with so many hosts, there are a few hosts recommended on WordPress.org. The recommended hosts are as follows:

- BlueHost
- DreamHost
- MediaTemple
- LaughingSquid

I've used several of the ones listed and have found them to be good, reliable hosts. Rest assured, you will find people who have had bad experiences with all these hosts (I've had bad experiences with a couple), but that is true for all hosts. If you go to http://wordpress.org/hosting/ and choose one of the recommended hosts, WordPress.org receives a referral commission from the host. So, by going that route, you can choose a host that you know will work well with WordPress out-of-the-box and support the WordPress community overall. Not a bad deal.

As you're checking out the hosts that your friends have recommended, take a look at the hosts' technical support area. Are there easy-to-read FAQs? Is there a search-able knowledge base? Do the answers make sense? Although you might not need to often rely on your host's tech support services, when you need it, you *really need it* (like when your website isn't working and so on). Being able to find a good, easy-to-understand answer is going to be critical to bringing your panic level from "make your head explode" to "palms a little sweaty."

One final bit of advice: See if your host lets you upgrade to a plan with more space and transfer without additional setup fees (and what the process is). Most hosts will "allow" you to buy more disk space and more transfer if you need it. Really good hosts will step you up to the next level of hosting when they see it would be cheaper than to just keep adding on one-off extras. The best hosts I've used will see how you're using your account and recommend to you when you might think about an upgrade.

TELL ME MORE   Media 1.1—How to Choose a Good Webhost

Access this audio recording through your registered Web Edition at
my.safaribooksonline.com/9780132182836/media

Working with Your Host

Your webhost is a business service you pay for just like any other service, but it's complicated by the fact that you might not feel comfortable with talking with your host or understanding what you get for your money. (Don't feel bad—I feel the same way about cars.) Your webhost is run by people who are (hopefully) trying to do the best job they can, and chances are in any given day, the front-line tech support people are getting yelled at every few minutes. (I know, because I've been there.)

For the most part, you're only going to need to interact with your webhost when something goes wrong (not the best way to forge a good working relationship), so here are some hints for working with your host (especially in a crisis) that should help you out:

- If you received an email from your host that you don't understand, reply to it (unless it says Don't Reply to This Message) or call the host's technical support to ask for an explanation.

- Though it's common sense, be cheerful and polite in emails and on the phone. Honestly, nothing greases the wheels of tech support better than a simple "please."

- If you are receiving an error message, try to copy it down *exactly* (this is important), take a screenshot, or copy and paste the error message into a document or email. If you email support saying "I got this error message; I don't know what it said, but now my site doesn't work," they are only going to email back to try to get more information from you.

- Speaking of information, provide as much information as you can about the problem you are having. Include your operating system, what web browser you use, what you were doing at the time the error occurred, your name, your user ID, and your contact information. I don't recommend giving your password. Tech support *shouldn't* need it to check out your account or site for issues.

- Be as patient as you can with tech support's questions back to you. They are in a position where they are trying to figure out the problem, maybe without being able to see it or re-create it. Yes, they might take some shots in the dark to try to figure it out and ask you to do some obvious (to you) things. Bear with them.

- Finally, if you feel like you aren't being helped, ask to be bumped up to a supervisor. At least that person might have more years of experience under their belt and might also be able to give you compensation, like a free month, if your site is down for an extended period of time because of their error.

Should you ask one of your geeky friends first? Depends on how geeky your friends are and how familiar they are with your host. When I'm asked to fix things for friends, sometimes I'm stumped only because I'm not familiar with how a particular webhost does something. Although a lot of webhosts work in a similar fashion and use similar management tools, people likes to tweak their service for their needs, preferences, and clients.

All this said, I'm not a typical client or particularly easy customer for tech support people. I'm already pretty savvy, so when I'm having a problem, chances are it's a doozy. I try to always be especially polite and give as much information as I can. Being snarky and saying something like "If you were a real host, you'd do it like this" doesn't help matters. (And I guarantee it will make things worse.)

Don't be afraid to start looking for a new host if your host isn't working out for you. If your host is putting tight restrictions on you or complaining that "The WordPress site is just too resource heavy for a hosted service and you need a dedicated server," you might start shopping around and get some independent expert opinions on the problem.

Remember, if you're using shared hosting, it's just like an apartment building. If someone is always hogging the elevator or having loud parties all weekend, they might get kicked out. Your webhost wants to make sure the server you are on works great for all the other customers on the server as well. If your host shuts down your site or throttles it back somehow because they say your WordPress install has gotten out of control, this is the time to find a WordPress geek to help you.

I've helped scores of people with this problem, and 90% of the time just using site caching (more on this in Chapter 6, "Finding and Using Plugins") and turning off a few plugins (there are a few extras that do tend to use a lot of system resources) fixes the issue. That said, aside from growing beyond a host's capabilities, having these kinds of issues with a host are the main reasons most people I know switch hosts.

Editing Your DNS Settings to Work with a Webhost or WordPress.com

I'm going to be honest here: Editing your DNS settings isn't hard at all, but it also isn't something that I can show you *exactly* how to do. Each domain registrar handles DNS updates a little differently. One service might refer to it as Manage DNS but another service calls it Edit DNS. The two registrars I frequently work with (my personal one and a client's) have similar-looking words that do *completely different things* regarding DNS. So, as I often teach in my classes, if there is one time I'm sure to check the help files on a service, updating my domain's DNS is the one.

Some hosts offer a free domain name with sign-up. If you took them up on that offer and registered your domain through them, you can skip all this—you're ready to go! Also, if you use WordPress.com and select the option that you didn't have a domain already and registered through them, you're good to go as well!

 LET ME TRY IT

Update Your DNS Settings

Here is the basic process you will be following to update your DNS settings:

1. Log into the Control Panel of your web host, and find the option to add a domain name. Go through the steps (usually a simple form) and finish.

2. In the welcome email from your host, there should be a section of the email that says something like this:

    Note: If you are using your own domain name, please update your domain name servers to

    ns1.yournewwebhost.com

    ns2.yournewwebhost.com

    This is the information you are going to need for step 3. If you have opted for using your own domain on WordPress.com, it will give you its DNS settings when you sign up for its domain service.

3. Log into your domain registrar and find the place where you can update the DNS settings for your domain. Mine looks something like what is shown in Figure 1.3.

Figure 1.3   *Example of updating a domain's DNS settings on a domain registrar*

4. Click the button to submit the changes.

5. Wait.

SHOW ME   Media 1.2—Updating Your DNS Settings
Access this video file through your registered Web Edition at
my.safaribooksonline.com/9780132182836/media

Sorry—more waiting. Updating the DNS for a domain takes as little as a couple of hours to as many as 48 hours. There is no way to gauge how long it will take, *but* there are easy ways to find out when the change has been made! The first and easiest way to know is to just enter your domain name into your browser's address bar and see what comes up. Truthfully, you should do this *before* you make the switch so you know what the default This is a Brand-New Domain looks like from your domain registrar; then you can check to see if it's different later. After you see the page has changed, you're ready to go.

The second way to see if the domain updates have been made is a little more geeky than the first, but it's a lot more exact. Go to a site like www.network-tools.com or www.who.is (yes, .is is the TLD, not .com), enter your domain name, and choose a "whois" lookup. This will give you what servers on the Internet at large recognize as your DNS. This check is independent of your Internet service provider (often, ISPs are some of the last folks to update their DNS servers with new or updated entries) and gives you a double-check that things are progressing or have progressed. It is common, especially if you move a website, to have different people see different versions of your site at the same time. This is because one person's ISP hasn't updated his DNS and another has. This discrepancy is perfectly normal, totally unavoidable, and completely maddening.

To avoid the hassles of your ISP not updating its DNS frequently enough, try a service like OpenDNS, which maintains a large number of DNS servers around the world and updates them frequently. You can set your computer or router at home to use OpenDNS instead of your ISP's default DNS settings. This little trick might save you hours of waiting to get a site ready, as your ISP takes its sweet time updating its DNS.

 **LET ME TRY IT**

Checking Your DNS from the Command Line

Sure, you can use various services online to see if your domain's DNS settings have changed, but there are a lot of great tricks and tools you can learn to do from the command line. We're going to use the nslookup command because it works the same for Macs and PCs.

1. On a PC, go to the Start menu; click Run. Type **cmd** and click OK. On a Mac, go into your Applications folder and then into Utilities and launch Terminal.

2. At this point, on a PC or a Mac, you have a window with a command prompt sitting in front of you. At the prompt, type **nslookup** and press Enter or Return.

3. At the > prompt, type **set querytype=ns** and press Enter or Return.

4. It won't *look* like anything has happened because you'll get another > prompt. At the prompt, type the domain name you'd like to check and press Enter or Return. You should get something that looks like this:

```
SSBN-643:~ trishussey$ nslookup
> set querytype=ns
> usingwordpressbook.com
Server:    208.67.222.222
Address:   208.67.222.222#53
```

```
Non-authoritative answer:
usingwordpressbook.com        nameserver = ns1.dreamhost.com.
usingwordpressbook.com        nameserver = ns2.dreamhost.com.
usingwordpressbook.com        nameserver = ns3.dreamhost.com.

Authoritative answers can be found from:
>
```

5. Type **exit** and press Enter or Return, and that's it. You have your answer!

If you're not sure you're getting the right answer (maybe your friends are seeing your new site, but you aren't), you can quickly flush out any addresses your computer is storing (the DNS cache) with one simple command from the command prompt (since you have a terminal window open), as follows:

PCs: **ipconfig /flushdns**

Macs 10.4 and lower: **lookupd -flushcache**

Macs 10.5 and higher: **dscacheutil –flushcache**

I've had to flush my DNS cache when I've been impatiently waiting for a server to come up when all indications are that it *is* up, but I can't seem to get to it. Yes, rebooting will also do the same thing, but who wants to reboot when you can enter cool commands at the command line?

 SHOW ME   Media 1.3—Checking the DNS for Your Domain Name with nslookup
Access this video file through your registered Web Edition at
my.safaribooksonline.com/9780132182836/media

How to Manage Settings and Features on Your Webhost

Before I wrap up this first chapter, I want to talk about one of the most important but also potentially most frustrating parts of your webhost: the Control Panel. The introductory email you received from your host gave you a link to your web-based Control Panel and to your hosting account. Through this tool, you'll be able to manage just about everything to do with your webhost and hosting, except for your WordPress site itself. There are several different Control Panel software packages that hosts deploy for users; man hosts happen to use cPanel, and some hosts even make their own Control Panel packages. What Control Panels are *supposed* to do is to make common tasks easier for nontechnical users. Poorly written Control Panels can do the exact opposite, but considering the alternatives (doing everything through a command line or, worse, having to call support for the smallest change), I think we can all learn to use Control Panels.

Here are the common tasks that you should be able to do on your host:

- Set up to use new domains and subdomains with your host.

- Use the web-based file manager to create empty files and folders and set their permissions.

- Create, edit, and maintain databases.

- Use a one-click install package (if your host offers it) to install WordPress or other tools.

- Manage additional FTP accounts.

- Create and manage email accounts.

When I start using a host that has a Control Panel set up that I haven't seen before, I look for the help or tutorials section and find where I can learn how to do these basic tasks. Sure, you might have to do some additional things later (like generate a key for SSH), but those tasks are going to be the core.

 SHOW ME   Media 1.4—Using Your Control Panel
Access this video file through your registered Web Edition at
my.safaribooksonline.com/9780132182836/media

Although you can do a lot of the file-based tasks through a good FTP client, you have to log into your Control Panel to manage databases, accounts (email or FTP), or manage domains. This is one area where skipping the help files isn't a good idea.

By the end of the chapter, you will know how to install WordPress on your webhost's server and start becoming familiar with how WordPress works.

2

Installing WordPress on Your Own Server

Now we get to the good stuff: installing WordPress on your own webhost using your own domain. If this is the part of the book you've been dreading because you think it's beyond your comfort level of geekiness, don't worry. Installing WordPress is simple. Sure, there are geeky things to do, but how often do you get to say to your friends, "Yeah, I set up a MySQL database, FTPed up my server, edited my config files, and installed a CMS...."? My friends would just reply, "You installed WP again, didn't you?" but I hang out with a bunch of WordPress and web geeks. Just wait until we install a working server on your own home computer and run WordPress there...yeah, now that's some bragging rights.

In this chapter, we go through this step by step. First, we double-check that your host can support WordPress (almost all can, but it's always good to double-check); then we download WordPress, set up a database, and install WordPress. Minus the time to download WordPress and upload to your host (and I even give you some shortcuts on that), installing WordPress should take you 15 minutes or less. Seriously. I don't think you can make a pot of coffee in the time it's going to take to get WordPress installed. Put the coffee on anyway, because after you get WordPress set up, you'll want to browse the Net for great themes for your site. (We save that for Chapter 7, "All About Themes.")

Installation Requirements for WordPress

Many hosts today specifically note in their feature set that they support WordPress, and some hosts have even started to offer "WordPress Hosting," which means the webhost has completed the grunt work of installing WordPress for you ahead of time. That said, you should have in your head (or on a piece of paper) what the core requirements for a WordPress install are so that you can zip through this chapter and get to the good stuff. Installing WordPress might be fun for some of us, but tweaking the site and getting it ready to show to the world is *much* more fun, I think.

WordPress runs best on what we geeks call a LAMP stack. No, this is not a sculpture made from the lighting section from the hardware store. LAMP stands for Linux Apache MySQL PHP. We call it a "stack" because on a server, they all work together and build off each other.

What's in a LAMP Stack?

Most of the websites in the world run on a LAMP stack that is just an acronym for Linux, Apache, MySQL, and PHP, which comprise all the parts on which you build a website. Think of these as foundational elements.

Linux is the operating system (like Windows or OS X). Apache is a webserver software package. MySQL is a free relational database program. And PHP is a scripting language for building dynamic websites. All of these parts are free because they are either open source technologies or they have a GPL (general public license).

You won't have to worry about what version or variety of Linux the webhost is using, nor do you have to worry about the version of Apache. The only requirement for Apache is that the mod_rewrite module is turned on. Saying "Huh?" to yourself here is normal; mod_rewrite is a basic but nitpicky part of the server module. Most hosts already have it turned on, because it's a handy function that allows the server to "rewrite" URLs on-the-fly. It allows WordPress users to have "pretty permalinks" by changing the default URLs from something like www.usingwordpressbook.com/?p=123 to www.usingwordpressbook.com/2009/11/welcome-to-the-book/. I discuss making your permalinks pretty in Chapter 4, "Configuring WordPress to Work Its Best."

As for PHP, you need version 4.3 or greater and MySQL version 4.0 or later. PHP and MySQL are both standard parts of a LAMP stack and are also included on many Windows-based servers as well. As of the time I'm writing this book, both PHP and MySQL are at versions 5 and greater, and many webhosts might have already updated to those versions.

It is becoming more common for newer WordPress plugins to require PHP 5 or greater to work. Often webhosts make PHP 5 available, but it's not the default version that is active. I cover how to make PHP 5 active for your WordPress install in Chapter 15, "Troubleshooting Common Problems."

If you have any questions about whether your host is good to go, the folks at WordPress.org have a handy, little email that you can copy and paste to send to your host's support people:

I'm interested in running the open-source WordPress <http://wordpress.org/> blogging software and I was wondering if my account supported the following:

- PHP 4.3 or greater
- MySQL 4.0 or greater
- The mod_rewrite Apache module

Thanks!

Nine times out of ten, the reply will come back that you're good to go. What if you're not? That depends. If your host replies that the rest is okay, but mod_rewrite is the issue, your install will go fine; however, you will be stuck with ugly perma-links, and most caching plugins will not work. In practice, I haven't had a host or system administrator balk at having this turned on (unless they were just lazy or trying to annoy people on purpose).

Although WordPress runs best on Linux- or UNIX-based servers, it *can* run on Win-dows-based servers as well. It *can*, but the server administrators often have to do a good amount of geek trickery to get it working all ducky. My experience is that when someone says "Windows server" and "WordPress" in the same sentence, I expect to hear a horror story of trying to get core functions running. This experi-ence includes my own experience in trying to get this done. So, if you have a choice, go with a Linux- or UNIX-based server set up. If you're not sure what the host is running, just ask. It's not silly or a stupid question; we're talking about your time and money here, so be 100% sure before you give that credit card number.

After you sign up with your host, log into your control panel, and check the ver-sions of MySQL and PHP that are installed. Figure 2.1 displays a view of the seg-ment from my host (which uses cPanel).

Note that on my host, it *says* it's running PHP 5.2.9. I'll get to why you can't always go by what you see there in Chapter 6, "Finding and Using Plugins." That's it for making sure that you can install WordPress; now let's get to the good stuff.

SHOW ME   Media 2.1—Web Host Compatibility with WordPress
Access this video file through your registered Web Edition at
my.safaribooksonline.com/9780132182836/media

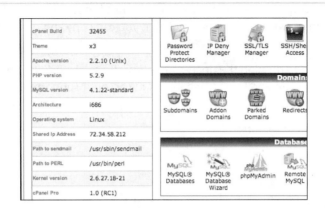

Figure 2.1   *Checking the versions of MySQL and PHP on a host running cPanel*

Downloading WordPress to Install Yourself

Downloading WordPress is going to start in one place: www.wordpress.org. That is the *only* place from which you should download WordPress to make sure the copy you download is the real deal (and not a hacker-exploited or modified version). When you go to WordPress.org, you will see a large button called Download WordPress [the current version] (as shown in Figure 2.2).

Figure 2.2   *The Download WordPress button in the lower-right corner of the WordPress.org home page*

When you click that button, you go to the actual download page, where you click a second blue button, and a ZIP archive of WordPress will start to download to your computer. The download page is shown in Figure 2.3 and offers links to more resources to help you with the installation process.

Figure 2.3   *The WordPress.org download page, where you download the ZIP (or tar.gz) archive of WordPress*

Do I Have to Run WordPress on a Server?

No, you don't. You can install everything you need to run WordPress on your own computer. Why would you *want* to do that in the first place? Running WordPress on your own computer gives you a little playground, a sandbox, to experiment, learn, and test things. Test in an environment that isn't on the Internet but can pretend like it is.

It isn't as hard as you think, and there are several free software packages to help you do this. XAMPP (www.apachefriends.org/en/xampp.html) for PCs and Macs or MAMP (www.mamp.info) for Macs makes having your own private WordPress install as simple as installing a single application. Using either of these two apps, you can have your own local WordPress installed in less than 15 minutes!"

After the archive is downloaded, unzip the archive so you have a folder called wordpress with all the files within it.

Installing WordPress on Your Webhost Yourself

We're in the home stretch now for getting your WordPress install up and running. Just three steps are left, as follows:

1. Upload the WordPress files to your host.

2. Create the MySQL database for WordPress to use.

3. Run the web-based WordPress installer.

Like everything we've done so far, nothing here is going to be complicated or require you to learn arcane commands. WordPress is built on a philosophy of making technology and publishing easy for everyone. Making a democratizing technology misses the mark if people have a hard time installing it, or there are a lot of prerequisites to make it work.

Before you start, make sure you have a few things at the ready:

- The ability to log into your host's Control Panel

- A text editor like NotePad (PC) or TextEdit (Mac)

- Your web browser of choice (for example, Firefox, Internet Explorer, or Safari)

- An FTP client for uploading the files

Uploading WordPress to Your Server

Let's get the uploading process going while we do the rest of the behind-the-scenes work. You've already *downloaded* WordPress to your machine and should have unzipped it by now. Find the folder named wordpress and open it; it should look something similar to what's shown in Figure 2.4.

Open your FTP client and use the FTP information your host gave you to log into your account (see Figure 2.5).

If you don't already have an FTP client, here's a list of some free FTP applications for Macs and PCs:
- FileZilla filezilla-project.org (Macs, PCs, Linux)
- FireFTP (Add-on for Firefox)
- CyberDuck cyberduck.ch (Mac only)

Open the folder called public_html or "www" in the listing. This is the "root" of your website. If you have only one domain associated with your webhost, and this is your first venture up to your host, the folder is going to be quite empty. I have a lot of extra files and directories in my public_html folder because I host more than one website from my account.

When you install WordPress, you have the choice of installing it at the root of your website or as a subdirectory of your site. If your WordPress install is going to be just a part of a larger non-WordPress website, you might want to install it as a subdirectory. If it's not going to be part of a larger website, install it in the root directory.

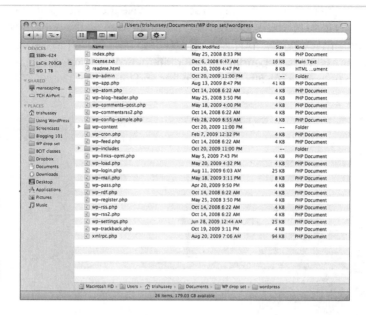

Figure 2.4   *Contents of the wordpress folder after unzipping the downloaded copy of WordPress*

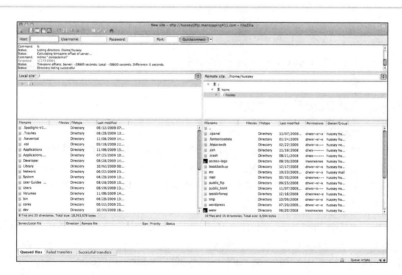

Figure 2.5   *Basic file listing for a webhost through FTP (using FileZilla)*

On the left side of Figure 2.6, you can see that I have the contents of the wordpress folder on my *local* machine selected and the empty site on the right (called UsingWordPressExample). You just drag and drop from the left to the right, and the upload process starts. Depending on your Internet connection, it will take a few minutes to upload all the files. (There are lots and lots of files.)

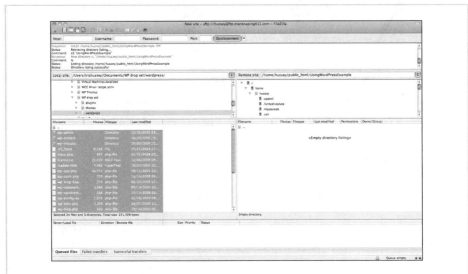

Figure 2.6 *WordPress files on my local machine selected on the left, ready to be dragged and dropped onto the waiting server on the right*

If you want WordPress as a subdirectory instead, just drag that whole folder over.

MySQL Database Setup

While the WordPress files are uploading, it's time to create the MySQL database for WordPress to use. This is where logging into your webhost Control Panel comes in. My host uses cPanel, so after logging in, I scroll down to the section called Databases. This is where I find the tools I need to create and manage my databases (see Figure 2.7).

If your host offers, like mine does, a MySQL Database Wizard, go ahead and click the icon for the wizard. This can walk you through the process in a few easy screens and achieves the same thing as clicking MySQL Databases. (Don't worry—I'll show you that option, too.)

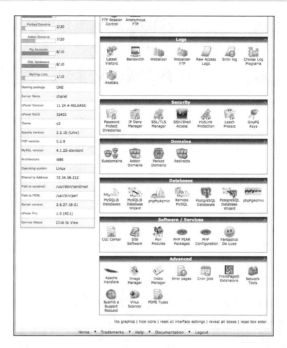

Figure 2.7   *My host's cPanel scrolled down to the Databases section, where the MySQL tools are located*

 LET ME TRY IT

Using a MySQL Database Wizard

1. Give your database a name (see Figure 2.8). (Choose something like blog or wordpress.) Then click Next Step.

2. Create the user who will use the database and the password for the account. The username can only be seven characters long, so don't go crazy here. Using something like blog is fine. The key is the password. I have the server generate a completely random one for me; just don't forget to copy down that password. (I copy and paste it into a blank file or Stickies.) When you're done with the username and password, click Next Step (see Figure 2.9).

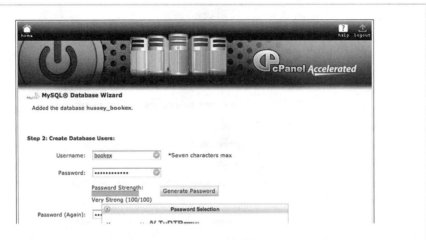

Figure 2.8   *Giving your database a name in the MySQL Wizard*

Figure 2.9   *Creating the user bookex to use the database being created*

3. Check the ALL PRIVILEGES box. Before moving on to the next step, make sure you have the username and database name noted *and* the password. When you have it all down, click Next Step.

4. Review the information on the confirmation screen.

 **LET ME TRY IT**

Using MySQL Databases

If you don't have the Database Wizard (I'm sorry), using MySQL Databases is just as easy:

1. Click the icon and create the database at the top of the page, as shown in Figure 2.10.

Figure 2.10 *Top of the MySQL Database screen where you create the database*

2. Scroll down to the users section, and like in the Wizard, you pick a name and a password (see Figure 2.11).

3. Add the user to the database by selecting the user from the top menu and the database from the bottom; then click Add. A screen similar to Figure 2.12 opens.

4. Click ALL PRIVILEGES and then click Make Changes.

Congratulations—you have just created a MySQL database!

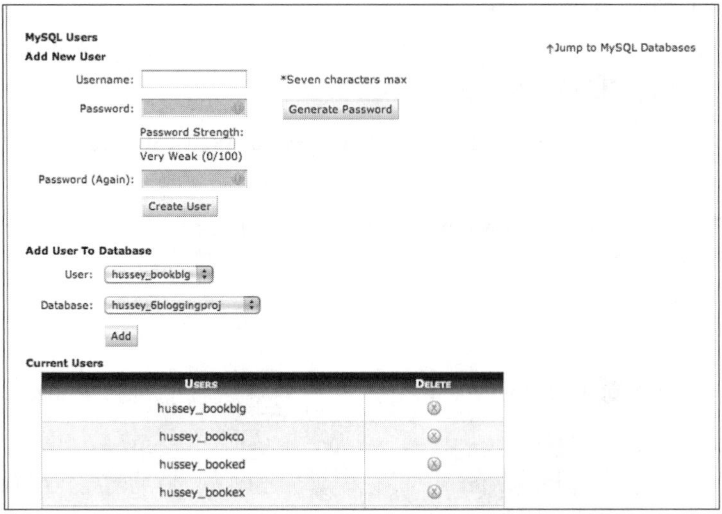

Figure 2.11 *Creating a user under MySQL Databases*

Figure 2.12 *Adding a user to an existing database under MySQL Databases*

Have all the information handy for the database? Great, because we're about to start the WordPress "Famous Five-Minute Install."

In the preceding section (and figures), I illustrated how creating a MySQL database works for *that* particular host. Given that there are thousands of different webhosts out there in the world, what you see might look *entirely* different. This is okay; don't panic. Just follow the steps your host recommends. Remember the tasks to follow are

1. Create the database (and give it a name).

2. Create a user (with a password) that can access the database.

3. Make a note of the database name, database user, and the password.

Famous Five-Minute Install

You're so close to being done. All that's left is to actually "install" WordPress, which is actually WordPress editing the database to create all the stuff WordPress needs to run. In reality, the "guts" of WordPress are already installed; you uploaded them already! Right now, they are just kinda limp and lifeless. Just like the Frankenstein monster, WordPress needs a little jolt to come alive, and in this case, it's a database connection.

WordPress *can* create and edit the files it needs, but that depends completely on your host's server configuration. There is a good chance that just trying to let WordPress create files isn't going to work, so we're going to edit the configuration file and upload it first. It takes only a minute to do and will make sure your WordPress install does its thing first try.

 LET ME TRY IT

Installing WordPress by Hand

1. Go to the wordpress folder on your local machine and open the folder. Look for a file called wp-config-sample.php (shown in Figure 2.13). Right-click (or Control-click on Macs) the file and choose Open With. On a PC, if you aren't offered Notepad (or your preferred text editor) as one of your choices, click the Browse button and find Notepad.exe. On the Mac, choose TextEdit if you don't already have a preferred text editor already.

2. Enter your database name, username, and password where you see database_name_here, username_here, and password_here. Make sure that the text you enter is still surrounded by single quotes.

Figure 2.13 *Opening wp-config-sample.php in TextEdit*

3. Scroll down and copy https://api.wordpress.org/secret-key/1.1/salt/ to the clipboard and paste it into the address bar of your browser. You'll get a result something like what's shown in Figure 2.14.

Figure 2.14 *Generating random keys and salts for WordPress logins and security*

4. Select all the lines on the web page and copy them to the clipboard.

5. Back in your wp-config.php file, select all the text in the similar looking block (except that they say "put your unique phrase here") and paste the new keys and salts in their place. These salts allow WordPress to generate random passwords and cookies to help keep your install more secure.

6. Choose Save As from the File menu and name the file wp-config.php. Click Save.

7. Upload this wp-config.php file to the root of your WordPress files on your server.

8. In your web browser, you'll go to the WordPress installation script at a URL something like this (use your domain name instead of mine): http://usingwordpressbook.com/wp-admin/install.php or http://usingwordpressbook.com/wordpress/wp-admin/install.php. This will get the ball rolling, and you should see a screen like the one shown in Figure 2.15.

Figure 2.15 *First (and only) screen before WordPress is installed and running*

9. Give your blog/site a title (which you can change later) and put in your email address (use a real address because it will be important for admin functions later); then click Install WordPress. New in WordPress 3.0 is the ability to both set the first username to something other than admin and set your own password. I suggest picking a new username such as Administrator or using your own name. As for the password, I like secure and random passwords, which is exactly what you'll get if you leave those password fields blank. And, ta-da! You should see a confirmation screen like the one shown in Figure 2.16.

Yep, really, that's it. The password you see there is randomly generated, and although it should be emailed to you, you need to copy the password or write it down. It's the only time you're going to see it on-screen like that.

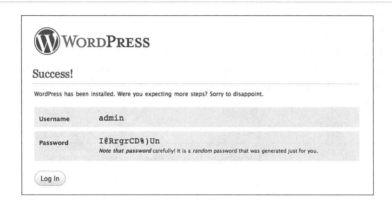

Figure 2.16 *WordPress is successfully installed, the admin account is created, and the random password is generated.*

Now you can log into WordPress by clicking the Log In button. On the next screen, enter your username (admin) and password and again click Log In. If all has gone well, you will see the WordPress Dashboard (see Figure 2.17).

If you get to the Dashboard, you've installed and logged into WordPress correctly. Believe me, it takes a lot longer to *write* about how to install WordPress than it takes to actually *do it*!

 SHOW ME   Media 2.2—Uploading WordPress to Your Own Server, Creating a MySQL Database, and Editing the Configuration File
Access this video file through your registered Web Edition at
my.safaribooksonline.com/9780132182836/media

 SHOW ME   Media 2.3—Running the Installation Script to Complete the WordPress Installation
Access this video file through your registered Web Edition at
my.safaribooksonline.com/9780132182836/media

Figure 2.17   *The WordPress Dashboard and a successful install and login. Hooray!*

How Your .htaccess File Works with WordPress and Why It's Important

Earlier in the chapter, I told you that WordPress runs on a LAMP stack, and that the A stood for Apache. Apache is the software on the server that serves the webpages to you. (Apache is webserver software.) One of the things people wanted to do early on was restrict access to parts of their websites to only certain people. We usually did this by setting a password on that section, and the username-password combination was stored in a file called .htaccess. The "." in front is critical, because under Linux/UNIX operating systems, putting a "." (or dot) in front of a filename made it invisible to general file browsing. Files like .htaccess are generally configuration files that you don't want people to stumble upon and edit (or delete) accidentally.

Although .htaccess files are still used for securing sections of websites, in WordPress, they do a far more important job: creating your pretty permalinks. I cover pretty permalinks in Chapter 4, but for now as part of your initial setup, you just need to know that it's there (or soon will be).

Throughout the rest of the book, I show you other things you can do with your .htaccess file, including blocking access to search engines and potential intruders, and running different versions of PHP that your server offers by default.

SHOW ME   Media 2.4—One-Click Install of WordPress
Access this video file through your registered Web Edition at
my.safaribooksonline.com/9780132182836/media

Setting Your Directory Permissions

Now that we have WordPress up and running, we're soon going to start configuring WordPress, installing plugins, installing additional themes, and later updating WordPress itself as new updates come out. You'll also, I'm sure, want to add pictures and other media to your posts and pages, and that requires you to upload them to the server (through WordPress) Most of the time, you can complete installs, updates, and uploads through WordPress via the Dashboard and your web browser. For many hosts and many users, the process will go smoothly, but sometimes it doesn't, and the reason it often doesn't is because of directory permissions. Before we get into configuring and customizing WordPress, I need to give you a crash course in UNIX directory permissions.

When you use your computer at home, you don't usually think about file and directory permissions, but you deal with them all the time. Everything on a computer (Mac, PC, or UNIX) has to have some notation of who can edit the files or run the programs. On your home computer, that is usually you, but if you have a shared home computer and each person logs into their own account, you have seen directory permissions at work. You can't see, much less edit, the files of another person who uses the computer, unless you are the all-powerful administrator. Your server works pretty much the same way. In UNIX, we talk about owner (you), group (a group of administrative users or programs on the server), and world (everyone) as the three levels of permissions, and the permissions given are **r**ead, **w**rite, and e**x**ecute.

For most webhosts, when you upload files into your public_html directory (or similar for your particular host), all the files are only writable (editable) by you, but other people can read and execute the files. This is a safe way to have your files, because people can see your website (because the world can read it), but they can't change anything. In the UNIX world, we're never satisfied with having just one way to describe things, so we give each kind of permission a number value and the sum of the numbers indicates the level of permissions for the file or directory. Confused? Don't worry—it took me a while to get it too when I was starting out. Here are the values:

- Read = 4
- Write = 2
- Execute = 1

For the case where the file owner has all privileges, but group and world only can read and execute, it works out like this:

- Owner = 4 + 2 + 1 = 7
- Group = 4 + 1 = 5
- World = 4 + 1 = 5

This is all expressed in shorthand as 755. Now let's see how this actually looks in real life. Figure 2.18 shows the directory listing for UsingWordPressBook.com, where you can see the file and directory permissions clearly.

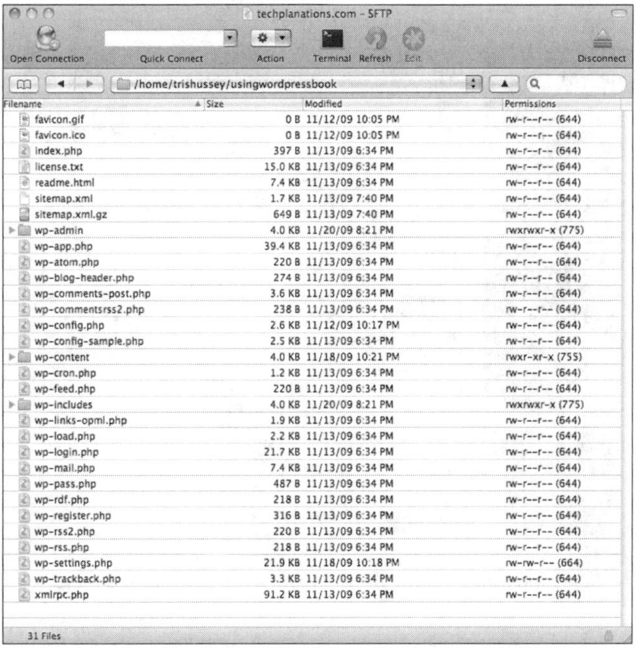

Figure 2.18   *Directory listing for the root of UsingWordPressBook.com. The far-right column shows the permissions for each file and directory.*

The notation you see like rw-r—r— or rwx-r-x-r-x refers to the permissions I explained earlier. The order is owner, group, world. You can see that most files are 644, 755, or 775. These settings let WordPress function properly—most of the time.

Sometimes when you install some plugins, it asks you to *temporarily* set a directory (like wp-content) to 777. This means that anyone and anything can make changes there. This is safe if you work with a plugin that is trusted *and* if after you open up that directory, you close it back down to 775 or 755.

Changing file permissions is easy to do through an FTP client, and *generally* easy to do through your host's web-based file manager. I prefer to do it through FTP or command line. Because chances are that you won't have command-line access to your host, let's make the change through FTP.

If you want to change the permissions on your wp-content directory, do this:

1. Open an FTP connection (if one isn't already open).

2. Find the directory you need to change and select it. (Click once.)

3. From the File Menu (in general for most FTP clients), choose Get Info or Info (see Figure 2.19).

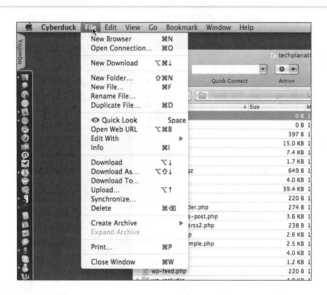

Figure 2.19   *Selecting Info from the file menu for my wp-content directory.*

4. In the resulting panel, check the empty boxes to enable write for all users *or* if you can, enter the permission number (777).

5. Click Apply if needed and close the info window.

When I'm done, I repeat the process, but change the permissions to 755. (On my server, I have them safely set to 775.) It is *essential* not to leave your wp-content directory open with 777 permissions longer than you need to (which is usually the short period of time you need to get the plugin configured). Although it is *unlikely*, it is *possible* that this security weakness could be exploited to allow malicious people to delete plugins, themes, or uploads or worse, to *upload* malicious content to your server without you knowing it.

There is one other case when a lot of WordPress users run into directory permission issues: uploading pictures. This is a tough one to deal with because according to how things *should* work, you shouldn't need to do anything for WordPress to create the initial uploads directory and any other subdirectories that it might need. It *should* work, which means it doesn't work 100% of the time. The *correct* way for your uploads directory to be is for it to have, like all the other directories, 755 privileges (only the owner can write to it), but sometimes the *only* way to make it work is to have it set to 777. (Everyone can write to it.) This is not optimal or even recommended by any stretch of the imagination (see Figure 2.20). The consensus is that if the only way to get the uploads directory to work is to set it to 777, do it as a stop gap and then send in a support request to your host. Include in your email a link to this page of the WordPress Codex: http://codex.wordpress.org/Changing_File_Permissions. This explains how things *should* be set up. More and more hosts are making sure their servers work securely with WordPress, and if enough of a host's customers complain about having to open up security to make WP work, maybe they will do something about it.

Figure 2.20   *Checking the boxes to give group and others write permissions to the directory*

As we proceed through the book, we come back to directory permissions again. We update, change, and alter them for a few tasks, but for right now, you have enough to get going.

 TELL ME MORE   Media 2.5—What's the Right Way to Install **WordPress: One Click or Manually?**
Access this audio recording through your registered Web Edition at
my.safaribooksonline.com/9780132182836/media

3

Getting Around WordPress

Now that you have WordPress installed and running on your server, it's time to take a short tour around the Administration area so that you can become familiar with where all the settings and goodies are hiding. I'll get into the actual *settings* in Chapter 4, "Configuring WordPress to Work Its Best," but in this chapter, we're going to look at not only where things are, but also how to customize the Admin area to your liking. Although I'll try to keep the descriptions as version-independent as I can, this book is written using WordPress 3.0 as the example. If there are significant changes to the Administration area, or any part of WordPress itself, there will be updated information available at usingwordpressbook.com.

Becoming Familiar with the Dashboard

When I log into WordPress, I usually go to http://[websitedomain]/wp-admin; the first page that comes up is the Dashboard. The Dashboard gives you a heads up on what is going on with your blog. You can quickly see how many comments need moderation, if plugins need to be updated, if there are updates to WordPress itself, and if there is any WordPress-related news. The button bar on the left can be expanded (the default setting) or collapsed for a more compact look. Each of the boxes can be moved around, and by clicking the Screen Options button in the upper-right corner, you can select which boxes you see and how many columns you have in your Dashboard.

Some of the boxes, like Other WordPress News, can be configured individually as well. Because the Dashboard is a place where you'll come back to often as you work with your blog, feel free to make it your own. Figure 3.1 shows the Dashboard for the example blog for the book.

 SHOW ME Media 3.1—WordPress Administration Area: Dashboard and Content Block

Access this video file through your registered Web Edition at
my.safaribooksonline.com/9780132182836/media

SHOW ME   Media 3.2—WordPress Administration Area: Core Settings
Access this video file through your registered Web Edition at
my.safaribooksonline.com/9780132182836/media

Figure 3.1   *The WordPress Dashboard using a standard configuration and with the Screen Options panel open*

One of the important areas of development in the WordPress community is the Dashboard. Over the past two or three years, a lot of work has gone into improving the layout and functionality of the Dashboard. WordPress 3.0 is one of the last interim steps along a longer Dashboard design process. You should expect from WordPress 3.0 to 3.1 and beyond that the Dashboard will continue to be refined and improved. For comparison, here is a shot of WordPress 2.6.5, which was released on November 25, 2008 (see Figure 3.2).

From the Dashboard, you can quickly jump to any section of the administration portion of the site or even produce a quick post (although I rarely take advantage of it myself). Let's start with the top and work our way down what I call the "administration blocks" button by button to explain what is there and how it all works.

Figure 3.2   *The WordPress 2.6.5 Dashboard (late November 2008). Big change and significant improvements since then!*

Updates

Before we move from the Dashboard, there is a *very* important menu item that I need to draw your attention to: Updates. This item was previously buried under Tools and called Upgrades; under WordPress 3.0, it's been moved front and center. Updates is where you go to quickly update plugins or themes in bulk and when you go to update WordPress itself (as updates come out). Figure 3.3 shows the Updates screen. Your WordPress install automatically checks for new updates nightly. When there are updates available, you'll see a number next to the Updates menu item with the number of updates available.

Posts, Pages, Tags, Media, and More: Content Administration

The first block below the Dashboard button is the content block. This is where you manage everything to do with the content on your blog. Of all the sections of the Administration area of WordPress, this is probably the one you'll hit the most often. If you use the Dashboard to manage your content, there are several ways to

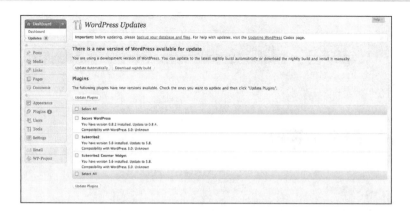

Figure 3.3   *The upgrade area, where you can update WordPress with one click. When plugins need updates, you can come here to update several plugins at once (new in WordPress 2.9).*

manage your content (and the Dashboard is just one of them), and you'll probably be clicking that Posts button often. Of course, if you are just looking to fire off a post, in the top left of the colored bar (right next to your login name), there is a New Post button you can click to jump right into the Post Editor. Let's start with the Posts button to see where it leads.

Posts Button

There are only really three real sections to the Posts button: Edit, Post Tags, and Categories. (If you click Add New, you jump to the Post Editor, so that's not like a real section.) When you click the Posts button, the Edit Posts screen (see Figure 3.4) comes up with a listing of all the posts saved to the blog's database. I stress *saved* instead of *published* because you can have posts that are unpublished, but drafts are published and scheduled to "go live" at a point in the future.

If you've used WordPress in the past, a new feature introduced in WordPress is the Trash section that you can reach through the Edit Posts screen. Deleted posts stay in the Trash until you empty it. Prior to the new WordPress Trash feature, when you deleted a post, it was not just immediately gone—it was *irrevocably* gone. I'm sure lots of posts were lost to the "oops" factor, so the brilliant coders behind WordPress created the Trash and deleted posts stay there for 30 days or until they are proactively deleted.

Our next stop is the Post Tags section. I'll delve into the differences between Categories and Tags in Chapter 8, "Organizing The Content on Your Blog," but for now, just note that this is where you go to manage tags. As you can see from Figure 3.5,

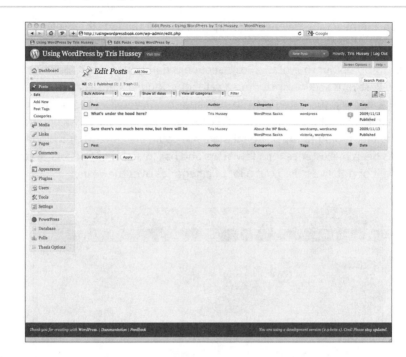

Figure 3.4 *The Edit Posts section. Note the new Trash item. Very, very handy!*

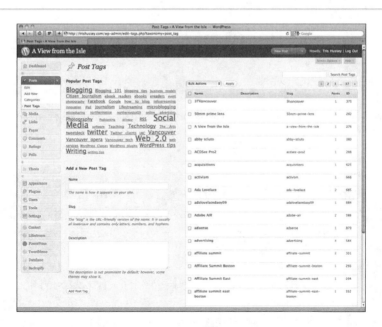

Figure 3.5 *Tag manager in the Post section of the content block. The larger the word in the Popular Post Tags section, the more often the tag has been used.*

you can add new tags, delete existing tags, and edit the tags themselves (change the names and so on).

The last stop on our tour of the Posts section is Categories. Yes, it looks very much like the Post Tags section, including a category cloud; because categories can be nested (category, sub-category, sub-sub, and so on), you also see one or more dashes in front of the category name. For Figures 3.5 and 3.6, I switched from my demonstration blog to my personal blog, so I could illustrate what a blog looks like after it's been in existence for a few years and has lots of tags and lots of categories. (Believe it or not, I've culled out a lot of categories over the years.)

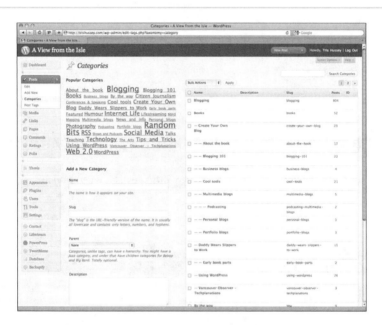

Figure 3.6   *Category manager showing the primary and sub-categories on my personal blog*

Getting the Words Out on How the Post and Page Editor Works

If you've used web-based email services like Gmail, Hotmail, or Yahoo! Mail, the post editor in WordPress (and the page editor as well, since they are essentially the same) shouldn't look too alien to you. WordPress, like many other web-based blog engines, uses the JavaScript component TinyMCE (pronounced "tiny mice") to give us an editor where we don't have to type HTML code in our posts for bold, italics, links, or images. To make things easier on myself, and gain access to all the features of the editor, I always click the (poorly named and even worse icon) "kitchen sink" button (see Figure 3.7).

Opening the kitchen sink (as in "everything including the kitchen sink") gives you access to buttons to embed videos, clear extraneous formatting, and, my personal favorite, the Paste from Word button. It's worth your time to explore the post window. When you start not only *writing* content, but also *editing* and *fixing* content, you'll become very familiar with the ins, outs, and quirks of this great little tool.

The New Post version of the editor has a place to set the category and add tags to the post. The New Page version of the editor (see Figure 3.8) doesn't have categories or tags, but does have Parent, Template, and Order spaces.

You will read more about the ins and outs of creating content using these two editors in Chapter 9, "Creating and Managing Content with WordPress." In the meantime, however, just note that this is where you get to these editors and what they look like.

Figure 3.7   *The Post Editor in WordPress. The Page Editor looks essentially identical to this screen.*

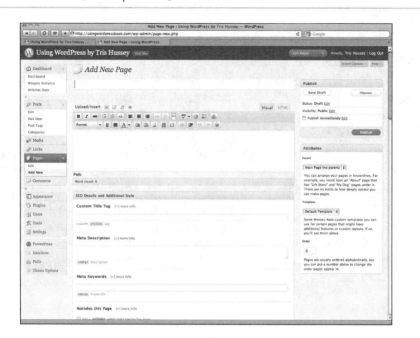

Figure 3.8   *Page Editor in WordPress. Note the major difference between this and the Post Editor is the Attributes panel.*

Media Button

The Media button brings up a list of all the media (pictures, movies, "regular" files, mp3s) you have uploaded to the blog. In Figure 3.9, you can see a few pictures that I've uploaded to the demonstration blog.

Clicking on the name of the image brings up the image's properties, where you can edit the title (name) of the image and other metadata like the description or caption (see Figure 3.10).

The Edit Image button was one of the big new features introduced in WordPress 2.9. Clicking that innocuous little button brings up a basic image editor that will let you crop, rotate, flip, and scale your images right in WordPress, *and* the changes can affect some or all of the auto-generated image sizes WordPress creates for you (see Figure 3.11).

Figure 3.9 *Media Library listing on the demo blog. Each file has a thumbnail and properties.*

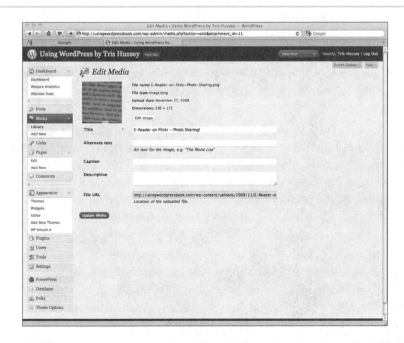

Figure 3.10 *The Edit Media panel after clicking on the name of the picture in the library*

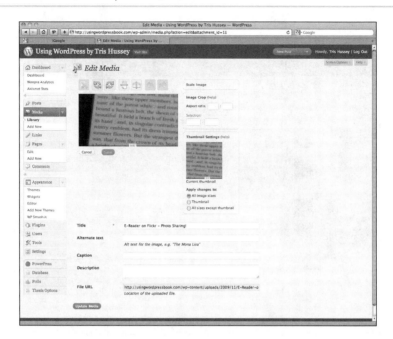

Figure 3.11   *The new image editor in WordPress 2.9. The scale, crop, and thumbnail settings sections all have helpful descriptions to explain how each of the tools work.*

Using the New Built-in Image Editor

The new image editor in WP 2.9 was one of the most anticipated features that users were looking forward to trying out. To be completely clear, this is not an image-creation tool or anything like Adobe Photoshop online. The WordPress image editor is a very basic tool that will let you make very basic changes to images.

The image editor will be perfect for times when you uploaded an image that is pretty large, but it turns out you could make the image better if you crop some of the image away—or if the image is too big (dimensions), and all you need is to resize it quickly. Often, themes use images of a particular size for thumbnails, or previews; maybe you thought you had the image right, but it turns out you didn't. A little resizing and cropping could be just the thing you need.

Because the image editor is so basic, there isn't much to learn, but it's not a bad idea to try it out a few times just to see what the results look like. Maybe you like how it scales screenshots but not photos. If you want to have a copy of the original photo and a modified photo, the image editor might not be a good choice for you. There isn't a Save As function, so although you can update just the thumbnail, all versions, or everything *except* the thumbnail, there isn't an option (right now) to Save and Make a New Copy.

Links Button

The Links button brings up the list of links to other websites and blogs that you can use as part of your blogroll. When you first install WordPress, a default blogroll is created for you with links to several WordPress sites and resources (see Figure 3.12).

Figure 3.12   *The default blogroll created when you install WordPress*

A *blogroll* is simple a list of links to other blogs and sites that you enjoy reading, support, or just like in general. I use my blogroll to link to all my other websites.

You don't have to keep any of these links, and you can delete some or all of them as you wish. To create links of your own, just click the Add New links and enter the name of the site in the top box, the web address (URL), and other information; then click Add Link (see Figure 3.13). Link Categories are ways to organize your links into logical groups—Friends, Coworkers, Must Reads, or My Other Sites are all categories you can use. The benefit of using link categories is that you can choose which groups of links to display on your site (or not). If nothing else, if you list all the links in all the categories, the list will be broken up by category, so it's much easier to read.

Figure 3.13   *Adding a new link to your blogroll through the Add New Link screen*

Are Blogrolls Dead?

It wasn't that long ago ("way back" in 2004, to be exact) that your blogroll was one of the most important parts of your blog. It not only helped people find new blogs, but it also showed the world what groups you affiliated yourself with. Even more important was getting *listed* on a top blogger's blogroll. Being listed on a high-traffic blog could be just the break you needed to make it big in the blogging world.

Now it's a different story. Conventional wisdom is that people aren't paying much attention to blogrolls anymore. Many blogs don't even have them on their sidebars. The thinking is that it's now more important to be linked to within a post than to be on someone's sidebar.

I'm on the fence on the issue. I don't disagree with the fact that blogrolls have become less important than they once were, and that links within posts are of greater value (especially as far as search engines are concerned), but I still maintain at least a small blogroll of my own sites and a few friends. Maybe it's nostalgia, or maybe it's just keeping connections alive, but I think that there is still an important place for blogrolls in the blogosphere. My advice: Just go ahead and do it. It can't hurt, and you might even find yourself linked to as well.

Pages Button

The Pages button works just like the Posts button, except it's for, well, pages. Without getting too much into the differences between posts and pages, pages are intended for *static* content like About pages, Contact Me, and similar content that doesn't change often *and* is intended to stand by itself. Don't worry—I'll cover this *ad nauseum* in Chapter 9, and it will all fall into place.

The Edit Pages list is much simpler than the similar Edit Posts list, because Pages don't have Categories or Tags assigned to them (see Figure 3.14). There are more options whether or not the page is published, draft, pending review, scheduled, or private, but you won't see that until you're in the Page Editor, which you'd get to by clicking New Page or editing an existing Page.

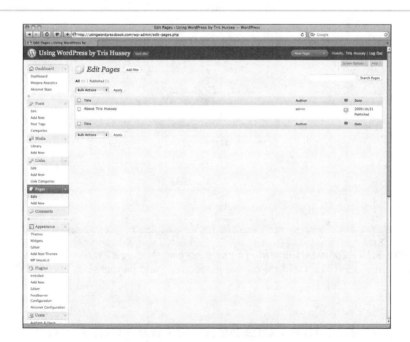

Figure 3.14 *The Edit Pages screen, which has far fewer options than the Edit Posts screen because Pages cannot have categories or tags*

Comments Button

The Comments button reveals the list of all comments. What you will find most interesting is each comment's status (see Figure 3.15). When comments come into your blog, they have to pass through the moderation and spam filters. Both of these run pretty automatically, but when a comment comes in from someone who doesn't have a previously approved comment, the comment will go to the Moderation Queue to approve the comment. Comment management has been made much easier and smoother in the recent versions of WordPress. Where there used to be several different list and screens to go through, now you can view the comments together or broken down on one screen. I'll cover how to manage comments in Chapter 9.

Figure 3.15   *Comments page from my personal blog showing a few recent comments. From here, you can manage all the comments, good and bad, on your blog.*

Tapping into the Core Settings for Your Blog

If there is a section of this book that is about how the "guts" of WordPress works, this is it. This block of settings described in this section controls how your blog work, how it looks, and who gets to do what on the blog. There are lots of settings here that you'll probably only touch once when you set up your blog and others that you'll come back to update often. Like all things WordPress, most settings here are simple radio buttons, check boxes, and pull-down menus. Even though I'm just going top down, the Appearance button is probably where I might have started regardless because being able to change the look of your blog with one click is just too cool to leave until later!

Appearance Button

The Appearance button is where you manage everything related to themes. The default when you click the Appearance button is to show you the themes you have installed (see Figure 3.16). The thumbnail that you see is provided by the theme designer, but when you click the thumbnail, you'll see how *your blog* would look with that theme applied. Sure, you can just click Activate to immediately turn on a theme, but if you're trying out a new theme, it's smart to check to make sure the theme will behave like you expect. It's pretty common to find a theme that looks great in all the previews and examples you find online, but when applied to your blog, it just doesn't look right (or good). Sometimes the conflict is with a plugin or how your images are formatted, but you won't know until you see the preview.

Figure 3.16 *Clicking on the Appearance button brings you to the Manage Themes section by default. Here are some of the themes I have installed on my blog.*

When you are looking at the preview, you can click Activate [theme name] to switch to that theme. Then you just go to your blog and refresh the page, and you should see the new theme in action. To learn more about themes, read Chapter 7, "All About Themes."

Widgets

The next item in the Appearance sub-panel is the Widgets link (see Figure 3.16). Widgets are the little placeholders or blocks that can be put into your sidebar, such as your recent posts or comments and all those great badges and interactive bits.

In Figure 3.17, you can see that there are spaces on the right (the sidebars) where widgets go, and the different widgets on the right. You can add the widgets with drag-and-drop, so it's really easy to put them on your blog. You can pick from the predefined widgets that come with WordPress, special ones your theme might offer, and widgets managed by plugins; if that isn't enough, you can also paste code into blank widgets to make something entirely your own.

Figure 3.17   *The Widgets section from my blog with all the active widgets on the right and inactive widgets on the left*

Menus

The ability to create and edit your own custom menus is a new and extremely handy function in WordPress (see Figure 3.18). I'll cover Menus in great detail in Chapter 7, but for now there are a couple things to note and understand about the new Menus function. First, this new function isn't supported by all themes out-of-the-box. The good thing is that *adding* support for the new Menus function is very easy. The other thing to know is that while this might seem pretty crazy to look at, the Menus function will make having completely customized menus a breeze. You'll be able to not only have menus and submenus for your primary navigation bar, but also specialized menus to appear in the sidebars as widgets.

Try to keep your excitement in check for a few more chapters, but if you feel compelled to skip ahead to Chapter 7 just to read about using Menus, I completely understand.

Figure 3.18 *The new Menus section in WordPress where you can create and edit custom menus for your site*

Editor

The Editor link opens WordPress' built-in theme editor, which has improved a lot over time; although this is potentially convenient, I've found that it can be more trouble than it's worth. I'll cover this in more detail in Chapter 7, but for now, part of the problem is that you have to set the directory for the theme you want to edit (or all the themes within wp-content) to world write (777 or 666). If you remember from the previous chapter, that is a potential security hole (although not a huge one) and the best practice is to keep all the directories set to 755 (best) or 775 (acceptable if you need to for your server). The other reason I don't like to use the theme editor is that if I am also working on the theme using a local copy on my laptop, I have to remember to download this modified copy to my drive and make sure I don't lose any changes in the interim. For me, it's just not worth the effort.

Figure 3.19 shows you what the built-in theme editor looks like for the theme that is active on my blog. So, although it is *possible* to edit themes here, it isn't something that I recommend.

Figure 3.19   *The built-in theme editor, which is only available on self-installed versions of WordPress*

Like the Plugins section that I will be getting to shortly, WordPress enables you to download and install themes without ever leaving the administration screens. Figure 3.20 shows you what you start with to browse for *approved and tested* themes. Sometimes if you're too picky about colors and other features, you'll find yourself with few (if any) choices, so start broad and narrow it down only if you have too many results to go through.

Plugins Button

The plugins section is, obviously, where you manage the plugins you are using to enhance your WordPress installation (see Figure 3.21). From this section, you can

Figure 3.20   *The Install Themes screen, where you can select the parameters you are looking for and see what themes match*

turn plugins on and off (activate/deactivate), update, and add new plugins to your WordPress install. Day to day, most often you'll be updating plugins, and now in WordPress 3.0, you'll be able to update several plugins at once via the Updates section of the Dashboard panel.

Installing plugins used to be a lot more difficult than it is now. Previously, once you found the plugin you wanted to try (usually through WordPress.org), you had to download the archive to your computer, unzip it, upload the plugin to your site, and then activate it. Now clicking the Add New link (or button at the top of the plugins list), you can choose from a list of Featured, Popular, Newest, or Recently Updated plugins, as well as search for plugins using the search form (see Figure 3.22). If you have already downloaded the plugin archive, you can use the Upload link to upload and install that plugin (see Figure 3.23).

In Chapter 6, "Finding and Using Plugins," I'll cover all the different ways to find and install plugins, as well as how to configure some of the more popular (and useful) WordPress plugins.

Figure 3.21 *The Manage Plugins screen, where you can turn plugins on and off as well as update or delete them.*

Users Button

Blogs just don't write themselves; users have to manage them. Clicking on the Users button brings up the current list of users for the blog. As you can see, this blog has *two* users. When you install WordPress, the Admin user is automatically created and a random password is generated for the account. The Admin user has the keys to the kingdom with Administrator privileges on the blog. When I start a new blog, I also create another user who has Administrator privileges, and then demote the original Admin user down to a lowly Subscriber (or delete it entirely), as shown in Figure 3.24. This is just one of many little security measures you can take to protect your WordPress install that I'll be talking about in Chapter 14, "Understanding WordPress Security."

As you would expect, Add New under Users enables you to create new users for the blog. An important note here is that although *names* can be re-used, *usernames* and *email addresses* must be unique. So, you can have two Bill Smiths, but they must have different usernames for logging in ("Bill" and "bsmith" would work), and each has to have a different email address. What about creating a dupli- cate account for yourself? How do you manage the unique email problem? For me,

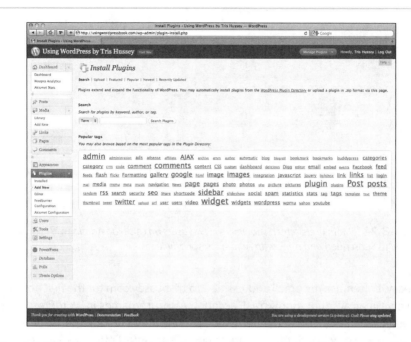

Figure 3.22 *Main install plugins screen showing the tag cloud of the various types of plugins you can choose from, as well as popular, new, and featured plugins*

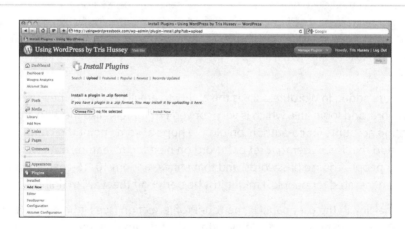

Figure 3.23 *Upload screen for when you have a plugin archive already downloaded to your computer and you'd like to upload it to your blog*

Figure 3.24   *Main users screen showing the two users on this blog Admin (with privileges reduced to Subscriber) and mine with Administrator privileges*

it's easy. I often use my email address tied to trishussey.com for the first account and my Gmail account for my "real" account. Also, usernames in WordPress are *case sensitive*, so Bill and bill are different and are considered unique usernames. You can also have a two-word (or three-word, I guess) username; I often use variations of my name as login names.

Gmail doesn't care about periods! If you created a Gmail address like bill.smith@gmail.com, billsmith@gmail.com *is exactly the same email address* as far as Gmail is concerned, but to WordPress, they are different! You can also mix it up with bill.smith+WordPress@gmail.com—this is not only unique, but you can also use it to filter emails!

A feature added in WordPress 2.8 is the ability to email new users their username, password, and login link, which is very convenient for folks like me who are often creating accounts for co-authors on blogs. I hope at some point the WordPress folks add the "force user to reset password on next login" feature, but given how poorly people choose passwords, and that I have random 10–15-character passwords generated for people, I might just be better off the way I'm doing it now.

The final link in the user panel is the Your Profile section (see Figure 3.25), which enables users to update and edit everything to do with their profiles/accounts on your blog *except* for their usernames. Sorry, usernames are set in stone. There is a lot that can be done with the information users put into their profiles, but the funny thing is that few people actually *do* anything with the data. I just set my name and display name, and leave it at that. That said, more themes are adding

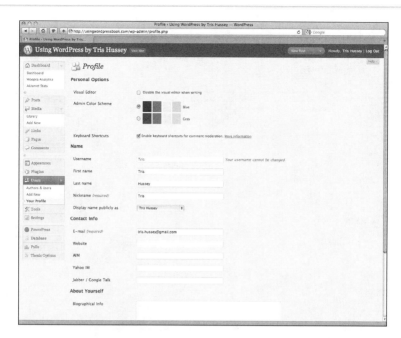

Figure 3.25   *User profile page where you add information about yourself, update your email address, and change your password*

"About Me" support that could pull from the biographical info field and into your theme. If you find a theme that uses that info, then by all means fill it in!

Tools Button

The Tools button brings you to a pretty interesting set of WordPress, well, tools (see Figure 3.26). You won't need to go to this section of the Administration area very often—maybe only when you first install WordPress and, after that, only if you need to convert tags to categories (or vice versa), import new content into your blog from another blog or export your content to a file. The Import and Export sections work just as you'd expect and have improved significantly over the last several versions of WordPress. So, let's get down to business and check out the Tools button.

Press This

Have you ever wondered how some bloggers seem to be able to crank out a *ton* of content in a day? How can they switch back and forth between browser windows or tabs to do it? They don't. What they do is either use a blog editor or a quick-posting

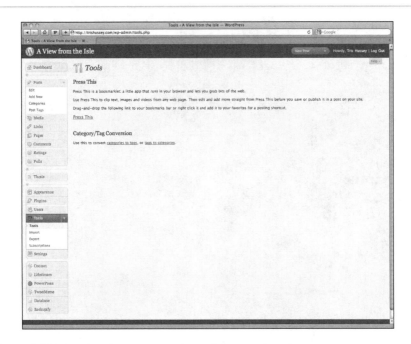

Figure 3.26   *Main tools screen Press This and Category-Tag Conversion sections*

bookmarklet like Press This (as in WordPress This). To start using Press This, just drag the link to your browser's bookmark/favorite bar, and when you're on a site or article you'd like to blog about, click Press This; you'll get a new window (or tab) where you can start the post (see Figure 3.27). When you're done, click Publish and, well, it's published. I used this kind of tool for years and years when I first started blogging. Calling it "handy" doesn't nearly do Press This justice.

Category/Tag Conversion

If you found that you have some categories that should have been tags or tags you've used so much that you really want to make them categories (so they can be on a menu for example), this is the place to start. Clicking on either of the links will bring you to a section of the Import area that handles Category-Tag conversions. Figure 3.28 show the Categories to Tags window from my blog. The Tags to Categories screen looks identical to this one and works in the same way.

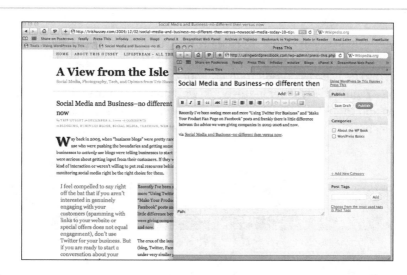

Figure 3.27   *Press This in action, creating a post based on one of my other posts*

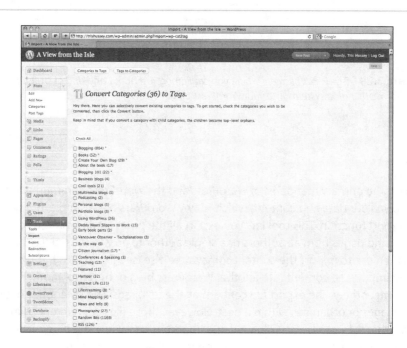

Figure 3.28   *Categories to Tags conversion screen. I'll talk more about this in Chapter 8.*

Import

Clicking the Import link brings you a page with a list of all the different ways to import content into your WordPress-powered site (see Figure 3.29). These are intended to be used as one-off tools and not as ways to feed content into your blog on a regular basis. Later in the book, we'll go through the different ways that you can and should use these tools to not only consolidate or import websites into your site, but also to manage categories and tags.

Figure 3.29 *The import screen, where you can import just about any kind of structured data from other blog systems into your WordPress blog*

Export

One of the primary mandates of WordPress and the WordPress community is that you own your data and content, which is why WordPress has a simple, but powerful, Export function. This tool lets you export all the posts (and comments on those posts) and pages from all authors or a single author to an XML-based file that you can then use to import the content somewhere else (see Figure 3.30). You can take it and import the content into another WordPress blog or move to another blog platform entirely. The export file contains all the text, tags, and categories but not any images or other files within a post. However, those files are referenced in such a way that they can be downloaded and imported into your next blog platform. This seems only fair, since you own your data and all.

Figure 3.30 *Simple and straightforward export screen. You own your content, not the blog system you happen to be using.*

Settings

Settings is the meat of what you'll adjust to make your WordPress install walk, talk, bark, dance, twirl, and do whatever you want it to do. Will you be mucking about here often? Probably not; most these settings are the "fire and forget" kind. Also, I'm not going to detail the settings you should use here, just *what's here*, because this is simply a tour. Chapter 4, "Configuring WordPress to Work Its Best," is where I'll delve into the nitty-gritty of the settings and why I choose the settings I use.

General

When you click the Settings button, you drop into the General settings first (see Figure 3.31). This panel covers the blog name, tagline, time zone, date format, and other basic settings. Once your blog is set up and going, you'll come here once to get things in order and then probably never look at it again.

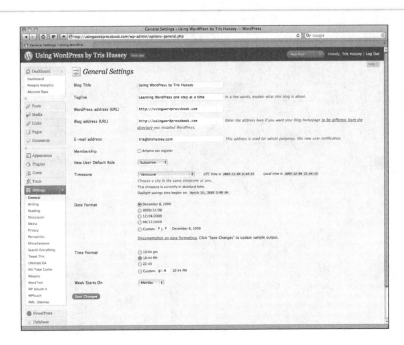

Figure 3.31   *General settings screen—one of the many settings you'll set once and rarely ever come back to adjust*

Writing

The Writing link is a little deceptive in its wording. There isn't too much about "writing" per se, but more like "what do I do with posts." The settings here cover default post and blogroll categories and setting up remote posting either through a blog editor or email (see Figure 3.32). You guessed it...another "just visit once then probably never again" type of panel. This is good, really—lots of these basic settings within WordPress are "fire and forget," which is great for me, because I forget stuff a lot.

Reading

The Reading section covers not only how many posts appear on the front page of your blog (from one to many) and your RSS feed, but also if the home page of your blog displays a static page or your posts (see Figure 3.33). Being able to make your home page a static page enables you to turn a WordPress "blog" into a website powered by WordPress with just a few clicks. I'll cover this coolness in Chapter 10, "Creating Sites with WordPress." Creating a site with WordPress is so easy and popular that it is the class I am most often asked to teach (generally about one a month, at least).

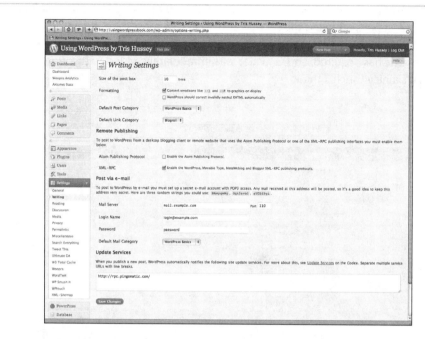

Figure 3.32 *Writing settings that have less to do with writing as they do with publishing*

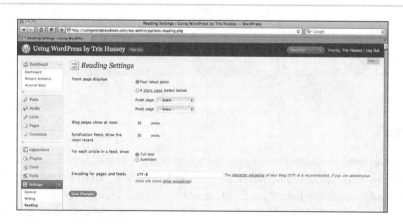

Figure 3.33 *Reading settings, which are more about your RSS feed and how people see your blog than about text or reading (that is, covered by Appearance)*

Discussion

Heading down to Discussion settings gives you the most cluttered-looking settings screen so far (see Figure 3.34). Don't worry, though—you'll rarely need to come back here, and the number of settings you will have to change here are minimal. The coolest part, I think, is the section at the bottom for setting the avatars for people when they leave comments. The Gravatar service is one of the groups that Automattic has acquired, and Gravatar was immediately added to the WordPress core. It's a nice touch, I think.

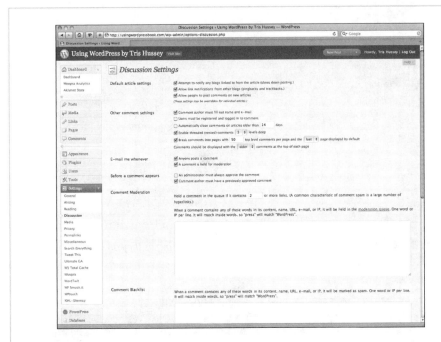

Figure 3.34   *Discussion settings—lots of options here, but really only a few settings to change*

Media

We now come to another semi-poorly named section, Media, which has more to do with how to *display* media than *adding* it (see Figure 3.35). In this screen, you'll set the size for the automatically resized versions of all the images you upload (which, by the way, is a *supremely* handy function that you'll make use of *a lot*). New in WordPress 2.9 is the ability to use oEmbed and set maximum embed sizes. These handy functions are ones that you'll probably just enjoy using without really knowing you're using them. Media embedding and image resizing fall under the category of *automagic* because they work not only automatically, but so automatically that it's like magic—hence, "automagic." Yes, this is a real word in geekdom. Feel free to drop it into conversations to impress your friends at home with how geeky-cool you are.

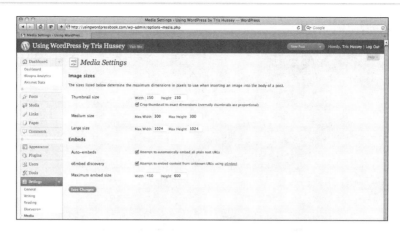

Figure 3.35 *Media settings. Very rarely will you need to adjust things here, but if you do, the options are clear and straightforward.*

Automagic (n): A process carried out automatically in such a clever way that the result appears to be magic. Related to Clarke's Third Law: Any sufficiently advanced technology is indistinguishable from magic. *(Source: Wikipedia)*

Privacy

The Privacy panel should really just be dumped in with General, I think. There is just one option, and 99% of people never change it (see Figure 3.36). Yes, I would like search engines to find my blog, thank you.

Permalinks

Permalinks is one of the fire-and-forget panels, but it is also *essential* that you not forget to go there and change the settings. This one setting will probably do more to help your site's effectiveness with search engines than any other. (If you block it from search engines, however, the point is a little moot.) It's here that you determine how the URLs will look to both users and search engines on your blog. As shown in Figure 3.37, the default is /?p=123 (the number being the post ID number), which doesn't tell anyone anything about the post or page. Compare this with the Day and name or Month and name options. It's pretty obvious that you'll be able to give everyone a good idea of the post topic with a halfway-decent post title.

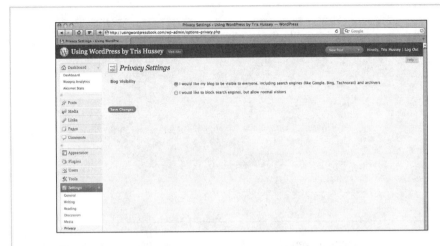

Figure 3.36   *Privacy settings*

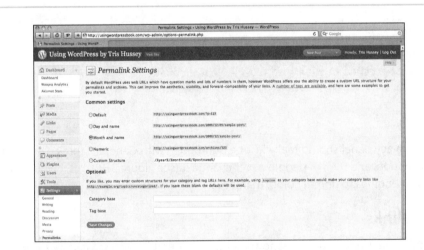

Figure 3.37   *Permalinks might seem daunting, but the setting is easy and essential.*

Other Settings

As you've seen from the screenshots throughout the chapter, I have *a lot* more settings under the Settings button than I've talked about here—not to mention the
buttons *below* Settings that you might be wondering about. These settings are for
the various plugins and themes I'm using on this blog. When you add and activate
a new plugin or theme, check Settings first; then glance down to see if there is a
new button at the end of the column.

Plugins

When you install a plugin, 99% of the time it's going to include a settings area, and most of the time, you'll find these settings under Settings. Some plugins put their settings under Plugins (Akismet is one of those), and WordPress 2.7 plugins can add their own button to the Administration panel. Having a button of its own lets the plugin (and now theme) author have a more compact and elegant way to offer multiple settings options than if they were just under Plugins.

Themes

Since WordPress 2.8, theme developers have also been able to add their own buttons to the Administration area. This has been a bigger boon to them than plugin authors, I think. Themes are now offering more and more user-customizable options through the Administration area—things we could only achieve with editing the theme files themselves. Several of the themes I like to use are taking advantage of this, including the Thesis theme, which I'll be covering in-depth in Chapter 7.

 SHOW ME   Media 3.3—Secrets of the Dashboard
Access this video file through your registered Web Edition at
my.safaribooksonline.com/9780132182836/media

WordPress.com Notes

As you can see in Figure 3.38, the blocks, buttons, and sub-menus are very similar between the version of WordPress (left and blue) you install yourself and WordPress.com (right and gray). Keep in mind that the example WordPress installation I've been using for this chapter includes many of the core plugins that I'll be talking about in later chapters. Note that under Appearance, there is no "Add New" link on WordPress.com (because you can't add additional themes), and there is no Plugins button at all (because you can't add plugins to WordPress.com).

I think one of the keys to notice are the overwhelming similarities but also the important differences. WordPress.com is a *hosted* blog platform; this means that to maintain stability for all users, a common feature set has to be agreed upon. New themes are only added after they have been vetted for not only aesthetics, but also ease of use and stability. New features are added (like iPhone compatibility and polls) only after the system administrators at Automattic know that the features work well, but don't compromise security in the process.

Figure 3.38   *WordPress (my install) compared to WordPress.com menus—very similar, but different, too*

Throughout the remainder of the book, I'll end the chapters with WordPress.com notes if there are significant differences between the experience of using WordPress.com and a self-installed version.

TELL ME MORE   **Media 3.4—Do WordPress Settings Make Sense?**

Access this audio recording through your registered Web Edition at
my.safaribooksonline.com/9780132182836/media

Learn all the settings to help your site run its best
and stay secure from hackers.

4

Configuring WordPress to Work Its Best

Now that you have the roadmap around the administration area of WordPress, it's time to get things going to configure and tune your WP install. As I'm sure you noticed when going through all the various parts of the administration area in WordPress, there is *a lot* that you *don't* have to configure. Unlike a lot of CMS systems, WordPress works pretty darn well out-of-the-box. Sure, a tweak here and there will whip it into shape, but overall WP is good to go from the moment it's installed.

In this chapter, we're going to walk through the few things you will have to configure (maybe *tailor* is a better word) in your WP install. From there, I'm going to get into managing comments, because although there aren't really any settings *per se*, a few things you set up from the start will help you manage the deluge of spam that will start hitting your site all too soon enough. We'll also discuss managing authors on your blog. Whether you are going to have the occasional guest poster or regular contributors, you don't have to open up your blog and all its inner workings just so someone can post.

The last part I'll cover is the semi-controversial topic of caching and page compression. Although WP is a pretty efficient CMS, if your site starts getting hundreds of visits an hour, you might start having problems serving content to all your visitors, unless you set up some very basic (and easy) caching methods that can keep your site up and running as you enjoy your 15KB of fame.

So, let's kick things off with the basic WP settings you'll need to worry about.

Choosing the Right Settings for Your Blog

The basic settings we're going to talk about in this section are under the General, Writing, Reading, and Discussion parts of settings. For the most part, the default settings for Media and Privacy are fine as they are. All of the settings are going to be very easy—just simple form fields, radio buttons, menus, and check boxes, until we get to Permalinks. If your host is one that works well with WordPress, changes on that screen will take effect without issue or intervention from you. If not, that's

okay; you'll just get to put another notch in your geek belt by creating your first
.htaccess file. Don't worry—if you've gotten this far, you're going to be fine with
.htaccess. All you need to know how to do is copy and paste, save, and FTP the file.
Not much different than what you needed to do to set up WordPress in the first
place!

 SHOW ME Media 4.1—What Are the Best Settings for WordPress?
Access this video file through your registered Web Edition at
my.safaribooksonline.com/9780132182836/media

Basic Settings

I hope you're not expecting a long, drawn-out series of steps to get all the settings
down for WordPress, because frankly, there aren't any. When you click the Settings
button, the General Settings screen is what you start with (see Figure 4.1). There are
only a couple things that I always make sure are set right.

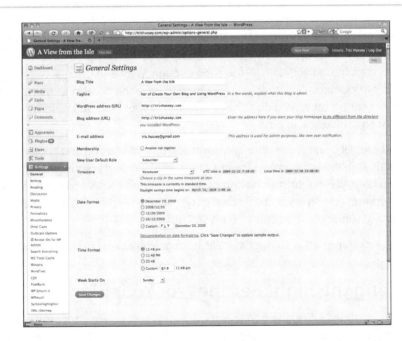

Figure 4.1 *General settings—just the basics here, and ones that everyone should visit and
adjust*

The first is the Blog Title. You might have just dashed off a title when you installed WordPress, but now is the time to think about a better title. No, my title isn't a great one, but that is because of some extra goodies I have installed with my template (Thesis). Generally, your title should be descriptive enough to give people a good idea of what your blog is about. The field right below your Blog Title is your Tagline. The Tagline is like the subtitle of a book. It gives a bit of information and context to really put your site's topic firmly in people's minds.

My Blog Title is "A View from the Isle" and my Tagline is "Social Media News, WordPress Info and Opinion from Tris Hussey author of Create Your Own Blog and Using WordPress." My blog has been called "A View from the Isle" since I started it in 2004 (when I lived on a small island of 10,000 people); although I don't live on an island anymore, I'm loathe to change it after all these years. My Tagline *has* evolved over the years, depending on what my focus was and what I learned from various search engine optimization gurus. As you can gather, I'm associating my name with terms like WordPress and social media. I look at my Tagline every few months just to make sure I like what it says. Looking at it now, I'm thinking it's going to need a change in a short while.

The next, and last, setting I manage is setting my Timezone. Depending on your server configuration, you will see either a list of cities organized by region (like the Americas, Europe, and Asia) or UTC +/– some number. If you've selected the UTC (coordinated universal time) option, North America is all negative UTC, and Europe is positive UTC. For example, New York and Toronto are –5 UTC, whereas LA and Vancouver are –8, unless it's daylight savings time. If you are lucky enough to have the city option, you never have to worry about daylight savings time—your time relative to UTC is adjusted for you (Vancouver is –8 during standard time and –7 during daylight savings). If you just have the +/– UTC option, you'll have to make the switch manually.

If you'd like to adjust the time and date formats and which day of the week your week starts on, that's up to you. (I just leave them as is myself.) Changing the day your week starts on only affects how the calendar widgets are displayed for you. (If you set it to Monday, Monday is the first column.)

Always remember to click Save Changes when you're done modifying settings.

Writing

The Writing Settings screen has a few options to work with (see Figure 4.2), but a couple of them you might not be ready to deal with at the moment (which is fine, don't worry). When you first set up WordPress, your Default Post and Link Categories will be Uncategorized (Post) and Blogroll (Link), and this is just fine for now.

You haven't created or edited your categories yet, so stick with the defaults for the moment. After you read Chapter 8, "Organizing the Content on Your Blog," you'll have a much better idea of how you'd like to organize your content, and you can come back here to change the settings. That said, the only change I make is to click the check box to enable XML-RPC. Just trust me on this—click the check box and then click Save Changes.

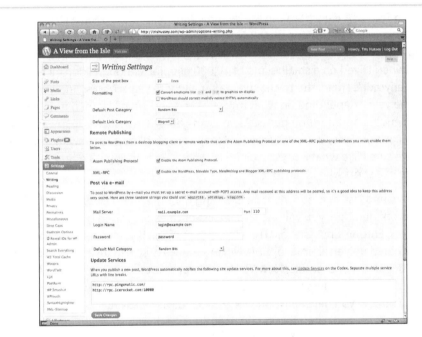

Figure 4.2   *Writing options with my core settings set (allowing XML-RPC and Atom posting)*

Another setting that some people like to modify is for the size of the post box. Some people increase the size beyond 10 lines (I find 25 to be a nice amount), but that is a personal preference. I'd stick with the default for now, and then increase the number if you feel cramped when you're writing a post.

Reading

The Reading Settings page is another interesting one because you don't have to change it from the defaults, and it isn't until you have had your blog around for a while that you might be interested in tweaking these settings (see Figure 4.3). The Front Page Displays setting is something that I'll cover in Chapter 10, "Creating

Sites with WordPress," because that setting lets you make your home page be more static and informational than "bloggy." It's a *very* powerful and handy feature and is the reason why I build a lot of "regular" websites using WordPress. The defaults for showing the number of posts per page and number of posts in your feed are both set at 10. You can increase or decrease these numbers to have different effects. On my blog, I have 11 posts showing because that keeps my layout even at the bottom (three featured posts and eight teasers). I set the Syndication Feeds Show the Most Recent option to 15 because 15 *used* to be the standard number, and out of nostalgia, I like to set it back to that. All it does is give my readers more content at once when they first subscribe to my feed.

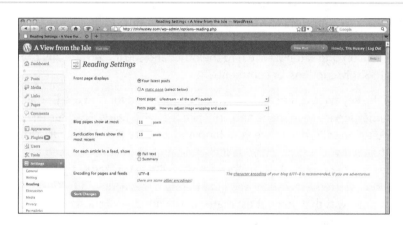

Figure 4.3   *Reading settings, full-text feed, and my non-standard settings*

RSS stands for Really Simple Syndication and is a computer-readable version of the posts on your blog. RSS is a structured file format that has been developed over the years to allow for simple checking for new content. RSS is essentially foolproof now, so you don't have to worry about configuring anything. Although RSS feeds from sites aren't intended to be read by people, using an RSS reader lets you keep up with the updates from hundreds of blogs without having to visit them. An RSS Reader takes the RSS feed and formats it into something easy to read. The best explanation of RSS is from my friends Lee and Sachi LeFever: http://www.commoncraft.com/rss_plain_english. Oh, and don't miss "Surviving a Zombie Attack in Plain English."

The RSS section in the Reading pane has a *huge* amount of baggage associated with it. There have been debates raging for *years* whether you should have the entire text of your post (full text) or a portion (Summary) in your RSS feed. It comes down to this: traffic to your website. When people read your RSS feed in their RSS feed reader (which is like an email program and Google's Google Reader is the current favorite RSS reader going); if there is an excerpt, they have to click to visit your blog to read the rest of the post instead of viewing the whole post in the feed reader. If you are getting money from advertising or just want more traffic to your actual website, using excerpts makes sense. On the other hand, by providing a full-text feed, you let people choose to do what they want. They can read the whole post in the email or click through. I've experimented with both excerpted feed and full-text feeds, and I use full-text feeds—not because I don't care about traffic to my site (because I do), but because when I'm reading feeds in my feed reader, I prefer full-text feeds. I *like* to be able to read the whole post. Often I still click through because I want to share the post in some other way (blog it, share it on Twitter, or bookmark it for later). My advice is choose one setting and then use it on your blog for a month or two (maybe three, if your blog is new). After you have a good baseline of data on one setting, switch to the other and see if there are any changes in traffic, RSS subscriptions, or comments.

One of the key tweaks that a lot of WordPress users go for is to use Google's FeedBurner service to manage and enhance their RSS feeds. FeedBurner works like this: You tell FeedBurner where your blog and feed are (FeedBurner is smart enough that if you just give it your site's main URL, it will find the feed for you) and then FeedBurner republishes the feed for you with extra features. When FeedBurner started a few years ago (and before being acquired by Google), the biggest draw was that you got estimates of the number of subscribers you had. This was critical data in the days when we were trying to understand the reach and power of blogging. In addition to metrics, FeedBurner also provided formatting and features to help make your feed compatible with all RSS readers and bots, as well as subscribing to your blog updates via email. These days, some of the compatibility features aren't too important, but the metrics are still important (and perhaps more so now that more businesses are using blogs for marketing and so on).

The key to making FeedBurner really work for you is to set up your blog so it serves the FeedBurner feed to your visitors instead of serving the "default" feed. There are several ways to do this. One is a WordPress plugin that, lo and behold, you'll be offered as you complete the FeedBurner sign-up process. You can also edit your theme's header.php file to do the same thing, and many themes offer a FeedBurner substitution built in. For my time, I go with the plugin route. When you edit the theme to make the switch, if you change themes, you might forget to make the change and have some people subscribing to one feed while other subscribers use another feed, which wouldn't matter with regard to your content. This discrepancy, though, would matter to your metrics. You'll have data from some readers, but not from others. Even if you remember to flip back, you'll still have readers on the old feed. You don't, however, want to break the connection to the original feed because that will certainly lose you RSS readers. Has this happened to me? You bet it has, and it takes a while to build back readership. My advice: Set up with FeedBurner, use the plugin, and enjoy the data. You'll thank me later.

Discussion

The last of the easy changes is found under Discussion (see Figure 4.4). Again, WordPress has done a good job with making the default settings pretty much dead on for 99% of people. I'm one of those 1% who just feels like I *have* to make a change, so I do, but only one. Nested comments were introduced in WordPress 2.8, which means that you can reply to a comment on one of your posts so that your reply is below and indented to the one you're replying to. This way, instead of just having a situation where you reply several comments down from the original, you comment *right below it* so everyone understands the context. Why this isn't enabled by default I don't know, but I always turn it on and leave the max set to five levels deep. I'll talk more about managing comments and moderation later in this chapter because it will make more sense once we get into spam and comments and that whole rigmarole.

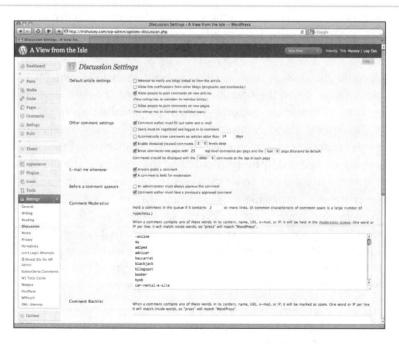

Figure 4.4   *Top half of the discussion settings, and the only ones I change—enabling nested comments*

Miscellaneous, Media, and Privacy

The Media and Privacy screens don't need changes, as far as I'm concerned. For some site designs, I've altered the default thumbnail size under Media settings, but that's pretty much it. The next, and last, basic setting we have to do is setting the (pretty) permalinks.

Permalinks

Before I get into how, and why, you set up your permalinks, you probably want to know what the heck a permalink is in the first place. Permalink is short for *permanent link*, meaning a link or webpage address (that is, the URL) that is permanent and bookmarkable. When websites first started to be run using databases to store content and templates to display the content, often you couldn't bookmark a link to a page. Back then, each page, essentially, existed only once and only for as long as a person was at the site. This also meant that Google and other search engines couldn't index the site well (if at all) because there were few real links to pages. All the pages were rendered when someone wanted to go there—something a search engine bot just couldn't replicate. From the beginning, blogs like WordPress, it was decided to fix that problem and create indexable, spiderable permanent links for all the content on the site. Even the technically dynamic content (like a listing of all the posts from a certain category) has a permanent link that can be bookmarked.

So, what could you possibly want to change about permalinks? What we want to tweak and change is how the permalinks are *formatted*. The default permalink structure in WordPress looks something like http://yoursite.com/?p=221. The 221 is the post ID number. Although this is okay, and can be bookmarked just dandy, it doesn't give readers, or search engines, much information about the post. The better way to do it is just supply more information that you have at hand in the link, like the year, month, and day on which it was posted and what the post title is. For example, on my site, permalinks look like http://trishussey.com/2009/12/09/ sometimes-you-just-have-to-write/. You can see when it was published (December 9, 2009) and the title (or at least part of it). That is a pretty (though rather long) permalink. Pretty permalinks not only are easier to read and understand in the *address bar*, but *search engines* also understand their contextual clues. Consequently, you have a much better ranked and easier-to-navigate site.

Changing your site's permalink is as easy as picking one of the options *other than* default; my suggestion is either Day and name (the setting for my blog) or Month and name (my preferred setting for new sites now), as shown in Figure 4.5. When you click the Save Changes button, you will see one of two messages: Permalink Structure Updated or You Should Update Your .htaccess File Now. The first means you're good to go, and you can move on to other configuration settings on your blog; the second means we have a little copying and pasting to do.

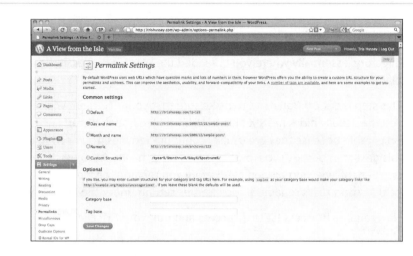

Figure 4.5 *Permalink settings, which seem simple but are essential to your blog*

LET ME TRY IT

If your permalinks don't automatically update and you get the You Should Update Your .htaccess File Now message, you'll need to edit the file yourself. Don't worry, it's a piece of cake.

To manually update your .htaccess file, you'll need your handy text editor (as mentioned in Chapter 2, "Installing WordPress on Your Own Server") and your FTP client:

1. Fire up that text editor with a new, empty file.

2. Select and copy the code at the bottom of the Permalink Settings screen. They should look something like this:

```
# BEGIN WordPress
<IfModule mod_rewrite.c>
RewriteEngine On
RewriteBase /
RewriteCond %{REQUEST_FILENAME} !-f
RewriteCond %{REQUEST_FILENAME} !-d
RewriteRule . /index.php [L]
</IfModule>
# END WordPress
```

3. Paste in the empty file open in the text editor and save. What to name the file is a bit tricky, but I'm going to suggest naming it **htaccess.txt** for now. You're going to need to rename it after you upload it to your server, but that's not hard.

4. Open your FTP client and connect to your server. Upload the htaccess.txt file to the root of your server. This is usually going to be in public_html directory, essentially where you uploaded the WordPress files in the first place.

5. This step is critical. You need to make sure that your FTP client will show you the usually hidden UNIX files. In UNIX, a filename that starts with "." isn't visible because they are usually configuration files. You need to do this next step because you're going to rename the file .htaccess; if you don't enable viewing hidden files before you rename the file, it will disappear as soon as it's renamed. Look for this setting under the "View" menu.

6. Now rename htaccess.txt to **.htaccess** and quit your FTP client.

7. Return to the Permalink Settings page and refresh your browser. If you did it correctly, the error messages you saw before will be gone.

Now with your settings all in place, we can move onto some of the other settings that help make your WordPress install work more smoothly. Next up—dealing with comments.

Moderating Comments and Comment Spam

Comments can be one of the best things about your blog. They continue the discussion, give solace, and turn your blog from a monologue into a community. There's a dark side of comments though: comment spam. Just like the spam you get in your email Inbox, comment spam has the same goal and same effect. There are two ways to manage comments. The first is simple moderation. Before a comment is posted, if the commenter is determined to be new (based on the email address) or the comment contains two or more links, or certain keywords are in the comment, you receive an email to notify you that there is a comment waiting for your approval (or disapproval).

Moderation works extremely well, except when there is a flood of comments and 99.9% of them are actually spam comments. That can clog your Inbox in minutes and take a lot of time to go through. It wasn't always like this, however; comment spam didn't kick in until 2006 or 2007, but when it did, it hit us all like a steam train. To combat the deluge of spam, anti-spam plugins were created to intercept all the comments coming in; if the comments match certain criteria, you never see them—they just go into the spam folder on your blog. Before I get into how to pick out comment spam when it squeaks through into the moderation queue, I'm going to go into moderation itself.

Moderation

The default settings for WordPress are good, and getting better. If someone hasn't left a comment before, you have to approve the comment before it will be posted. Not only that, if you happen to approve a sneaky spam comment, the door isn't completely open—if the later comments have lots of links (two or more) or certain keywords (the generally spammy ones), the comment is thrown *back* into moderation. Moderation is, in fact, your *second* line of defense against blog spam; your first line should be made up of one or more anti-spam plugins. Anti-spam plugins intercept all comments *before* they hit the moderation queue and see if they seem spammy, and if so, you never see them. Comments in the spam queue are automatically dumped after 30 days, but you can also manually purge the spam comments as well. One concern is having legitimate comments wind up in the spam folder, never to see the light of day. This does happen, albeit more rarely now, so I skim my spam comments folder just to double check. I might do this once or twice a week, unless I've written a tremendously popular post; then I'll check more often.

My anti-spam plugin of choice is Akismet, which is installed (but not activated) by default with all WordPress installs. When you activate Akismet, you'll be asked (well, nagged, I guess) to enter a WordPress.com API key. Don't worry; this isn't going to take a lot of time or cost you anything. All you need to do is go to WordPress.com and sign up for an account (you can choose just an account or create a WP.com blog as well, it doesn't matter); when you select Edit Profile from the My Account menu, right at the top of your profile is your API key (see Figure 4.6). Select the text, copy it to the clipboard, and return to your blog. Click on one of the messages telling you to enter the API key, paste it into the field, and click Update Options. All the red should turn to green, and then you're good to go.

Akismet works using a set of rules that indicate what is likely spam. Also, when a spam comment slips through to you, and you mark it spam as you're moderating comments, Akismet *learns* that the comment is spam. The same is true for legitimate comments that get marked as spam; when you "unspam" them, Akismet learns. Sure one blog marking one comment spam isn't going to help very much, but Akismet is used by millions of WordPress blogs and is automatically active for all WordPress.com blogs. This tremendous user base gives Akismet a huge dataset to work with to help us all pull out the wheat from the chaff.

Moderating comments is a one-click affair from either email or the Dashboard. When a comment comes in for moderation, you'll receive an email and have the option to approve, mark as spam, or delete. Just clicking on the appropriate link

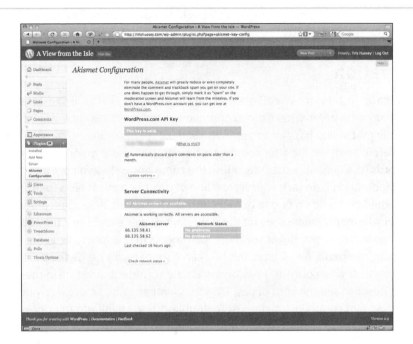

Figure 4.6   *Akismet configured with a valid API key that you get from WordPress.com*

will bring you to a confirmation screen on your blog; click your confirmation, and you're done.

If you visit your blog's Dashboard, you'll see the pending comments in yellow and a number beside the "Pending" in the "At a Glance" section. You can click the number and see all the pending comments or hover your mouse below a comment to see the options for that comment (Approve/Unapprove, Reply, Spam, Edit, or Trash). I generally manage comments by clicking the email link, unless I have more than more than a couple to deal with. Bulk management of comments? Not a problem. Like all WordPress listings (posts, pages, categories, and so on), you can select more than one comment and have WordPress complete an action for you.

A lot of spam is dead easy to pick out, but spammers are becoming very clever at masking that their seemingly "real" comment is actually spam. Picking out spam sometimes takes more than a casual glance; you need to know what to look for.

Comment Spam

SHOW ME   **Media 4.2—How to Pick Out Spam Comments**
Access this video file through your registered Web Edition at
my.safaribooksonline.com/9780132182836/media

It used to be picking out comment and trackback spam was dead easy. It isn't that spammers were less clever than they are now, they didn't *need* to be clever. Since moderation and spam filters were very new, a lot got through, at least for a little while, so that was good enough for them. Now, our filters and moderation tools are much better, so spammers are being, somewhat, more subtle. Following are a few comments that came into my blog recently—some are spam, and some aren't. Can you guess which is which?

1. Heh, you're funny! And yeah, do let me know...e-resources are always great to have.

2. How private is my computer (from gov't)? What about public library computers? Blithe assurances are not helpful. What can a person do to avoid privacy invasions?

3. I liked it. So much useful material. I read with great interest.

4. Are you a professional journalist? You write very well.

5. This is cool news. Thank you.

6. Yes, I absolutely agree with you, I am working on it too! Thanks.

7. Interesting and informative. But will you write about this one more?

8. Any updates coming?

Only comments 1 and 2 are real (I wonder about #2 actually, so I'm watching for strange comments posted); all the others are from spam bots. What gives them away? Spelling errors? Bad grammar? Nope. For all of these comments, the "name" submitted was either random characters, a drug name, or in non-English characters. The email addresses were from Russia (.ru), or the domain names were made up of just random letters, or there was something like a drug name as the email. Finally, the site they link to was either a spam site or google.com (an age-old trick). The comments with links in them are more obvious because when you mouse over the link, you see the destination in your browser's status bar, and the website URL looks pretty suspicious. I *do not* recommend that you click on the links to "just check them out myself" because often these spam sites can also deliver a payload of spyware to visitors as a bonus. I only visit suspicious sites when I am really, really not sure if they are spam. Figure 4.7 shows a selection of spam comments from my blog. Charming aren't they? Not.

Fun, huh? Okay, not so much, but Akismet is solid enough now that most of the time you won't ever see this stuff at all. Once in a while, there is a spam storm, and Akismet needs to be significantly updated to manage the new tricks. Again, don't worry—this doesn't happen very often, and when it does, clicking the Check for Spam under the Pending area will clear out the newly identified spam for you.

Figure 4.7 *Some spam comments are obvious, and others aren't. I tend to err on the side of caution instead of letting borderline comments through.*

Part of the secret sauce of Akismet is that there are some high-traffic blogs in a neutral zone of spam on the edges of Akismet's protection; these blogs will bear the brunt of the first wave of a new spam storm for the rest of us. The logic is that those sites receive so much traffic, when a new storm approaches, they would be high on the list of targets; by making them the first line of defense, the *rest* of us are spared the worst of the storm. These weather-glass blogs mark the new spam as "spam." Akismet learns and updates automatically for everyone else.

If it's any consolation, when you start getting comment and trackback spam, it means that Google has crawled, indexed, and listed your blog. There is always a silver lining, even to comment spam.

Managing Additional Authors on Your Blog

SHOW ME   Media 4.3—Picking the Right User Roles for Security
Access this video file through your registered Web Edition at
my.safaribooksonline.com/9780132182836/media

Most people have single author blogs and won't add additional users, except for disabling the admin user for security reasons, but there are a lot of multi-author blogs or blogs that have occasional guest authors, so let's get into the ins and outs of user management. The key for user management is understanding the capabilities that each role has assigned to it. Making sure someone doesn't have too many privileges on your blog is far more important than them having too few. There are five levels of user roles in WordPress, ranging from Administrator (keys to the kingdom) to Subscriber (can only read and leave comments). The WordPress codex goes into mind-numbing (but essential for developers) detail on each role, but here is a good summary of each one:

- **Administrator:** Administrators have access to all functions of the blog. This is the master controller account, and you should only give Admin privileges to users who can be trusted with them. A user with Admin privileges (there can be more than one user with the role of Administrator) can take down a blog by accident or on purpose. In the wrong hands...well, you can guess. Giving the wrong users Admin accounts is what gives guys like me ulcers and keeps us up at night.

- **Editor:** Editors have an all-access pass to everything content related, but no settings. The Editor role can read, publish, and delete posts, pages, links, categories, and tags. Essentially, if it has to do with content, a user with Editor privileges can manage it. There are many security experts who recommend that you create an account for yourself with Editor privileges and use that account for your day-to-day writing and posting—the theory being if that account is compromised, the blog can't be completely wrecked, whereas a compromised Admin-level account can be a very bad thing indeed. You'll still need the Admin account to manage the blog, but only log in with that account when you need that level of access. The Editor is also a great role on a multi-author blog for a person who you not only trust to publish, but can also manage other peoples' work as well.

- **Author:** Authors can write and post their own material, but they can't edit anyone else's or add new categories or links to the blog. This is the kind of person who you trust can write and publish on their own without you worrying about what he or she is writing about.

- **Contributor:** Contributors can write their own posts, but they can't publish the post to make it live on the blog. This is the good level for a guest author. Sure, you asked her to write a post or two, but you'd really feel better if you can just give the post a once over before it goes live.

- **Subscriber:** Subscribers can only read the blog and leave comments. The only time I've found this role to be handy is if I'm using a mailing list plugin (so new subscribers will receive the email) or using a plugin to restrict access to registered users only. A Subscriber is a registered user, and that's about it.

Managing users in WordPress is, thankfully, a very easy process (see Figure 4.8). First, those privileges reside *only* with the Administrator role, so make sure you're logged in as Admin before trying to manage users. (You won't even be able to find the options, actually.) Clicking the Users button and then Add New will bring you to the screen to enter in all the details. The only *required* fields are the username, email address, and password. The rest the user can submit herself through the Your Profile link. Just above the Add User button is the menu to select the role; if you want the person to be anything more than a Subscriber, now is the time to change that.

Figure 4.8   *Adding new users to a WordPress blog*

If you need to make changes to existing users, clicking the Authors & Users link will give you a list of all the users on the blog with their role. As you can imagine, you can't edit your own *role* when you're logged into your account, but you can change your password, email, and other profile information. The only thing that cannot be changed, without deleting the user account entirely, is the username. Should you need to delete a user, you will be offered the option to delete all of that user's posts or assign him to another user. Unless you're going for the "you're dead to me" level of user deletion, I'd just reassign the posts to someone else.

Remember that the key to managing users is *trust*; you need to be able to trust the people with privileges high enough to post things live to the blog. Sure, an author can't really muck around with someone else's content, but he can certainly wreak havoc enough if the post gets you into hot water.

While we're on the subject of trust and what people post, let's spend a little time on passwords. I am pretty tough on passwords, even though I haven't always been. I expect people to use passwords that are considered "strong" or better (WordPress has a great little password-strength meter in the Add User and Your Profile sections), especially if they have Editor and higher privileges. The Administrator's password should be darn near impossible to guess or crack. I use a password manager to generate very long (15 characters) random passwords with letters, numbers, and symbols and then have one master password to unlock all the individual passwords. No, I don't know what the passwords are for individual sites, but I do know that all of the passwords are complex enough that it would take a very long time for them to be cracked. Why is this so important, even for just authors? Once one password is cracked, there is a chance that the hacker could find a way to do more damage than just delete a few posts. Maybe that author uses the same password for email, too; then their email is compromised, which could lead to other breaches in security. In 2009, the microblogging service Twitter was hacked because one person, and not even a core developer, used a weak password for email. From there, the hacker was able to get into Twitter's Google Docs account and learn other more-sensitive passwords (like to servers and so on). It was very embarrassing for Twitter and could have been a lot worse than it was. Yes, it seems overkill to have tons of unmemorable passwords, but it's important to me to set a high standard for security. I'll really get security crazy in Chapter 14, "Understanding WordPress Security." After that chapter, I know you'll think I'm a bit nuts—but it's better to be nuts than hacked.

How to Make an Easy-to-Remember, but Very Strong, Password

It's fine if you don't want to go to my extreme of random password generation; it does get cumbersome when I need access to some sites on the go, and I haven't a clue what the password is to a site or service. So, in addition to my random passwords, I have a few key passwords I create using the method I'm going to show you now. It's a fact of life that you *will* need to have at least a few passwords that you can remember, so let's make the ones you have to remember also extremely hard to guess.

What I do is to think of a word or phrase that I can easily remember. Something like "I like dark chocolate" is a good one to start with. If I put all those words together into ilikedarkchocolate, that's a pretty good password because it's long (eight characters is considered the minimum length for a strong password), but it uses common words, so hackers throwing every word in the dictionary at it will eventually succeed. The trick is then to start swapping out letters for numbers and symbols and adding things like "!" to make it even more complex, but easily remembered. I would take ilikedarkchocolate and turn it into 1l1k3d@rk(h0(0l@t3! making it seemingly random, but easy to remember. So letter i = 1, e = 3, a = @, c = (, and o = 0, which isn't hard to remember but scores as "best" according to a Microsoft online password tool found at http://www. microsoft.com/protect/fraud/passwords/checker.aspx and "Strong" in the WordPress password-strength indicator on the Profile and Add User screens.

See? Not hard at all. That's such a great password, I'm disappointed that I can't use it now myself!

TELL ME MORE   Media 4.4—User Roles and Security

Access this audio recording through your registered Web Edition at
my.safaribooksonline.com/9780132182836/media

Caching and Other Tune-Ups

One last part in our initial configuration of WordPress: tuning WordPress for best performance under pressure (high traffic). There is a little controversy surrounding this topic because Matt Mullenweg feels that WordPress can handle a lot of traffic without any help, whereas other folks think (as I do) that setting up a little caching on any site is a good thing to help it perform better and lessen server load. WordPress does have some built-in caching available by adding one little line to your wp-config.php file, as follows:

```
define( 'ENABLE_CACHE', true );
```

Although, technically, this works and will enable caching, I think I'd be remiss if I didn't give you a little more info on caching.

Here's the deal: When you go to a WordPress-based site, the page you're looking at is generated by running PHP scripts that call the MySQL database and pull everything together in seconds. Because webservers are so powerful now, we don't really notice any lag, but what if your site or post is featured on CNN? Well, all those sustained simultaneous requests will likely overwhelm the server because it has to serve out a fresh page to every visitor. Now with caching, there is a static version of that page that is stored until something on it changes (like a new comment, new post, or edit). Although the built-in WordPress caching might do a decent job, most of us turn to plugins like wp-supercache, wp-cache, or W3 Total Cache; these plug-ins not only cache the pages, but provide easier configuration options and additional features like compressing CSS files, PHP scripts, and other goodies (see Figure 4.9). In practical terms, all caching systems work by creating a copy *only when it is requested*, so the caches aren't creating a duplicate version of your site, just of the pages that are being requested often. Even then, the cached copy "expires" after a period of time so that the page is automatically refreshed in the cache.

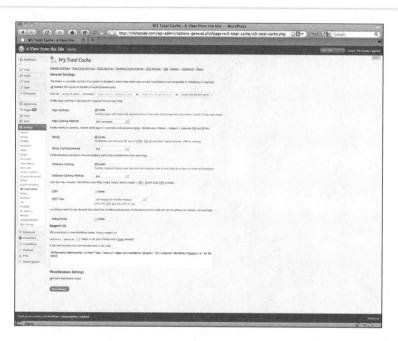

Figure 4.9 *My W3 Total Cache configuration screen. Doesn't look like much, but it protects my server from sudden traffic spikes.*

Okay, you're probably right; most sites *don't* need serious amounts of caching. However, I set up caching on all the sites I set up just to be ready. If nothing else, the site loads faster for visitors, and you're ready for a "just in case" moment.

For most WordPress users on shared hosting, setting up wp-supercache or W3 Total Cache is as far as you can go. There are some additional steps you can take, but these require setting up functions and features on the server you just won't have access to. Remember, this is okay because most WordPress users won't ever really need to have caching set up (I still recommend you do it, though), and if you run into a situation where you need that kind of high-end server performance, you'll have more server resources at your disposal.

WordPress.com Notes

On WordPress.com, your settings are going to be, for the most part, cosmetic tweaks. You can't change the permalinks (don't worry—your permalinks are pretty by default) or set up caching, but the same things apply for comments and users as with self-installed versions of WordPress. In Chapter 5, "How WordPress.com Is Different Than WordPress.org," I'm going to cover all the nuances of WordPress.com. The rule of thumb is that if I'm talking about uploading anything other than a picture, that's the realm of self-installed WordPress.

This chapter covers the difference between WordPress.com and WordPress.org—similarly named, but rather different parts of the WordPress family.

5

How WordPress.com Is Different Than WordPress.org

In the Introduction, I told you that WordPress.com and WordPress.org are related, but different, versions of WordPress. In Chapter 2, "Installing WordPress on Your Own Server," I talked about the WordPress.org side of things—that is, downloading and installing WordPress on your own web hosting account to run and manage yourself. In this chapter, I'm going to cover WordPress.com, how it differs from installing WordPress yourself (let's call it DIY WordPress), when it is a good choice over DIY, and how to tweak and tune your WordPress.com blog to work the best for you.

I think you'll find that DIY WordPress and WordPress.com blogs are complementary systems that you can use together to have several rich blogging environments at your fingertips.

As free blogging services go, WordPress.com is my hands-down favorite. Yes, I've tried others, but WordPress.com not only has a great balance of features, it also managed to do something that Google has yet to be able to do with its Blogger service: Keep it virtually free of spam blogs. Keeping WordPress.com free of spam blogs (that is, blogs with little or no original content and littered with ads) hasn't been easy, but the benefit to users has been that Google adds WordPress.com hosted blogs to their index very rapidly. Why? Trust. Google can trust that blogs hosted on WordPress.com are written by people.

WordPress.com and WordPress.org: Complementary Differences

If you remember from the Introduction, WordPress.com is a service run by Automattic that provides free, hosted blogs based on the WordPress Multiuser engine. There are two important parts to stress in that description: free and hosted. A hosted blog service is where someone else takes care of the server end of things, and you just log in and manage your own piece of the Internet. Essentially you skip what we covered in Chapters 2–4 and jump right into the writing and blogging part. You are probably familiar with other hosted services like Blogger, Gmail, AOL,

Hotmail, Yahoo! mail, and Google Docs, where you sign up for the service so you can do something online without having to know how you'd actually put it all together in the first place or bother with getting a web host or domain.

WordPress.com grew out of a very basic need that lots of people had: the need to run multiple blogs controlled with some central administration. Although DIY WordPress was designed to be a one-install, one-blog system, from nearly day one, people want to be able to run multiple blogs from one installation of WordPress.

From the outset, WordPress.com was intended to *complement*, not replace, DIY WP. Although WordPress.com is a fantastic place to have a free blog powered by the WordPress engine, because it is a hosted system, there are limitations to what you can do. You can't pick just any old theme and use it; there are a select number ("select" meaning more than 90 at present) of themes that you can use, you can't install your own plugins, and not all widgets or Flash-players are allowed within posts or in your sidebar.

The reason for these restrictions is simple: In a shared environment, stability and security have to be paramount (think of it like living in a college dorm). There can't be features that don't work flawlessly, themes that cause problems for readers, or JavaScript widgets that, although cool, might jeopardize the security of the whole system. Don't think for a moment that hosted systems are any less *powerful* than their DIY brethren—hosted systems are just as powerful, but they might not be as *flexible* as a system you'd install yourself. For example, on WordPress.com, you have to choose from specific, approved themes; if you install WordPress yourself, you have the choice of hundreds if not thousands more themes. It is the same powerful WordPress engine, but just limited in the fact that you can't just upload any old theme you'd like. Fair trade-off? Yeah, I'd say so.

Let's talk about the fact that WordPress.com is free for a moment. WordPress.com works off what we call the "freemium" model. There are core features and functions that are free, but if you'd like more storage space, or have the site use your own domain name or edit the style sheet, you need to pay for those options. For example, on WordPress.com, "free" means that you can't upload video or audio files and are limited to 3GB of storage for other files. It also means that once you pick your theme, you can only customize the look to a certain point. If you want more storage space or to edit the style sheet of the blog to change fonts or colors, you can pay for those privileges. Honestly, I think it's a good deal, and the prices that Automattic is charging for these extras are extremely reasonable. (When you look at them, you have to notice that the prices are *per year* and not *per month*.)

If you want a free blog, based on WordPress, but don't want the hassles (or cost) of a domain and webhost, WordPress.com is a great option. If you need more flexibility (like a 100% custom theme or specialized plugins), going DIY is the best option to consider. Don't worry, however: You can start a WordPress.com blog and then move to DIY with export-import functions and domain name magic. So, what are you waiting for? Let's sign up now.

Creating Your Account

When you go to WordPress.com, you'll see an ever-changing array of posts from some of the millions of blogs housed on WordPress.com, but what you're looking for is the big orange button to the right (see Figure 5.1).

Figure 5.1   *The Sign Up Now button on WordPress.com*

 LET ME TRY IT

Here are the steps to sign up with WordPress.com:

1. Click the Sign Up Now button.

2. Fill in a username, which will also be part of your blog's URL (for example, *username*.wordpress.com).

3. Pick a good password. (Refer to Chapter 4, "Configuring WordPress to Work Its Best," if you need some suggestions on picking a good password.)

4. Enter a working email address that you can access to confirm your account setup. (This is *essential*.)

5. Click Next (see Figure 5.2).

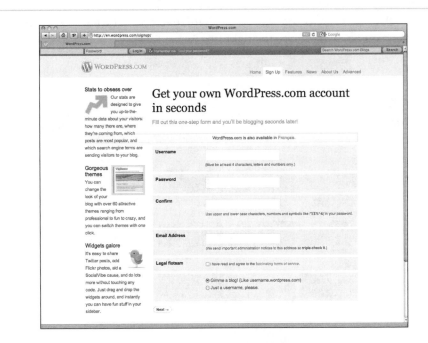

Figure 5.2   *The sign-up screen for WordPress.com. This is, essentially, the only hoop you'll have to jump through (except for confirming your email address).*

6. The name of your blog will be pre-populated with your username, but you can pick a different name now if you want. Don't worry about the title of your blog; you can change the title at anytime. Click Signup when you're done (see Figure 5.3).

7. While you're waiting for your confirmation email to arrive, take a moment to fill out your profile a bit (see Figure 5.4). Click Save Profile when you're done.

8. When you get the email from WordPress.com (check your spam folder if it doesn't show up in your Inbox), open it up and click the link to activate your blog. After clicking the link, you see the active account page (see Figure 5.5).

Figure 5.3   *Setting the URL and name for your blog on WordPress.com*

Figure 5.4   *The basic profile information at WordPress.com. Once your account is verified, you can put in more details (if you want).*

9.   Click Login to see the Dashboard of your new blog. Clicking View Your Site will bring you to your new, and rather empty, new blog (see Figure 5.6).

Through this account, you can use your API key to activate Akismet on your DIY-installed blog and also create other WordPress.com blogs.

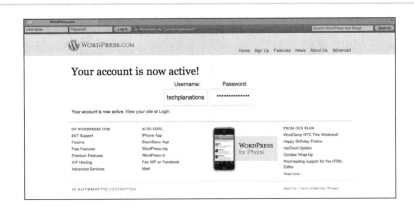

Figure 5.5 *Ta da! Once you click the link in the verification email, you get to this screen. Clicking View Your Site brings you to the home page of your new site, Login to the Dashboard.*

Figure 5.6 *You'll receive a second email that confirms your confirmation. Keep this email for future reference.*

Setting Up Different Blogs

After you have your WordPress.com account, you can create as many new blogs as you want, all tied to the same account. For example, I have a couple blogs on my primary account (I transferred the techplanations.wordpress.com blog back to "myself" so I don't lose track of them), as you can see in Figure 5.7.

Figure 5.7   *My primary WordPress.com account with two blogs associated with it*

If I need or want an additional blog, I just click Register Another Blog, and I come to a screen like step 6 when you created your account. You just need to pick another blog domain and click Create Blog. If the name is available, you'll get to a confirmation screen, as shown in Figure 5.8.

Figure 5.8   *Confirmation of adding another blog to your WordPress.com account*

And you're done. Now when you go to WordPress.com or through the toolbar at the top of the screen, you can jump to any one of your blogs. Unlike setting your blog/account for the first time, you don't have to click a confirmation message to have this new blog up and ready to go. That's because you're already a confirmed user in the system and have passed the Turing Test as a person and not as a bot.

> The Turing Test refers to a question posed by Alan Turing (considered the father of modern computing) on whether computers could "think." The Turing Test essentially checks to see if a series of questions are being answered by a computer or a human.

Becoming Familiar with the WordPress.com Dashboard

 SHOW ME   Media 5.1—WordPress.com Dashboard and How It's Different from DIY WordPress
Access this video file through your registered Web Edition at
my.safaribooksonline.com/9780132182836/media

Like all things WordPress, the Dashboard is the key interface to your whole WordPress.com world. Unlike DIY WordPress, on WordPress.com, you have at least *two* Dashboards: your Global Dashboard and a Dashboard for each of the blogs tied to your account (see Figure 5.9).

The Global Dashboard is designed to be a central hub for your WordPress.com experience. From the Global Dashboard, you can jump to any of your blogs and see what else is going on throughout the larger WP.com universe. The Dashboard button gives you the global options that you will also find under the same button at each of your individual blogs' dashboards: things like stats, checking out other blogs you like, announcements, and other interesting bits. The individual blog Dashboards are almost exactly like you'd see on a DIY WordPress install, with a few additional options and a few things left out. If you're familiar with one Dashboard, you should be able to maneuver around the other just fine (with a little hunting around for something now and again).

Global Dashboard

As I said earlier, the Global Dashboard is supposed to be a unifying element at WordPress.com. It might not be the *perfect* central hub, but it's pretty good at what it needs to do, which is let you get information that applies to all your blogs quickly so that you can drill down to the blog you really want to publish to or work on.

Figure 5.9 *My WordPress.com Global Dashboard—showing the menu with my individual blog dashboards as well*

If you have only one blog, do you still have a Global Dashboard? Yes. Although this seems strange, consider it from a computer standpoint. If you have one blog, you might very well have another. It's easier, programmatically, to have everyone have a Global Dashboard than for people to have just a Blog Dashboard until they had one blog, and then switch if they got another. It doesn't really matter because most people are going stick with their Blog Dashboard most of the time.

The Global Dashboard Dashboard button has the following options:

- Dashboard
- Blog Stats
- Blog Surfer
- My Comments
- Readomattic
- Tag Surfer
- My Blogs
- Subscriptions

Let's look at each of these options in detail.

Blog Stats

Blog Stats quickly gives you an overview of the stats for each of your blogs. Instead of having to go to the stats pages for each blog, you can just select them from the pull-down menu and switch between them. Because these same options are available from all your individual blog dashboards, the effect is the same. View the stats for one blog, select the next blog from the pull-down menu, and so on. Remember that just because you're looking at the stats for one of your blogs, it doesn't mean that you are on that blog's dashboard.

Blog Surfer

The idea behind Blog Surfer is that you can use it to "subscribe" to WordPress.com blogs—and only WordPress.com blogs—that you're interested in following. The real benefit here isn't following "normal" blogs, but private ones. WordPress.com happens to be a great place for kids to have a private blog so they can express themselves and learn about blogging and writing without being exposed to the wilds of the Internet.

My Comments

My Comments lets you track the comments you've left on other blogs within the WordPress.com universe. My Comments lets you look back at things you've said, and maybe wish you hadn't.

Readomattic

Readomattic is for updates and announcements from Automattic and the crew behind WordPress.com. You can find service updates, new features, and other important news here. Don't worry: If it's really important, you'll see a link to the announcement in a yellow bar toward the top of the browser window.

Tag Surfer

Tag Surfer is related to Blog Surfer, but instead of subscribing and following specific blogs, you're subscribing to specific *topics* that could be talked about on a multitude of blogs. Chapter 9, "Creating and Managing Content with WordPress," explains more about tags, but for now think of tags as search terms. So, if you subscribe to "knitting" or "fly fishing" or "wine," you will see posts that have those tags associated with them. Tags are deliberately added to posts by the authors, which can also mean that you'll get some posts that you don't think relate at all to that tag.

My Blogs

Clicking on My Blogs gives you what you'd think it would give you—a list of all the blogs associated with your account on WordPress.com. If you don't have *any* blogs associated with an account, you have to go out to WordPress.com and register a blog to see a blog listed under My Blogs.

Subscriptions

The final section, Subscriptions, is like Blog Surfer, Tag Surfer, and My Comments in that it enables you to track blogs that you receive an *email* from when a new post is posted. To subscribe to a blog like this, you have to put the Blog Subscriptions widget in your sidebar. (I'll talk about widgets shortly because they are a special case on WordPress.com.)

Profile and Users

The last button is Profile, which links to your personal profile across all of WordPress.com (and associated services like Gravatar). You will also see My Profile under the Users button in each of your individual blog Dashboards. These two links connect to the same thing. Yes, if you have several blogs on WordPress.com, all of them will share your same profile information. If you want to have a different profile on a particular blog, you'll need a different account for that blog.

Blog Dashboard

If you read Chapter 4, looking at the WordPress.com Dashboard might give you deja vu. Yeah, it looks familiar, but there is something subtly different. The Plugins button isn't in the WordPress.com Dashboard, but there are Ratings, Polls, and Upgrades buttons instead. (If you have the PollDaddy plugin installed on your DIY WP install, you'll see the same Ratings and Polls buttons; see Figure 5.10.) Because the WordPress.com Dashboard isn't that different than the DIY install Dashboard, I'm going to cover only the differences on WordPress.com.

Upgrades

Because WordPress.com is based on the freemium model, having the option to upgrade your WordPress blog (upgrades are on a blog-by-blog basis) only makes sense. Clicking the Upgrades button gives you the suite of available upgrades that Automattic offers. The upgrades are always improving as the service continues to grow. I'll detail each of the upgrades later in the chapter. One thing you should notice is that Domains is listed here and will also be listed under settings. With the option under the Settings button, you can to manage all the domains you have

Figure 5.10   *The menu panels on the Dashboard of WordPress.com blogs*

mapped to your blog. The option here is to *purchase* the option for that particular blog. Upgrades are purchased on a blog-by-blog basis so you can have extra space and domain mapping on one and domain mapping paired with Custom CSS on another.

Ratings

The Ratings button and the related Polls button enable you to manage whether people can rate your content (using the stars or thumbs up/down model) on posts, pages, and comments. In its default screen (see Figure 5.11), you just see the enable check box (it's off by default) and where you'd like the ratings to be. (I like following the post myself.) Clicking the Advanced Settings link brings you the "good stuff" for changing how the ratings actually look. When you click Advanced Settings, you'll notice *two* Save Changes buttons. The top one only updates the settings for those two options above it. The Save Changes button to the right in the Advanced Settings section updates only the Advanced Settings. Just make sure you click the Save Changes button that goes with the area you're working on and you'll be okay.

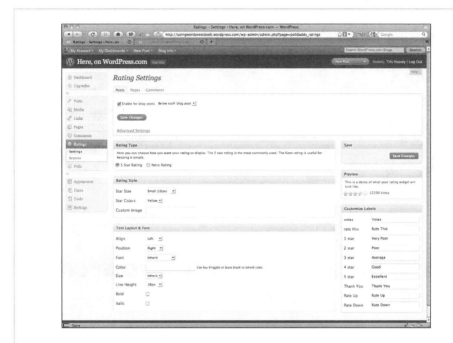

Figure 5.11   *Ratings settings showing the advanced options*

Of course, ratings aren't much good without reports, so the Reports link enables you to see reports of your ratings. Interestingly enough, Ratings and Polls are places where WordPress.com users have an edge over DIY people. Right now, the Ratings feature is only available for WordPress.com (although a plugin for WordPress.org is said to be in the works).

The Ratings options and Polls (which I'll cover in a moment) come from the PollDaddy service that Automattic acquired in October 2008.

Polls

The Polls button, as you'd expect, brings you to a screen to create new polls, after you have set up PollDaddy. I recommend the option of having your WordPress.com credentials sync with PollDaddy so that you don't have another login to manage. If you click the Add New link, you come to a simple screen for setting up your poll and picking from one of the 20 different built-in styles (see Figure 5.12). If you don't like one of the 20 styles, you can delve into a little CSS and make a custom style all your own. Why would you do this? If you have a very distinct blog layout, having a custom style allows the poll to better match the style you have already established.

Figure 5.12   *Adding a new poll using the built-in PollDaddy support*

Appearance

The Appearances button is the first of the overlap buttons from WordPress.org where we need to highlight a couple differences: Extras and Typekit Fonts (see Figure 5.13). WordPress.com users have a few additional options under appearance that can be applied to your blog regardless of the style. Because WordPress.com users cannot install additional plugins, Automattic tries to incorporate as many cool (and requested) features as they can into the core of WordPress.com. Believe me, this is no easy task, but when they do add something new (like Ratings and Polls), you can rest assured that whatever techie goodie they added will work.

Extras enables you to turn on and off mShots site previews (when you pass your mouse over a link to another site, you get a little preview of what the site looks like), the mobile theme (it makes your blog more friendly to iPhone and other mobile device users), and related links (this puts links at the bottom of your posts, linking to similar posts on other blogs, and vice versa).

Typekit Fonts is a service that enables you to use custom fonts on your blog. This is a really amazing service and feature, and I'll cover it in a lot more depth in the section about choosing themes for your blog.

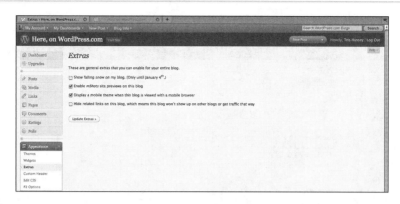

Figure 5.13 *Appearance Extras on WordPress.com; the default settings are fine, but this screen doesn't exist on WordPress.org installs.*

Users

The Users panel is a little interesting because at first glance it doesn't *look* like much is different, but in reality, *a lot* is different behind the scenes. For now, note that you can add a new author or user to your blog by either adding someone who already has a WordPress.com account *or* inviting them into WordPress.com. (This used to be the only way to get a WordPress.com account when it first launched.) Getting into the mechanics of user management in WordPress.com is the topic for the next section.

Tools

After Chapter 4, you might think the Tools screen is going to be boring. Ah, but you'd be oh so wrong! Because WordPress.com users can't edit their themes or upload files, it was very hard for them to claim their blogs for services like Google's Webmaster Tools (an absolutely invaluable toolset, by the way). The main tools screen (see Figure 5.14) provides WordPress.com users with the ability to insert the meta data that Google, Yahoo!, and Microsoft's Bing search engines need to verify that the blog you say is yours *is* really yours.

I think this kind of addition is something that helps set WordPress.com part from other free blog services. Like WordPress.org, you have the same import-export options, following the overall philosophy held by the WordPress community that you own your content. Last but not least is "Delete Site." This is unique to WordPress.com because in the DIY world, if you want to delete your WordPress site,

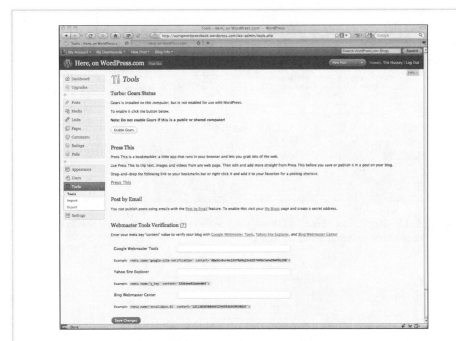

Figure 5.14   *WordPress.com Tools with additional features to claim your blog for Google, Yahoo!, and Bing Webmaster tools*

you just delete the files and database associated with it. Because you can't get to those files on WordPress.com, they had to provide another way to achieve that end. I'll give you a word of warning, however: If you delete your site on WordPress.com, you can never, ever, ever have that URL again (and neither can anyone else). I had trishussey.wordpress.com and foolishly deleted the site; now I can't get it back. Of course, neither can anyone else, but it's rather annoying to me that *I* can't. So, remember: If you delete the site, not only is the content gone, but the URL is too—forever.

Settings

Under the Setting button, there are three new options not present in WordPress.org installs: OpenID, Domains, and Webhooks.

OpenID is a system using the username and password from another trusted site on a new site. OpenID is part of a larger effort to make linking services together easier and to make the web more secure. It hasn't quite caught on yet, but you can use your blog URL as an OpenID credential to log into other sites. How OpenID works and why it's one of the "next big things" is the topic for a different book entirely.

Domains is where you manage all the domains that point to your blog. Yes, you can have more than one, but at $10/year for each domain. I think it's best to have one domain point to your blog.

The last section is Webhooks, which is a setting that slams the geek-o-meter to an 11, maybe a 12. This section is for a very, very small group of users who want to send content from your WordPress.com to other places like Twitter or as a SMS to your phone. To use this section, you're going to need to use and rely on other services outside of WordPress.com to send the data to. If you're confused by reading this, don't worry. This is a really geeky (and new) part of WordPress.com that only a small fraction of people will take advantage of.

Now, let's get into the nitty gritty of each of these sections and their settings.

Getting Your Settings Right for WordPress.com

From the 30,000-foot level, there is little difference in the settings you'd use for a WordPress.com blog versus WordPress.org blog. Essentially, all the same rules for search engines and clarity work the same. The main difference is that on WordPress.com, you have some different options to work with as well as some you don't have to worry about at all. I'm going to approach the settings with you assuming that you read Chapter 4, and that you understand the basics of what you're going to need to tweak, what you *might* want to tweak, and what you won't have to worry about at all.

The Reading setting, oddly enough, has *more* options on WordPress.com versus WordPress.org installs. There's a good reason for this: WordPress.com users don't have as easy ways to redirect their feeds to FeedBurner as WP.org users do. To alleviate this potential problem, you can add options to include additional information, such as how many comments a post has or options to share the post on other social networking sites like Stumbleupon or Digg.com. I suggest you set the options for comments count, Stumbleupon, and Digg.com so that you don't crowd the footer of your feed with a ton of distracting options.

The last setting on WordPress.com to worry about initially is Privacy. Under WP.com, you have three options (compared to two for WP.org): visible to everyone, public and visible but shielded from search engines, or private. The first two are basic options that don't need much explanation; it's the third option that I like. If you want to have a private team or client blog, maybe a blog to share family photos on, having a blog that only a select few people can see, and only with your *explicit* permission, is a really handy option. In Chapter 10, "Creating a Site with WordPress," I'm going to talk about not only using WordPress as a blog or "normal" website, but also as a private extranet for collaboration.

In the Users settings, WordPress.com handles things a little differently than WordPress.org installs. To add someone as an author or administrator of your blog, the person needs to have a WordPress.com account. The tricky bit that I've found is making sure you invite the person using the email address that she uses with WordPress.com (if she already has an account). So, step one is to ask if the person has a WP.com account already. If she looks at you with a blank stare, assume that the answer is no and click the Invites link under Users (see Figure 5.15). Make sure you check the box Add User to My Blog as a Contributor so the person will then appear under your Authors & Users area (after completing the sign-up process, of course).

Figure 5.15   *Inviting people to your blog if they don't already have a WordPress.com account*

SHOW ME   **Media 5.2—Core Settings on WordPress.com**
Access this video file through your registered Web Edition at
my.safaribooksonline.com/9780132182836/media

Picking the Right Theme for Your Blog

I go into a lot of detail about themes in Chapter 7, "All About Themes," but the difference between the discussion here and in Chapter 7 is that your customization options in WordPress.com are much more limited compared to DIY WP. So, picking a theme here is just a little more difficult. You have to choose something that you like, and you have to be okay with how the theme is arranged because you won't have ability to change it.

A final tip I have for picking a theme is to put at least some content, even if it's just placeholder content, into the site so you can see how the theme looks as a site or blog. Just the one default post and page isn't often enough to judge if the theme is right for you and your site.

Configuring Sidebar Widgets on Your Blog

There are far, far more widgets for WP.com than are available by default on WP.org-based blogs (at least without installing additional plugins), but it's the custom widgets you add via the Text widget that causes some problems. Text widgets are fantastic, because with a quick copy and paste, you can have an additional poll, or quiz, or top-ten list of your best tweets except...on WordPress.com, there are filters that block most widgets that include JavaScript. Yes, this means that a lot of widgets don't work, but before you start complaining, you need to think about what's important to Automattic and the admins of WordPress.com: keeping all the blogs and the whole network up and running. That is no easy task, believe me. I've been keeping sites up and running for more than 15 years. A rogue widget could open security holes, spread malware, and even cause unforeseen server load that jeopardizes the whole kit and caboodle. That isn't going to go over well with either the millions of WordPress.com users or the VIP users of the servers that expect them to run, run fast, and run securely. So, some widgets won't work. Take heart, however: Although you might copy and paste a widget today and it may not work, if enough people request a new function, it often appears. Sooner or later.

When you're tricking out your WordPress.com blog with widgets, start with just a few. The more widgets you add, especially custom text widgets, the slower your site will load. Sticking to fewer than 10 widgets on your sidebar is a really good idea (too bad that I rarely take my own advice).

When to Add WordPress.com Upgrades to Your Blog

 SHOW ME   Media 5.3—What Are the Upgrades Available to Me on WordPress.com and How Do They Work?
Access this video file through your registered Web Edition at
my.safaribooksonline.com/9780132182836/media

Up until now, I've only talked in passing about the upgrades available to you on WordPress.com. Before I wrap up this chapter on WordPress.com, it's important for you to not only understand what upgrades are available, but also why you'd want them and why they are being offered in the first place.

Why WordPress.com Upgrades?

You should be asking yourself by now, "if WordPress.com is free, how do they make money?" Good question. They make it in two ways: upgrades on WordPress.com (see Figure 5.16) and VIP services for large clients. (VIP support *starts* at $15,000 per *person*, and VIP hosting on their servers is so exclusive that you have to *apply* for it.) Because I don't think many of you are going to be going for VIP support or hosting (although given how good the servers are, I wish I could afford it), let's talk about WordPress.com upgrades. There are lots of great reasons to pay for WordPress.com upgrades, using your own domain, hosting videos, and adding space. All of them are priced per year per blog, and although these upgrades aren't free, they are very competitively priced. As I'm writing this, the most expensive upgrade is 100GB of extra space at about $290/year. (That's a lot of space!) For a person just starting out with blogging or a site, a smart way to ease into things without risking a lot of money is to begin with a free WordPress.com blog and adding small upgrades over time (although if I were starting a professional business blog, I'd start with the Add a Domain option right away). Let's go through the options one by one so you can understand the whys and wherefores of each one.

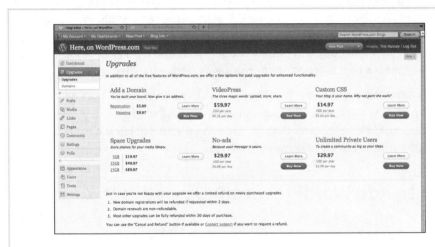

Figure 5.16   *The upgrade options available for WordPress.com blogs*

Domain Hosting

Adding a domain to your WordPress.com blog is one of the first upgrades I'd suggest that someone make on their site if they are starting to get even remotely serious about the site. Having your own domain means that you care about your image and you want to look professional. Domains are inexpensive to purchase from a number of domain registrars (if you remember from Chapter 1, "Domains and Hosts: Getting the Foundation in Place"), and WordPress.com makes it even easier. If you don't have a domain, you can register it through Automattic for $5 a year and then map that domain for $10 a year. If you already have a domain, it's only $10 a year for you. Once you buy this upgrade, your blog usingwordpressbook.wordpress.com can become usingwordpressbook.com—simple, easy, instantly more professional, searchable, and a lot easier to type in.

Although I said that this is the upgrade I would recommend the most, I wouldn't recommend buying a lot of domains and paying to point them all to your WordPress.com blog. To do that, I'd register the domains with someone else and have them redirected or point to your site. You can save money that way, and it might be easier to manage in the long run.

Extra Space

Extra space and VideoPress go hand in hand, but you don't have to have both. Each WordPress.com blog is allocated 3 gigabytes (GB) of space for free. That's a lot in the web world. Most image uploads should be pretty small, and that's what is going to take the biggest chunk of space. However, you can only upload images and documents with a free account. Video files, MP3s, and music are not allowed. Why? Well, I think it's for two reasons. One is that videos and MP3s do take up a lot of space, but more importantly, they take a long time to upload and download. Having a person with a bunch of videos on his servers can cause a significant drain on his bandwidth, so the solution is to allow only those bandwidth-intensive files if you pay extra.

If you just want more room for more pictures (or more high-resolution pictures) or a podcast, all you need is a space upgrade. Starting with 5GB will give you not only the breathing room you might need, but also a very powerful platform for podcasting. If you'd like to upload videos, meaning not uploading them to YouTube, but into your media library on WordPress.com, you need the next upgrade: VideoPress.

VideoPress

VideoPress is a relatively new option for Automattic and WordPress.com. This option enables you to upload files to your WordPress.com account *and* stream it from there as well. If you, for example, can't put video on YouTube because it's too long (YouTube's maximum length is 10 minutes), you could register a WordPress.com blog and host the videos there, but still embed them in another website. You don't *have* to buy additional space with VideoPress, but I bet you'll go through the 3GB pretty fast if you don't. I'd wager that you should move to at least 5GB, if not 15GB, right away if you're going to use VideoPress.

Editable CSS

What if you *love* the theme you have, but you really don't like some of the font choices or color scheme? If you've installed your own blog, you'd whip out your handy CSS editor and start tweaking the CSS style to get something more to your liking. You can't do that on WordPress.com, however, unless you opt for the Custom CSS option. I suggest approaching this option with some caution if you're a newcomer to the web. Editing your CSS isn't hard, and it doesn't take long to learn, but CSS and style sheets are *fiddly*. They take time and patience to tweak just right. Being able to edit your CSS isn't a panacea for getting a theme to the point you want it. You can't edit what appears in the navigation bars through CSS or change how many sidebars it has. You can change how big the header is, the background, and some of the sizes of columns, but before you venture into this area, you should know a little about what you're doing. You don't want to waste your money and wind up going back to the original theme's style after a lot of swearing and yelling at the computer.

If you want to see what your tweaks might look like (or if you are getting in over your head), you can go to Appearance -> Edit CSS and make the changes you'd like. When you click Preview, you'll see what the changes will look like, but they aren't saved or visible to the public unless you purchase the Custom CSS Upgrade.

Unlimited Users

If you want to have a private WordPress.com blog, as I talked about before, you have to create an account for each of the people who will have access to the blog. But you can only have 35 users on a free, private blog. If you're running an extranet, you can add Unlimited Private Users. I will say that if you're going to the extent of paying for unlimited private users, you might be pushing into the realm of just getting your own hosting account. Still, if you like WordPress.com and the fact that you don't have to worry about the server, it might be worth it.

Ad Free

The final upgrade is No-ads. In addition to the revenue from upgrades and VIP services, Automattic places ads on blogs. They only show ads occasionally and only if you aren't logged in as a WordPress.com user. I'm often logged in, so I rarely see the ads, but if they bother you (or rather, the *thought* of them bothers you), you can opt to have the ads never appear at all. It's a nice upgrade, but not one I'd person-ally worry about.

The Final Word

Here's my final word on these upgrades. Before you start going beyond adding a domain and getting a wee more space (say $35/year for registering a domain, adding it to the blog, and 5GB of space), keep an eye on the monthly costs. Sure, $35 per year is less than $3 a month, and you *can't* get good hosting for that price anywhere, but if you're getting to 15GB of space and domain and maybe throwing in VideoPress, you're paying *more than* the cost of hosting (estimating between $10–20/month for good hosting). It still might be worth it to you to have every-thing on WordPress.com—that is a decision you'll have to make—but having a hosting account and doing a little site management now and then isn't too hard, and there are always people willing to help you out.

Just something to think about....

Summary

TELL ME MORE   Media 5.4—WordPress.com Versus WordPress.org
Access this audio recording through your registered Web Edition at
my.safaribooksonline.com/9780132182836/media

Here are a few final thoughts on WordPress.com. It is a great freemium host. I have no hesitation recommending people use it for their blogs and sites. It has enough features for most users, and if you need to upgrade, there are enough features to make sure you look professional. There isn't a "but" in all of this—there is a "just so you know," because as you've learned in this chapter, free and hosted services come with limits. You might not have infinite themes to pick from, and you might not be able to embed all videos, slides shows, or other coolness in your posts or sidebars because of content restrictions. Also, you can't have ads. If you want to be the next person to get rich using Google Adsense, WordPress.com is not the place for you to be.

My recommendation is to try it out. See what you think. It's free, so there is no risk there. If the restrictions and theme limitations (this might come into play if you're trying to make a "regular" website) don't work for you, then getting a host, domain, and WordPress.org are the best fit for you. I'd still keep the WordPress.com site around, though. It's always good to have another place to test and practice.

This chapter is about learning how to use plugins to extend what WordPress can do.

6

Finding and Using Plugins

Now that you have WordPress installed and the basics configured, it's time to *really* make your WordPress install walk and talk—it's time to install some plugins.

Remember, if you've decided to go with a WordPress.com blog, installing plugins isn't in the cards for you. Don't worry, however—the folks at Automattic are adding new features all the time.

When people ask me about WordPress and why I choose it over other blog engines or light CMS platforms, my answer is the availability of plugins and themes. Instead of trying to develop *everything* that users might need, WordPress is designed to be *extensible* so other developers can build the additional parts that people needed. Those additional parts became plugins. Some plugins eventually become part of WordPress itself (part of the core application), but most plugins remain separate things to add on yourself.

In this chapter, we'll be going through finding, installing, and upgrading plugins, as well as I'll tell you about a few of my favorite plugins and how to configure them. Throughout this chapter, you should think of plugins like adding a new stereo or sunroof to you car. Sure, the stereo that came with your car might be pretty good, but maybe you need some additional features, so you buy and install a new one. Like car stereos, there are good, bad, and mediocre plugins, so a little caution is warranted when downloading and installing plugins. That said, there are some amazing and fantastic plugins available, for free, through WordPress.org. When people ask me if they can do x, y, or z with WordPress, my answer is usually "I bet there is a plugin for that." Let's jump right into the first task—finding the good plugins to install.

Finding Plugins

When you're shopping for a plugin for your WordPress install, you don't have to venture any farther than the plugin section of your own blog's Dashboard. One of the features added into WordPress was being able to search for and install new plugins from within the administration area. Once in your plugins list, just click Add New from either the top of your plugins list or the link at the left, or click Install Plugins from the top menu bar. Choosing from a list of featured, newly updated, or popular plugins, you can find a plugin for almost any task, job, or tweak to WordPress you can imagine (see Figure 6.1). If you can't (quickly) find a plugin through one of these quick pick lists, you can search or use the tag cloud to narrow your search to something more manageable.

Figure 6.1   *The Install Plugins screen, where you can find new plugins for your blog*

Once you find the plugin you *think* you want, the next step isn't downloading or installing it, but evaluating if the plugin will work with your version of WordPress and if it's any good at all. It's important for you to know that although the WordPress.org is the *official* place to find plugins, there are few checks of the plugins for stability, security, or quality. Those checks are up to us, the user community. For this reason, there are star ratings, comments, and number of downloads to check against to see if the plugin is up to snuff. When I'm evaluating a new plugin, assuming I haven't been directed to a specific one, I look at *both* the star ratings *and* the number of downloads (see Figure 6.2).

A lot of great plugins, including ones that I'm going to recommend to you in this chapter, don't have 5 out of 5 stars. What these plugins *do* have instead are thousands of downloads. People don't download a plugin that doesn't work, nor do they recommend it to anyone else. Over time, and as you start to tune into the WordPress community, you'll quickly see what plugins are recommended and which ones are not. Some great plugins are great for everyone, and others only for experienced users who don't mind a little mucking about in code now and then. In

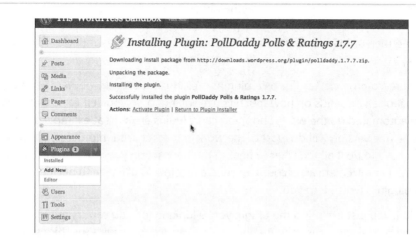

Figure 6.2 *Example of plugin information panel showing the star ratings and number of downloads for PollDaddy Polls & Ratings*

the world of open source software, the *community* is the essential part that will make an app successful. The people—who are mostly all volunteers to the "cause"—who create themes, write plugins, test code, and contribute to the project are the backbone of the project. Sure, Matt Mullenweg is a brilliant guy, and he has contributed a lot to WordPress (and still does), but he can't and couldn't do it all himself. It just isn't possible to manage something of the scale of WordPress alone. Where Matt can't do everything, the larger community takes up the slack. In this case, it's vetting good plugins from bad.

When you've found a plugin that *sounds* like it will do the job, you see that it has been downloaded a lot, and it is compatible with your version of WordPress, what's the next step? When I'm looking for new plugins after those first "sniff tests," I look at the documentation provided. I want to know if there are any special things I need to do to get the plugin to work. Does either the installation or configuration seem complicated and laborious? Follow your gut. If a plugin *requires* that your entire wp-content directory is world-writable all the time or if the plugin requires you to open an account at some obscure website to get a "free" access code, your gut might tell you to be wary. If you're still not sure, a quick search through the WordPress.org forums or the Internet might allay or confirm your suspicions.

Although searching for plugins through the administration area is easy and convenient, I often go to WordPress.org/extend/plugins/ and search from there. You get a lot of the same information, but I find it easier to parse through lots of plugins that way. In the end, it really doesn't matter too much. Searching through the admin area will enable you to install the plugin you find right away, if your host can work that way, but downloading the plugin from WordPress.org in one browser tab, and then uploading and installing it through your administration area, is just as easy.

Are there "commercial" or "for pay" plugins? Yes, there are, and whether they are worth it often depends on how much you're willing to do yourself versus let something automated do the work. Shopping cart plugins are a great example of this. Often, a free version will do *most* of the work in the transaction process, but you might have to tie it all together to finalize the transaction yourself (such as put it through PayPal, create an account, or send a receipt). You'll have to decide if paying for a plugin is worth it to you.

Finally, if you just can't find the plugin you're looking for, you can try to write one yourself or hire someone to write one for you. Myself, I'd go with the "hire someone" route (because I know several plugin developers and I'm a lousy coder), but if you'd like to learn a little PHP, go ahead and take a shot at it. Who knows—you could write the next über popular plugin!

One way or another, you've got your plugin. Now what? Time to install this puppy.

 SHOW ME   **Media 6.1—How to Find the Right Plugin for the Job**
Access this video file through your registered Web Edition at
my.safaribooksonline.com/9780132182836/media

Installing Plugins Quickly and Easily

Starting in WordPress 2.7, along with plugin search, came the ability to install plugins through the admin screens. Although this is easy, sometimes either your server or the plugin just doesn't like to be installed that way. For those times, there's the old-fashioned way: FTP.

Automatic Install

If you're installing plugins through the admin screens and your browser, you're going to go about it in one of two ways. The first way is if you have searched for a plugin, found it, and clicked the Install link. This will download a copy of the plugin to your server, put it in the correct place, and unzip it. If all goes well, the next screen you'll see is to activate the plugin or not (see Figure 6.3). Now, the other similar way is if you downloaded the plugin to your computer. In this case, you browse for the plugin on your local machine, and then it's uploaded, unzipped, and so forth. If all goes well, the next thing you'll see is if you'd like to activate the plugin.

What if it doesn't go smoothly? You'll know this if you don't see the Would You Like to Activate It? question. Don't worry—the alternative is just as easy.

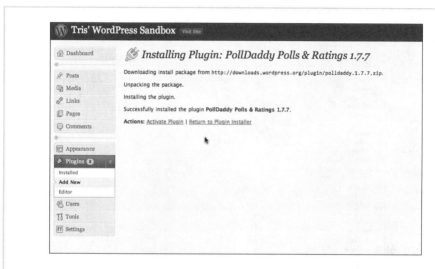

Figure 6.3 *Automatic install gone smoothly and the new plugin ready for activation*

Manual Install

You remember our friend FTP, right? I talked about using FTP in Chapter 2, "Installing WordPress on Your Own Server," when we were installing WordPress; here we're going to use it to install plugins. FTP is one of the geeky-sounding, but really pretty easy, tools that you should have in your WordPress arsenal and be comfortable using. Installing a plugin "the old-fashioned way" through FTP is very easy. By the way, we'll be revisiting FTP in Chapter 7, "All About Themes," when we manually install and update themes, and Chapter 13, "Maintaining WordPress," when we discuss updating WordPress. See, I told you it was handy!

 LET ME TRY IT

Installing a Plugin by FTP

1. First, you need to download the plugin archive to your computer through WordPress.org or the admin area of your blog.

2. Next, unzip the archive so you have a folder on your computer with the contents of the archive. Good? Great.

3. Open your FTP client and navigate to the root of your blog. It should look something like what's shown in Figure 6.4.

Figure 6.4 *Root of my WordPress install (first column), wp-content directory (second column), and plugins directory (third column)*

4. Double-click wp-content to open it.

5. Double-click plugins to open it.

6. Drag the plugin folder (the whole thing as a folder, not as a group of files) into the plugins directory on your server.

7. Once the plugin has finished uploading, go to your administration area of your blog and click the Plugins button.

8. Click the Inactive link.

9. Look for the plugin you just installed and click Activate (see Figure 6.5).

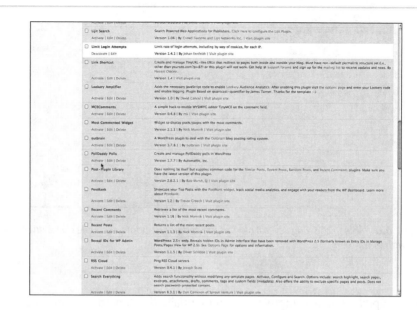

Figure 6.5   *List of plugins; the ones in gray boxes are inactive.*

That's it! Now just configure your new plugin (if there is any configuration at all), and you're all set.

In case you're wondering—no, manual isn't intrinsically better than automatic or vice versa. On some hosted servers, automatic installs don't work consistently. You might have no problem with one plugin, but no luck with another. The best thing is to know both ways of installing (and upgrading) plugins so you're never stuck.

SHOW ME   Media 6.2—Installing Plugins, Automatically and Manually
Access this video file through your registered Web Edition at
my.safaribooksonline.com/9780132182836/media

Upgrading Plugins

Throughout this book, both in the figures and the screencasts, you might have noticed a little number next to the Plugins button. That number is the number of plugins that have updates available. One of the benefits of the WordPress.org plugin repository is that WordPress periodically checks your plugins against the repository and sees if the versions match up. If there is a newer version, WordPress lets you know (see Figure 6.6).

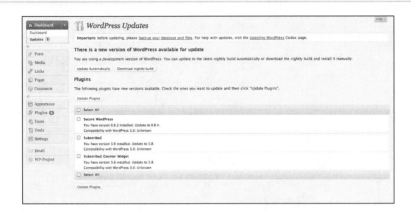

Figure 6.6 *Screen showing several plugins in need of an update. A couple clicks, and I'll be done with that.*

You can update plugins automatically or manually. If automatic updates work on your server, use it. I've found that the automatic update system for plugins does a great job at smoothly moving from one version to another. This is because WordPress goes through an automated process of entering maintenance mode, disabling the plugin, updating the plugin, re-enabling the plugin, and exiting maintenance mode. When I update a plugin manually, I often forget (or just don't bother) with those steps and just FTP a new version up to the server and overwrite the older version. That has worked for me 99% of the time, but other times I really wish I had taken a little more care and followed all the steps.

Updating a plugin automatically is as simple as clicking the Update Automatically link from the Plugins page. If you have more than one plugin to update, there is a handy feature in WordPress—being able to mass update plugins through the Update function under Dashboard.

Manually updating a plugin follows the exact same route as installing it in the first place. Again, you really should click the Deactivate link before updating. Most FTP clients ask, when you're dropping files or folders of the same name into a directory, if you want to overwrite or ignore. Choose overwrite; this *should* just overwrite the files of the same name. Before you take my word for it, do a test. I have known some FTP clients to first delete a duplicate directory and *then* do the uploading. This, technically, isn't overwriting, but replacing. Better programs know that what you really want is to just go through the directory (and subdirectories) and swap out individual files. If there isn't a duplicate file, either leave it alone (if it is on the server, but not in the set being uploaded) or upload it (if the file is entirely new). Exercise a bit of caution the first time you try this by downloading a copy of the plugin to your local machine *first* and then trying the upload and overwrite. This is actually good practice because you'll need some of these skills to update WordPress itself later! Once the upload is done, go back to the plugins page (you probably left it open) and reactivate the plugin. Your plugin should now be ready to go with an updated plugin.

Recommended Plugins

Get more than a couple WordPress users together, and eventually the subject of plugins will come up. People want to know a good plugin for this or how to fix a problem in another plugin or just how to update them safely. WordPress users are like any other kind of hobbyist—get enough of us together, and we'll start talking about our "hobby."

At WordCamps held all around the world, the topic of plugins is *always* on the agenda somewhere. In keeping with this, I would be remiss if I didn't suggest some plugins for you to try. Like many things in the WordPress world, there are often several plugins that do a great job at the same thing. I've grouped the plugins as follows:

- **Interface tweaks:** Plugins that help you with the look and feel of your blog, regardless of the theme.

- **Caching:** Various plugins aimed at improving your blog's performance by caching frequently accessed pages.

- **Search Engine Optimization tools.**

- **Metrics:** Stats, stats, and more stats about how much traffic you are getting on your blog.

- **Multimedia:** Handling audio and video files.

- **Comments:** Handling and styling comments.

- **Theme related:** Helping out your theme a bit (overlaps with interface tweaks).

- **Administration:** Plugins to help you manage your blog, databases, users, and security.

- **Integrating with social media:** Connecting your blog to Facebook, Twitter. and all the other social media sites out there.

- **Mobile users:** Making your blog look great for people using smart phones like the BlackBerry and iPhone.

- **Search:** Helping your readers find what they are looking for on your blog.

- **Miscellaneous:** Other tools that are just good to have around and do cool things.

This isn't, by any stretch of the imagination, a complete list of all the great plugins that are available for these tasks. There is always a certain amount of risk when anyone, but book authors especially, make these "recommended" lists. There are probably plugins that exist already, or will by the time the book is out, that are better than the ones I've listed here. I can deal with that, because I'm always on the lookout for better ways to do things. The one that makes me cringe is something that makes all "experts" duck for cover—when stuff doesn't work. Almost as sure I am that someone will find a better plugin, someone else will try one of these plugins and it will fail catastrophically, completely, and epically. This is why making any kind of recommendation is pretty gutsy. Saying, "yeah, this is awesome, go ahead and use it, it's okay," opens up that karmic risk that it will do everything *but* work. So, like software, cars, computers, and all other things—*caveat emptor*. Also, the features and availability of any of these plugins could change by the time you read this. For updates, please check this book's blog at UsingWordPressBook.com, especially my recommended plugins post: http://trishussey.com/my-must-have-word-press-plugins-any-to-add-to-the-list/.

As a final note, I don't recommend that you download and activate *all* of these plugins at once. If you don't run into numerous conflicts (which is extremely likely), your blog may also slow down to a crawl (very, very likely). Remember, plugins are like programs. They need memory and computing time to run. The more plugins you run, the more work the server has to do (in general); the more work the server has to do, the longer your blog will take to load. I've done this to myself on many occasions, and it's part of the testing process. So again, just take things easy, one plugin at a time. Good? Great! Now let's get to the fun stuff.

Interface Tweaks

Sometimes your theme might need a little help. The plugins in this section are some of my favorite interface-enhancing plugins that I tend to use for my blogs.

Before you add an interface tweak to make your blog/theme do something, just double-check that your theme (or an updated version of it) doesn't already do what the plugin does. Also, many themes are written expecting that certain plugins are installed and active, so just double-check that, too.

Here's my list of interface tweak plugins that you might want to check out:

- **Drop Caps:** This adds that extra-large and often stylized first letter to the beginning of a post. I like it, just for the look. Yes, you can achieve the same effect with CSS styling, but this is much simpler.

- **Simple Pull Quote:** Pull quotes are those short pieces of text within the body of an article that stand out. Usually it's a larger font, often bold, and maybe a line above or below. Pull quotes draw attention to a specific point or idea. If your theme doesn't have a specific style for pull quotes, this will give you that flexibility. You use this plugin within the post editor.

- **WP-Typography:** For typography geeks out there, this plugin lets you use all manner of proper and cool tweaks to your posts and pages *automagically*! You want correct typographer's quotes? Proper use of em and en dashes? Yeah, you got it here.

- **WP-Cumulus:** I love tag clouds on blogs. You have all the tags that are used in all the posts, and the bigger and bolder the word is, the more often the tag is used. WP-Cumulus does that, just like the default tag cloud widget, but it *animates* the cloud so it moves to focus on the tag your mouse is pointing at. It looks cool.

- **WP-Pagenavi:** This plugin is one of the many written by Lester "GaMerZ" Chan, who might be not only the most prolific plugin writer, but also his plugins are some of the most installed and most used within the WordPress community. PageNavi is used by a lot of themes to provide nicer, more styled, and advanced Next/Previous page navigation. It's a good, solid, core plugin.

Comments

Yes, comments can be a blog's lifeblood, but they can also be the bane of your existence if spam comments start overwhelming your moderation queue or, worse, you let one slip through; then you are awash with dreck that would make your mother faint. So, the cornerstone of all blogs should be an anti-spam plugin. With that out of the way, there are a whole suite of plugins that are intended to make your comments richer and cooler, and even connect commenters to all their other sites (like Twitter and Facebook). Here are some of my favorites:

- **CommentLuv, Disqus, and IntenseDebate:** These three plugins are all about making your comments cooler *and* easier to manage as well. Disqus and IntenseDebate are intended to connect a person's comments with other comments they've made on other sites as well as their larger "online identity." Disqus was the first plugin/service that tried to connect the discussion about a post to the various places it was happening online, as well as provide a "single sign-on" for people leaving comments across several blogs. Intense-Debate (owned by Automattic) also provides for a single sign-on as well as comment management via email (which I found to be very handy when I was on the go). CommentLuv provides many of these features, as well as a nice link back to the commenter's last post on their site (if they have one). So, do you *need* these plugins? Maybe not, but Disqus and IntenseDebate can certainly make your comment section richer. Personally I've had mixed results with all these plugins and choose to just keep my comments as they are. Like interface plugins, these comment plugins can slow down your blog if the connection to the services are slow as well.

- **Akismet:** Akismet is the king of anti-spam plugins. It's installed (but not activated) with WordPress by default. This is a plugin that you just activate, get your API key from WordPress.com, and use. If your blog is commercial, please purchase a license from Automattic for the plugin. The strength of Akismet is in *how many* people use it—the more people who sift through comments and mark them as spam, the better the filters get. This is one of the must-haves.

Caching

As I talked about in Chapter 4, "Configuring WordPress to Work Its Best," whether or not WordPress needs any kind of caching at all is debatable. Myself, I lean toward the "better safe than sorry" approach and use some caching to improve overall site performance. Here are some plugins you should look at for your blog:

- **WP Cache, WP SuperCache, and W3 Total Cache:** WP Cache and WP SuperCache are related plugins (SuperCache was built from Cache) that create a static version of frequently accessed pages so that WordPress doesn't need to call the database for the content, but they do have to still use PHP. W3 Total Cache adds "minifying," which is taking files like your style sheet and JavaScripts and compressing them so they download faster for visitors. W3TC also has optional connectors to database optimizers and content distribution networks that can improve performance by making content and database functions less reliant on a single server. In reality, most users will be just fine with no caching. Sites with moderate traffic should look at WP SuperCache, and if you have a more elaborate site, adding W3TC will improve site-loading performance. You only want to choose one of these two plugins, not both. Running more than one of these plugins together will potentially cause your blog to be unavailable.

- **WP-Smush.it:** WP-Smush.it serves one purpose and one purpose only—making your image files smaller. I think all of us have gotten pretty lazy about making sure our images are as small and optimized as possible. Ten years ago, every kilobyte counted (remember, we were all on dialup access then), and I spent a lot of time making sure that all of my images were as compressed as possible. Now I don't worry as much, which isn't a good thing, really. WP-Smush.it is based on Yahoo!'s Smush.it protocol to compress images for you. It works automagically as you upload images to WordPress. Once you install it, the only thing you'll notice is faster page loads. That seems like a good idea to me.

SEO

Most of us want our sites to be found by search engines, and although WordPress is awesome at search engine optimization (SEO) from the get-go, it can use a little help. Luckily, it really doesn't need much help at all!

All In One SEO Pack is one of the two killer, must-have SEO plugins to install. While many themes are incorporating many of its features, most users can benefit from its SEO tweaks. The primary thing it does is to make sure that individual post pages are formatted with the post title first instead of the blog name first. For some reason (which eludes me), it was standard practice for themes to have something like My Really Awesome Blog | Today's Post on Kumquats when the better way is Today's Post on Kumquats | My Really Awesome Blog. The reason is that you want search engines to index the post title first, instead of the blog name over and over again. The blog name isn't changing, but the post title will. Beyond that important tweak, All In One SEO Pack has some great tricks up its sleeve for making your home page more SEO friendly and making sure search engines don't over-index your site (yes, that's actually a bad thing). Trust me—install this one.

Google XML Sitemaps is the second must-install plugin for SEO because it creates a special index or map of your site especially for search engines like Google. Search engine indices *love* this. It's like candy to them. You're providing the search engines with everything they need to know about your site in one file, one gulp. Plus, every time you post or edit something on your site, not only is the file updated (as it should be), but all the major search engines are told that there is new content. Think of this like the ice cream truck and its little song. Kids can hear it miles away and just come running for it (okay, grown-ups too). You're creating a digital ice cream truck for search engines and just calling them over for free samples.

I make sure I always install both of these plugins on every blog or WordPress-powered site I set up. They are essential to ensuring that your site is properly indexed by search engines.

Metrics

Some folks say that if it can't be measured, it must not matter. Although I don't entirely agree with that sentiment, I do believe in webstats; however, I think you can also go too far and drive yourself bonkers in the process of gathering stats. I try to keep my metrics simple, and here are some of the plugins I use (or have used):

- **Ultimate Google Analytics:** Ultimate Google Analytics has one purpose in life: making sure that your Google Analytics tracking code is always on your blog. I highly recommend using Google's free analytics tools, but there is a (small) catch—you have to make sure the tracking code is in place for it to gather data. I've forgotten to put the code into the footer of a new theme enough times to make sure that this plugin is installed and configured. It just makes sure the code is there. That's it. Simple.

- **WordPress.com Stats:** WordPress.com Stats comes straight from the folks at Automattic as the stats solution that is built into WordPress.com blogs. This plugin gives you real-time stats and ties into your WordPress.com account. As an extra bonus feature, it also lets you generate shorter, more compact URLs for Twitter and so on. The stats are good enough for almost all users.

- **Woopra:** Woopra is a new breed of real-time stats tuned especially for blogs. After a long (and fantastic) beta period, Woopra has made their freemium stats package available to everyone. The folks at Woopra are closely tied to the WordPress community, and it shows in this great plugin. This is my go-to real-time stats tool now. The data and filtering it gives is very impressive. The free version is for sites with fewer than 30,000 visits a month, which is pretty much most of us.

- **PostRank:** PostRank is a different kind of metrics plugin because it doesn't track traffic, but does track engagement with your site and content. The PostRank service looks at your content all over the Internet, gauges how many times it is commented on and shared, and gives each piece of content a score from 1 (no engagement) to 10 (high engagement). Visitors can also subscribe a special weighted RSS feed that gives them from all to only the best (9-10 scored) content. I've been using PostRank to help not only see what content people like to read, but also to subscribe to "super feeds" on particular topics and only read the "great" posts.

If you're wondering how many metrics tools I personally use, the answer is three: PostRank, Woopra, and Google Analytics. I like the range of data I get from the three services. For most non-business users, I suggest just picking one, and WordPress.com Stats is a great choice.

Multimedia

If there has been one hallmark of blogging and Web 2.0, it has been the integration of audio and video into "ordinary" content. The ability to make any post a "multi-media-rich" post is something that I would have given my eye teeth for 15 years ago. Today it's just, *meh*, no problem. WordPress handles multimedia very well on its own, and the latest versions of WordPress make it even better, but even the best tools sometimes need a little help.

Viper's Video Quicktags is the king of the WP multimedia plugins. It made adding a video a two-click effort: Click the button for the kind of media you were embedding, paste the URL of the media into the box, and click okay. That's it. The plugin figured out the rest. Wait, WordPress does that now, doesn't it? Yes, and here is what Alex (aka Viper007Bond) says about that:

"Yes, WordPress 2.9 features native easy embeds. However, this plugin offers more customization than allowed without the plugin (player colors, etc.). It will work fine side by side with the new code, and you can opt to use either embed method.

"The plan for this plugin is to recode it from scratch to instead build upon the new embed API and allow for more customization. The new plugin will be backward compatible and keep your current videos working."

Yep, that's good enough for me too. Go ahead and install it, because if Alex's past work is any indication, the next version will probably be amazing. Oh, and yeah, he helped write the code for embedding multimedia into posts for WordPress.

Blubrry PowerPress is the most full-featured podcasting plugin we have right now. PodPress used to have that title, but the only development on that plugin has been to continue compatibility with WordPress updates. PowerPress doesn't require a Blubrry account, but if you do sign up for one, you can get stats on your podcasts (listeners, and so on). I find it to be pretty interesting that the *easiest* multimedia blogging (podcasting) has taken a back seat to video blogging. That's a discussion for another time (or book).

Theme Related

There are two theme-related plugins that I make sure I have around and available, though not always active. Theme Test Drive lets you try out a theme by making it active for only logged-in users of a certain level (generally just admins). This way, you can be working on your awesome, stylin' new theme but not let the rest of the world know until you're ready. The only risk is if you need to enable a specific plugin for the new theme that the *old* theme doesn't play nicely with. If that happens, you'll have to crank the geek-o-meter up a couple notches and do it all on your local drive.

The second theme-related plugin is called Theme Authenticity Checker (TAC), which goes through all your themes and checks for hidden links and links to known spam/malware sites. Yes, I'm sad to say that there are more and more free themes out there—and not from the official WordPress.org repository, mind you— that try to sneak spam links and other fun stuff into themes. TAC tries to make sure those themes aren't widely used.

Administration

There are lots of little things that you might like to keep tabs on and running smoothly behind the scenes of your blog. These admin-related plugins are just the trick:

- **WP-DBManager and WordPress Database backup:** Your MySQL database is the most critical part of your blog. Without it, you have pretty much nothing. Not only does the database hold all your settings, it also holds all your content, comments, file locations—yeah, pretty much everything that's important. Either of these two plugins will do a great job of regularly backing up your database for you. You can have the files backed up on your server, as well as emailed to you. WP-DBManager adds the ability to repair and optimize your database. Yes, this is built into WordPress, but in comparing both methods, I've found that the plugin is easier to use and faster in completing the tasks.

- **FD FeedBurner plugin:** If you're like many bloggers, you use Google's FeedBurner service to add additional features and metrics to your RSS feed. If you also use Google Analytics, your feed data is now being pulled into GA as well. There's a trick with using FeedBurner: You have to make sure as many users as possible subscribe to *that* version of your RSS feed and *not* the default version. To do this, you *could* edit your .htaccess file, hack your theme, or just use this plugin. Having done the other two (harder) methods, trust me—use the plugin. That said, like Google Analytics codes, more and more themes are providing for FeedBurner support automatically (Thesis does). So to be safe, just double-check that your theme doesn't have support for FeedBurner built in before you install the plugin.

- **RSS Cloud and PuSHPress:** These are a pair of plugins that are part of a growing movement to change RSS from a passive data stream (servers pull the information) to a more active one (the information is proactively *pushed* to servers). RSS Cloud and PubSubHubbub are two new ways to achieve this RSS push feature. You don't notice anything different when you turn them on, but they're there working away and making your blog work more efficiently. RSS cloud works with the RSS Cloud system and PuSHPress with PubSubHubbub. I use both plugins simultaneously on my blog to ensure that everyone gets my updates as soon as possible.

- **WordPress Exploit Scanner, Secure WordPress, and Limit Login Attempts:** This set of plugins help secure WordPress from hackers. Technically, WordPress Exploit Scanner (which is written by one of the key developers at Automattic) just checks for problems and doesn't fix them. However, coupled together, Exploit Scanner and Secure WordPress will help you stay hacker free. Both have simple and easy setup, so don't think you have to be a security expert to configure them. Because WordPress has become so popular, it has gotten the attention of hackers; this is just a fact of life, so be prepared. Limit Login Attempts helps you prevent hackers from just trying password after password to break into your blog. After a certain number of attempts, both the account being attacked and the computer (or network) doing the attacking are blocked for 20 minutes. If the account is attacked a few more times, the lockout time can be extended to hours or days. Although you might think it's annoying if you accidentally lock yourself out of your site, if hackers are trying a brute-force login attack on your site, you'll be happy you installed it.

Integrating with Social Media

Social media and blogs, like multimedia and blogs, just go seamlessly together—okay, seamlessly with the help of a few choice plugins. The important decision you're going to have to make is which social networks are you going to connect to and why. For me, the primary connector is Twitter. Twitter is contributing the lion's share of traffic to my blog (after Google) that is in no small part due to the fact that every post is sent out as an update to Twitter. Twitter, then, updates Facebook. I'm not alone in focusing a lot of attention on Twitter, which is why plugins to send updates to Twitter and allow readers to Tweet your posts are some of the most popular plugins in the WordPress plugin repository.

Some Twitter-focused plugins are as follows:

- **WordTwit:** This is my preferred plugin for sending out my posts to my Twitter stream. The authors have spent a great deal of time making sure that they keep up with Twitter *and* WordPress changes to make this a must-have plugin.

- **TweetMeme and Tweet This:** These are plugins that help your readers retweet (send via Twitter) your posts. You want to choose one or the other of these plugins. My choice is TweetMeme because it also shows the number of times the post has been tweeted/retweeted. The benefit of Tweet This is that you can include not only Twitter but links to other social networks as well.

- **Social media plugins:** In the class of social media plugins, ShareThis, and Sociable follow a common model—they make it easy for your readers to share your posts across many different social networks. ShareThis and Sociable are similar to Tweet This in how they offer a selection of social networks to be offered. ShareThis and Sociable have been around for years, and these plugins are found on thousands of sites.

SHOW ME   Media 6.3—Plugins for Social Media and Mobile Users
Access this video file through your registered Web Edition at
my.safaribooksonline.com/9780132182836/media

Regardless of which plugin you choose, the end goal is to help readers share your posts easily on Twitter, Facebook, Stumbleupon, and whatever new social networks crop up in the future. Once upon a time, much of a blog's readership was through RSS; now social networks like Twitter and Facebook are second only to Google for driving traffic to my blog. This is a critical piece of information because it means that those visitors will also see any ads I put on the blog.

Mobile Users

Making your blog mobile friendly is critical to getting and keeping readers. Not long ago, making your blog "mobile friendly" was a nice feature to have, but not anymore. As Apple's iPhone exploded onto the scene, more and more people are viewing websites on their mobile phones. Sure, on many BlackBerries and other smartphones, the experience isn't the greatest, but as more phones running Google's Android platform are in consumers' hands, that is changing fast. There are two plugins that are worthy of your consideration: WordPress Mobile Edition and WPTouch. WordPress Mobile Edition is written by long-time WordPress plugin author Alex King, and WPTouch is written by the same guys behind WordTwit (BraveNewCode; they are also friends of mine). Either one is an excellent choice, but I lean toward WPTouch because of the absolutely gorgeous way it renders a site for the iPhone. Don't take my word for it, however; Automattic chose WPTouch as the code-base for making all WordPress.com blogs iPhone compatible.

Search

When you need to find something on a blog, you look for the search box, right? Right. The problem is that the default WordPress search isn't so hot. It doesn't index categories, tags, author names, or a few other key fields. To overcome this, you can build a Google Custom Search for your blog (it isn't terribly hard), or just use a plugin or two and get some of the same benefits.

The first plugin that I think is certainly a great one is Lijit. Lijit can help you measure the traffic on your blog, but the *real* benefit is how Lijit connects the content you generate *all over* the Internet. I can have Lijit include in the search results posts I've written on other blogs, my pictures, and even Twitter. Why is this a good thing? Breadth. Giving your readers the widest breadth possible gives them a better chance of finding what they are looking for. On top of searching through *your* stuff, Lijit can also give readers results from your "network." Your network is defined by who you link to, whose posts you share through Twitter, Google Reader, and so on. Essentially, it's the people in your social and professional circle. With one search, readers can see not only your content, but how your content relates to other content on the Internet.

The other plugin that I like to use is called Search Everything. It has one simple job: Add all those things that WordPress's built-in search *doesn't* index into the index (the tags, categories, authors, and so on). A few check boxes (the default settings are fine, actually) and you're done. Even if I have a Google custom search set up for a site, I'll make sure this plugin is running so I have a back up. Redundancy is the name of the game in tech.

Miscellaneous

Just so you don't think that those are the only plugins I use, they aren't. The following are some that I couldn't fit into a category that I *also* rely on:

- WP-Polls is another plugin from GaMerZ that is so good, CNN used it for a long time. Yep, it's that good. It does exactly what you think: It lets you create polls. You can have the polls in your sidebar or in posts. It is nice, simple, and easy to set up. If you have a question to ask, this should do it for you.

- Contact Form 7 is one of myriad contact form plugins around. I've played with lots of them in the past, and I think all of them are harder than they should be to use. Contact Form 7 is good, as is cforms II (http://www.deliciousdays.com/cforms-plugin/), and is worth a try. If all else fails, create an image with your email address for people to read, but not spammers!

 TELL ME MORE   Media 6.4—Tris and Catherine Winters Talk About wp-Typography
Access this audio recording through your registered Web Edition at
my.safaribooksonline.com/9780132182836/media

For Advanced Folks—Editing Plugins

Sometimes, but not very often anymore, plugin authors will suggest editing the plugin files to change how the plugin works or unlocks other features. This isn't nearly as common as it used to be (not that it was very common before), because plugin writers have more flexibility and tools at their disposal now (and I think they are just getting more experienced overall).

If you run into a situation where you want or need to edit a plugin, you can do it in one of two ways: from within WordPress (see Figure 6.7) or externally in a text editor. I think you can guess which way I'm going to recommend—yes, externally. I'll probably repeat this over and over in the book, but it's an important fact that you always need to remember: Editing anything directly on the server is always a dangerous thing and is something you should do only if you know how to fix things if you goof.

Figure 6.7 *Editing plugin screen, not that you'll need it often.*

Why do I harp on not editing on the server or at least approaching it with due care and caution? Because, back when the Web was young, a hot-shot web developer working for an extremely large pharmaceutical company decided that he was cool enough to edit server configuration files live on the server. He was wrong, however, and all of the marketing websites disappeared from the Internet for about 20 minutes. Longest 20 minutes of my life. I got the sites back up only with the help of the hosting company. Let's just say, "lesson learned."

If you do want to edit a plugin through WordPress, the plugin editor is found under the Plugins button. Click Editor and you'll see the code editor and a list of your plugins on the right. No, I wasn't kidding; it is a little intense and not for the faint of code. A little less scary is downloading the plugin's folder from your wp-content/plugins on your site, *making a clean backup copy*, and then opening the file(s) you need to edit in your favorite text editor. The backup copy step is key, especially if you're editing through WordPress, so if you *do* mess up the plugin, you can quickly swap it out for a working copy. Oh, sure, you can fly without a net (no backup copy), but if something goes wrong, you'll be downloading a fresh copy from the repository anyway.

It goes without saying that if you're editing plugins, you're either A) following specific directions to change something or B) know about writing PHP scripts, in which case all the preceding warnings will be met with "Yeah, yeah, I know what I'm doing." In either case, good luck.

In this chapter, you will learn all about WordPress themes: how to find them, how to install them, and how to edit them to suit your needs.

7

All About Themes

If there is one part of using WordPress that I think is the most fun, besides writing and posting, it's playing with new themes. How often do you have the ability to change your website from dark, brooding, and professional to a hot pink Hello Kitty-themed site with one click? With WordPress, switching themes is just that easy and, even better, thousands and thousands of great-looking, professionally designed themes are available for you to use on your site for free. The range of styles, colors, features, and designs is truly mind blowing.

In this chapter, I take on the subject of themes head on and give you a huge brain dump on everything I've learned about WordPress themes over the past few years. Themes have come a long, long way since I first started using WP. Not only are they better designed with more features, but also themes can have their own settings pages that enable you to do significant customizations from within the admin area and without needing to know how to code at all. Believe me, even for those of us who don't mind coding, having simple check boxes and options is a lot nicer than having to edit theme files every time you want to change something.

Beyond picking and editing themes, we explore one of the most interesting new developments in the WP Theme world: theme frameworks. I'm excited to get into this topic because it's so new and so innovative.

A *theme framework* is the equivalent of buying a set of general house plans that have been architected to be customized to suit your needs.

By the end of this chapter, you'll be able choose, edit, and tweak a theme to your heart's content. Just don't get lost browsing for themes; you can lose days doing that! Let's start off by understanding how WordPress themes work in concert with WordPress as a whole.

Understanding the Structure of WordPress Themes

Unlike plugins, where you don't need (or generally want) to know about the files within a plugin folder, to understand and work with themes, you need to know what the core files are and how they work together with WordPress. Luckily for all of us, the filenames for WordPress theme files (generally) make sense. For files such as header, footer, comments, sidebar, index, archives, and style, it's quite easy to figure out what they pertain to, even if you don't understand the underlying code.

All themes start off in a folder with a name. Only two files are required to make a theme a theme: index.php and style.css. Of course, almost all themes have far more files, but WordPress needs only index.php to render the file as HTML and call The Loop to display posts and style.css to define a few theme variables and give the page some kind of look.

As themes get more complex, they handle different kinds of content in different ways. Archives handled one way, categories another, and search results another way. Each of these kinds of content can have different headers, footers, and sidebars.

Core Files

As I've already told you, all that themes need to "work" are index.php and style.css. Table 7.1 lists the standard files that generally come with a theme (I'm using the default WordPress theme Twenty Ten as my example) and shows what they do.

Table 7.1   The Most Common Theme-Related Files

File Name	Description
404.php	The 404 not found page, when visitors try to go to a page that doesn't exist. In its simplest form, it just says "try again." More clever versions can suggest possible pages that might match what the visitor was looking for.
archive.php	A core file that returns a list of all the posts from a given category, date, or tag. For example, if you have a category called Recipes and someone clicks a link to that category, all the posts with the category Recipes will be listed and use this template file to do it.
attachment.php	A template file to display files attached to posts (such as images or documents).
author.php	This file lists all the posts by a particular author (new in WordPress 3.0).
category.php	Special type of archive template file to display all the posts from a certain category.
comments.php	When your readers want to leave a comment, this is the file that is called that not only lets them do it, but also gives your comment form its own particular look. The only time you edit this file is if you need to change some particular details of the comments form (meaning, pretty much never).

Table 7.1 The Most Common Theme-Related Files

File Name	Description
editor-style-rtl.css and editor-style.css	Companion files (one for right-to-left languages) to style the Post and Page editors with special options when using this theme.
footer.php	As you can imagine, this file is called to close off all open HTML tags and to do nifty things such as put a copyright message on your blog. More and more often, the footer also contains a widget (or three) and is larger than what we used to like (often now called the new giant Web 2.0 footer).
functions.php	Probably one of the most mysterious, but crucial, files in the core template files. Within functions.php are additional functions, and that can take a theme from meh to wow. This is where a theme designer can put in special things like magazine-style layouts, sliding images, and anything else the theme designer might want to throw into the mix. If you're adding your own custom functions in a regular theme, this is where they would go.
header.php	This is where the header graphics and top navigation live (most of the time). If there is one file that people wind up editing, this is it. If you use WordPress to make a "regular" website, often you wind up editing the header file to include or exclude pages or links in your core navigation (unless the theme uses the new Menus options, that is).
images (directory)	Sure you can have images in the root of a theme with all the other theme files, but that gets to be messy and confusing. Most theme designers just use the good old images directory to stash all the images for a theme.
index.php	This is the home page of your blog. It calls The Loop, sidebars, header, footer, and all the rest to make your site look like it does when people first visit it. In the case of Twenty Ten, index.php just calls a special file called loop.php.
languages (directory)	Provides extra information so the theme natively supports other languages (as set under Settings -> General).
license.txt	The license terms for this theme.
loop.php	Called from a number of files in the template, this file runs through The Loop to display posts. Instead of having to edit The Loop in several files to make changes, editing this file will handle it for the entire site at once.
onecolumn-page.php	A special Page template without a sidebar.
page.php	Like its twin, single.php, this is the default template for how Pages look when you create them. You can use different templates for a page so that the features and look of the page matches the page's task. The most common template is the blog page, but you also have Archives, Links, and almost anything. We get into how you pull this off later in the chapter.
rtl.css	A stylesheet to handle languages that are read right to left.
screenshot.png	When you go to your Appearance section of your blog and see the pictures of each of the themes, this is where it comes from. Just a simple graphic that helps you remember which theme is which.

Table 7.1   The Most Common Theme-Related Files

File Name	Description
search.php	This file is used to format the results on a search page. This is not one of the common files to edit, but now you know what it's for.
sidebar-footer.php	This sets up the widgets for the theme's footer.
sidebar.php	It doesn't matter if your blog has one, two, three, or even more sidebars; this is where they are defined and laid out.
single.php	This might not seem like an important file, but this how your blog renders a post when readers look at it alone. Generally not a big deal to edit, but also not often needed either.
style.css	If you want your blog to look a certain way, this is the file that does it. All of the cascading style sheet information lives in this file. This file is often edited.
tag.php	A special archive template to display all the posts with a certain tag.

Because WordPress themes work modularly, you can have a lot more files and directories than what I've talked about here. A whole hierarchy of files exist that few WordPress users even know about. This "secret" hierarchy can give you some pretty cool capabilities and, believe it or not, there isn't even much coding needed.

Finding Themes and Choosing the Right One for Your Blog

It might be over-reaching to say that there are almost as many different themes as there are WordPress users, but I don't think I'd be that far off. This, of course, presents a bit of a problem—how do you choose from the 1,100+ themes available at WordPress.org?

The first thing I think about is what kind of style or feel I want my blog to have. Do you want minimalist and clean or colorful and cartoonish? Just having that idea in your head will help you narrow down the results that you find when you start searching. Like picking themes on WordPress.com (which is a great place to start checking out themes because there are far fewer to choose from there), I find that starting with color is a good start. Yes, in the end, you should decide on things like number of columns, SEO features, and design, but I've found that people gravitate to color first. If you really don't like green, then no green theme, no matter how awesome it might be, will ever be the right one for you. Let's, then, walk through this together.

You can start your search either in the search box or click the filter and tag picker (see Figure 7.1).

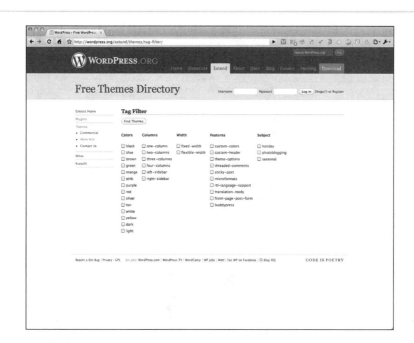

Figure 7.1   *Use the tag filter to search for themes.*

By checking blue (one of my favorite colors for blogs), I get a list of 333 themes to pick from (see Figure 7.2).

Then you narrow it down a bit. For example, I like three-column themes, and checking that box gives me 12 themes to pick from. At this point, I often sigh and start over again with different terms because I just don't like the options I'm presented with. This is okay, because often the theme designers haven't categorized their themes very well. I've sometimes found the perfect theme when browsing in more general ways. The drawback of self-categorization is that people often don't categorize things they way you want them to.

At this point, I'd pick about five themes that I think look good. I make sure that the themes have been updated in the last year or so; WordPress has many more theme tools and capabilities than it used to, so a newer theme has a better chance of supporting the new features over an older one.

Do the ratings or number of downloads matter more when picking a theme? I go for downloads almost every time. Ratings are a good indicator, but having 10 ratings and the average 4.5 stars suggests to me that the designer's friends did most of the rating. Downloads show how often people have picked a theme given all the other options. If a theme has been downloaded tens of thousands (or more) times,

Figure 7.2   *All the blue themes*

that's a good indicator that the theme has some legs. Of course, a brand-new theme might not have many downloads at all, so sometimes taking a chance on a new theme can lead to a fantastic surprise.

Themes are one of those things, like plugins, that you don't really know how good it is until you install it and use it. Yes, you can click the Preview button on the theme's information page, but that view gives you only a partial look into how the theme works. I've lost count of the number of times I've downloaded a theme with high hopes only to find that the content column is narrower than I like (I like at least 500-pixels wide) or that some of my plugins or widgets look strange on it. This is why I pick several themes that I think I like and try them.

One of the challenges you face when you start a new blog is that you don't have a lot of content to test the theme against. You might not run into a roadblock for a few weeks or months, but don't worry about that now—you can tweak the theme or change to a different one later. I tend to change my theme a few times a year so that I can try out new features, new styles of information flow, or just a new look. Again, that's the great thing about WordPress themes; you can change themes with little risk of you breaking your blog or wrecking content.

Be daring, be classic, be colorful—it doesn't matter because WordPress themes let your blog be anything you want it to be.

SHOW ME   Media 7.1—Finding Themes for WordPress

How do you find the right theme? This video shows how the tag filters and search work to find just the right theme for your blog or site.

Access this video file through your registered Web Edition at
my.safaribooksonline.com/9780132182836/media

Installing Themes on Your Blog

If you've installed a few plugins by now, you have everything you need to know about installing themes. Not only can you install them manually the same way (except themes go into the themes folder, not the plugins folder), but you can install them through the administration area the same way as well. There is a theme browser that connects to the WordPres.org repository to install directly and can upload a ZIP archive to install if you downloaded a theme already. If you need a refresher, head back to Chapter 6, "Finding and Using Plugins," and skim the installing plugins section. Just remember that you're installing *themes* in the themes directory, not plugins!

Why don't I browse for themes within the administration area (at least very often)? I find it harder to look at lots of themes quickly, and sometimes the results appear to be slower to come up through my admin area. It's just a personal preference, but if I'm helping someone and I *know* the theme I'm looking for, I'll use the admin area just to be more efficient.

Just like plugins, when you have the theme uploaded and installed, you need to activate it:

1. Click on the Appearance button to see all the themes you have installed. (The list is refreshed from what themes are installed when you click the Appearance button.)

2. You can activate the theme with one click, but if you try out a theme for the first time, click Preview first. Sometimes all I need to see is the Preview (which shows you what your blog will look like with the theme, using all your content and widgets) to decide that the theme just won't be a keeper.

3. If, on the other hand, you're happy with what you see, click Activate theme.

4. Go to your site and refresh the page to see your new look!

It's just as easy as that.

SHOW ME   Media 7.2—Installing WordPress Themes
A video about installing themes automatically and through FTP.
Access this video file through your registered Web Edition at
my.safaribooksonline.com/9780132182836/media

Configuring Extra Features on Themes

As themes have become more sophisticated and complex, it just makes sense that themes would start to have configuration options. The first, and probably still the most common, is to swap in a custom header image. Because a lot of themes come with a great header image (there are some great photographers out there), lots of folks didn't really want to change, but when the same header image is appearing everywhere, the luster wears off fast. Usually it's an easy form field to put in the URL of the new image. Sometimes there is a handy upload option, which makes it even easier to get a custom look with minimal effort. The only thing you should worry about is making sure your header image is the right size. Remember that themes are designed with certain sizes in mind, so parts mesh nicely together. Having a header image that is too long or too high might make your blog look rather strange (to say the least).

Let's look at changing the header image for the new default theme Twenty Ten as an example:

1. If it isn't already active, activate Twenty Ten under Appearance.

2. Click Header under Appearance, and you should see something like Figure 7.3.

3. To switch to any of the supplied images, click the radio button next to the image and click Save Changes.

4. If you'd like to use a file of your own, create an image on your computer that is 940 pixels wide by 198 pixels tall, (I'd suggest a PNG or JPG.)

5. Click Choose File, browse your hard drive for the image you created, and click Okay.

6. Click Upload.

7. On the next screen, you can crop the header to fit in the space (unless it's exactly 940x198). Remember that this is cropping (cutting/removing) and not scaling (shrinking). Click Crop Header when you finish (see Figure 7.4).

8. Your new header will be active! Now, you might not like the result on the first try (or two), so be ready to keep trying.

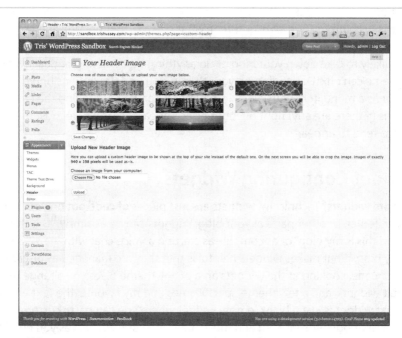

Figure 7.3   *Header image screen for Twenty Ten. As a side note, many of the pictures were taken by Matt Mullenweg.*

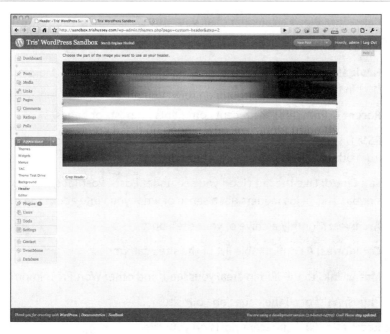

Figure 7.4   *My new header image (a long-shutter shot I took of traffic). The area within the dashed rectangle is the area I'm using.*

As for other options, it's becoming more common for themes to let you choose how many columns (one, two, or three), what size the columns are, and how they are arranged. Should you worry about any of these settings? No, theme settings aren't likely to take down your blog or do anything that deleting or deactivating the theme can't fix. Depending on your theme, you find the options under Appearance or as a menu item of its own. Sometimes it can be hard to find the custom settings (if there are any) right off, but under Appearance is where most of the new options tend to appear.

All About Configuring Widgets

What are widgets? Technically, widgets are just pieces of code put on your sidebar, header, footer, or other parts of your blog. Widgets can be as simple as just "Hi, I'm Tris and this is my blog" or as complex as starting a voice chat with me while visiting my blog. What makes widgets helpful is that they are managed as discrete units of code. Looking at the Widgets area of any theme gives you a range of default widgets, and a few theme-specific ones and my favorite: the Text widget. The Text widget is just a blank, empty widget where you can paste custom code (such as a Google Adsense ad) and move it around your sidebars as you need to. The Text widget is one of the several core, default widgets that are available to all themes. The other default widgets are as follows:

- **Akismet:** If Akismet is active.

- **Calendar:** Shows a calendar of all your posts.

- **Links:** For your blogroll.

- **Navigation menu:** This ties in with the new Menus feature. (More on this later in the chapter.)

- **Recent Comments:** The recent comments on posts or pages.

- **RSS:** Displays items from an RSS feed of your choice. Great for pulling in news from other websites.

- **Tag Cloud:** Like the tag cloud you see under Posts, Post Tags, but on your sidebar. This helps readers get a sense of what you write about the most.

- **Archives:** Monthly archive of your site's posts.

- **Categories:** A configurable list of the site's categories.

- **Meta:** Links to the admin area, your feed, and other WordPress information.

- **Pages:** A list of all the pages on your site.

- **Recent Posts:** Your recent posts on your site.

- **Search:** Basic search box for your site.

- **Text**.

These are some of the core items that a lot of people add to their sites, including me. Don't be afraid of trying these widgets and experimenting with various options they offer (like number of recent posts or recent comments to display) or setting your own titles (for the Archives widget on my site, I set the title to Blasts from the Past).

The problem with widgets is that they are addictive and fun to add to your blog, but you need to resist adding too many. Using too many widgets can make your blog load as slow as molasses for your visitors. The reason is that each widget is a little piece of code that has to be run before it can display. While all these widgets are loading, your blog might partially load (which looks strange) or not load at all (leaving visitors sitting and waiting at a blank page).

What is the "perfect" number of widgets? As you can imagine, there isn't one. Using all of the default widgets isn't too much of a drain on the system, whereas one giant live video chat widget could be all it takes to make your blog unusable.

 **LET ME TRY IT**

Adding Widgets to Your Blog's Sidebar

Before you are completely scared off of using widgets at all, let me show you how easy it is to add them in the first place.

1. Click the Appearance button.

2. Click the Widgets link. If you don't see a Widgets link, your theme doesn't support widgets. This is quite rare now, but if you come across one, I have a simple solution for you—find a theme that does support widgets. (It's called being "widget ready" and is one of the tag options available when searching for themes.) There is no point in you trying to add and edit code to make a non-widget-ready theme to be widget ready when there are so many widget-ready themes around.

3. Clicking the Widgets displays a screen where you have widgets on the left and places you can put them on the right. Note that I said "places" and not "your sidebars"—this is because you can now have "widget areas" in places other than the sidebars. You can have widgets in the header, footer, and even within the content portion of the page. We get to how to do that later in this chapter, but for now don't be surprised if you run into themes that have more than just sidebars as places you can drag and drop widgets.

4. Make sure the section (sidebar, header, footer, and so on) is expanded (more than the title of the area is showing) and then drag a widget from the left to the right.

5. Set widget options such as a custom title or number of posts or category for links (depending on the widget).

6. Click Save, and you're done!

It's as simple as that. If you have more that one widget, you can move the widgets around within a sidebar (for example) by just dragging the widget up or down in that section (or even to a new section). Removing widgets is just as easy, except you drag the widget to the left and into the not active or recently active section (see Figure 7.5).

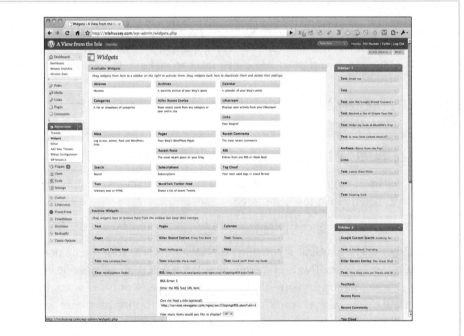

Figure 7.5 *Sidebars, available widgets, and inactive widgets on my blog*

As you move widgets in and out of sidebars, you notice the little "marching ants" dashed box, which lets you know where the widget will go. Sometimes as you're dragging, it takes a moment or two for the box to appear, so be patient. Unlike previous versions of WordPress, you don't have to save anything to ensure the widgets appear on your site; every time you put a widget into a space, it will appear there on your site automatically.

Common Widget Options

Many widgets come with their own options, and others enable only you to customize the title of the widget to something that you prefer over the default. For example, instead of Archives, I have Blasts from the Past and instead of Killer Recent Entries, I have The Great Stuff. How you want the categories widget or recent posts widget to appear is up to you, but just remember to click the Save button in the widget to make sure your changes are saved.

RSS Widget

The RSS widget might not be exactly what you think it is. It isn't, as I learned when it first came out, to display your RSS feed or buttons for your feed but to display another site's feed in your sidebar. Why would you want to do this? Well, let's say you write for more than one site or you are part of a larger network of bloggers, and you want your other posts and posts from others in your network to appear on your sidebar to help promote those articles. This is what the RSS widget is for. As you can see in Figure 7.6, I added the feed from my newspaper column to the widget. The RSS widget is an easy way to help promote other sites you are affiliated with or just plain like.

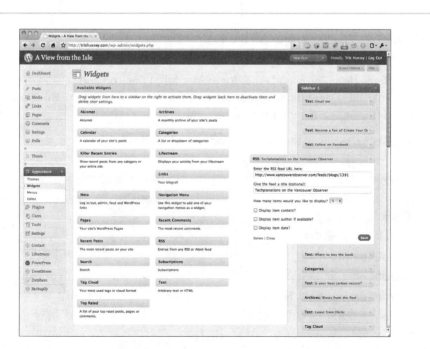

Figure 7.6   *The RSS widget with the feed to my newspaper column added*

 **LET ME TRY IT**

Setting Up and Adding an RSS Widget for Your Blog

1. You're going to want to flip between a couple sites for this exercise: your site's administration area and the site that has the feed you want to display. I suggest having your admin area open in one tab of your browser and the other site in another one (Command -> Control+T opens a new tab within your browser window in all major browsers).

2. Start in the Widgets section. Go to Appearance and then click Widgets.

3. Drag the RSS widget to the area where you want it to appear on your site (sidebar, header, footer, whatever is configured for your site).

4. As soon as you let go of the mouse and place the widget, the RSS widget options opens.

5. To configure the widget, you just need to copy the RSS feed for a site. However, this is sometimes easier said than done. What you need to do is look for the little orange RSS icon, as shown in Figure 7.7.

RSS FEED

Figure 7.7   *Example of the orange RSS icon.*

6. Right-click (Command+click for us Mac folks) the icon and select Copy link/URL. Depending on your browser and OS, it will say something a little different, but the intention is the same.

7. Paste the URL in the space on the widget for the RSS feed.

Learn your keyboard shortcuts! Below are a few basic keyboard shortcuts that *everyone* should know and use:

Control/Command+C: Copy

Control/Command+V: Paste

Control/Command+X: Cut

Control/Command+S: Save

Control/Command+N: New (new what depends on the program)

Control/Command+W: Close

Control/Command+T: New tab (for web browsers)

You can save so much time using those instead of going up to the menu bar with your mouse every time. Learn them—they are your friends!

8. You can put in a custom title or just let the automatic title for the feed come through, and then click Save. That's it!

> If you'd like to add the feed from my blog to your sidebar, it's http://trishussey. com/feed/.

Text Widgets

Up until now, we've been looking at widgets that are ready-made for you—stuff that just works after you drag and drop it. Text widgets are blank slates; you can paste just about anything into them, and it appears on your blog. It's the anything part that sometimes throws people. Not that it's hard, but it's easy to go overboard or to accidentally paste (or type) in code that doesn't work quite right. Here are common uses for the Text widget:

- Google Adsense ads
- Blog badges (awards, support, causes)
- Video/audio players
- Display Twitter, Facebook updates, or networks
- Just plain old, text information like "About me..."

Although you can hand type in code for text widgets, in reality you'll most likely be copying and pasting code from other places into your widget. When you do copy and paste, make sure you *do not* click the Automatically Add Paragraphs box. This will, nine times out of ten, break the code you are pasting into the widget. The only time to use that check box is if you type in a block of plain old text and don't want to have to worry about the code for new paragraphs.

Like all the other widgets, you move text widgets around in the same way, and you need to click Save or the things you added won't be saved. One handy feature is that if you drag a custom text widget to the Inactive Widgets area, WordPress keeps the code you pasted in there intact. This comes in handy for annual events or if you need to troubleshoot your blog and strip off all the widgets to test things.

I can't stress enough that although widgets are awesome, and I have lots on my own blog, it's easy to get carried away and have too many widgets on your blog. When people start mentioning how long it takes for your blog to load or that your blog "looks funny," it's probably time to take a hard look at those widgets, especially the custom text ones, and see what you truly need to have and what is just blog bling.

Using WordPress Custom Menus

Besides changing colors around on your blog or site, the other thing most people want to customize are the navigation menus in their themes. Most themes list all the Pages you have in the main navigation (About, Contact, or whatever Pages you created). A few themes let you use your Post Categories as well (or instead). Here's the rub: With the standard code to automatically generate menus and lists, you can't mix categories and pages together. For example, you can't have navigation that went Page, Category, Page, Page, Category. You have to list one and then the other. Let's not even get into working with submenus, shall we? That is a whole other world of hurt. Well, that is until now. WordPress 3.0 has introduced a new Menus feature that is nothing short of awesome.

We've gone through widgets already and have seen how easy it is to just drag and drop widgets around. Now imagine doing that for your navigation menus. Figure 7.8 shows the default navigation for my test blog (using the default theme Twenty Ten).

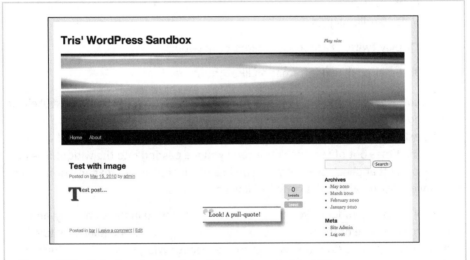

Figure 7.8 *Default navigation, default theme on my testing blog*

In Figure 7.9, I created a new menu for the site using the new Menus tool.

Notice that I have a link to the home page, then a Category, then a Page, submenus of the page are Categories, and then a few more Categories. I'll go through this in both a Let Me Try It and a Show Me section, but it's just a matter of dragging and dropping. How does it look? Check out Figure 7.10 for the results.

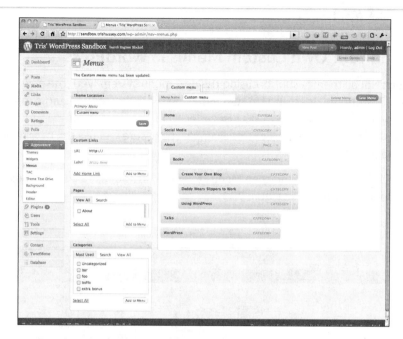

Figure 7.9 *The parts of my new custom menu using the Menus tool*

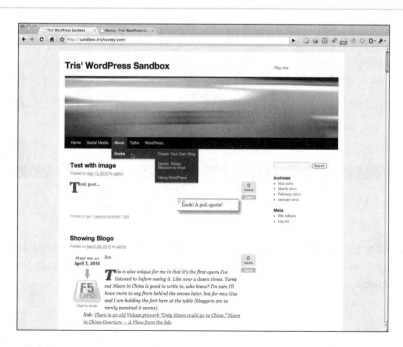

Figure 7.10 *My new custom menu, including submenus and mixing Pages and categories*

LET ME TRY IT

Creating Your Own Custom Menus in WordPress

Caveat: Not all themes support using the new menu system (yet). The new default theme Twenty Ten does, and I'm sure more and more themes will start supporting the new menus soon enough. It's just easier. I'll talk about adding support for the menus later in this chapter. For this example, make sure you use the new Twenty Ten theme for your site:

1. Click Appearance and then Menus to get to the Menus screen. It should look something like Figure 7.11.

Figure 7.11 *Default Menus area with no menus set up yet*

2. Click the text box labeled Enter Menu Name Here, give your menu a name, and click Create Menu. For this example, I've called my menu "custom menu."

3. You're now ready to add menu items. Most people want a Home link, so in the Custom Links box, click Add Home Link and then click Save Menu. Get in the habit of clicking Save Menu often to save your work as you go.

4. If you'd like to change what the menu says on the menu bar, click the small, gray triangle in the bar, and you can edit the link URL, name, and attribute (see Figure 7.12).

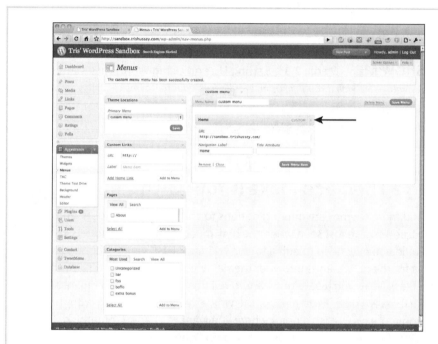

Figure 7.12 *The Home item in our new, custom menu with its options opened to be edited*

5. For Pages and Categories, just click the check box next to the name of the item you want to add and click Add to Menu.

6. You can click-and-drag the menu items to rearrange them and make submenus. When some thing is a submenu item of another, it will be slightly indented (see Figure 7.9).

That's it! Very easy, very straightforward, and you don't need to know one bit of code to make it all come together. You can create additional menus by clicking the plus sign next to your menu's name. If your theme supports additional navigation bar menus (say, for specific page templates), you can specify that under the Theme

Locations area. All menus are available to be used with Navigation Menu widget, so you can create special menus for your sidebars or wherever you can place widgets in your theme.

The code for menus came from a collaboration between the WordPress development community and the people behind the theme foundry Woo Themes (http://www.woothemes.com/). I think that if a theme uses the new Menus system and offers basic options for changing colors and similar things in a theme, most people never need to learn how to edit CSS or PHP files.

Of course, that's not going to stop me from teaching you those skills here.

SHOW ME   Media 7.3—Setting Up and Using WordPress Menus
A step-by-step walkthrough of using WordPress Menus for themes.

Access this video file through your registered Web Edition at **my.safaribooksonline.com/9780132182836/media**

Editing a Theme to Make It Your Own

More and more themes are offering options to change colors, layouts, and other settings, and you've just seen when the new menu system and widgets can do. So, why would you *ever* need to edit a theme by hand? First, you might need to add support for the new menus into your theme (which requires editing a couple of the theme files). Next, you just might want to roll up your sleeves and dig into a theme to make it really yours. Regardless of the why, as you start working with themes more and more, you reach a point where you want to change something. This is when you either A) look for a new theme or B) figure out how to make the changes.

Before you start worrying that you can't possibly edit WordPress themes, relax. It's not hard. Really. I'm not going to get into creating themes from scratch (although with the kernel of knowledge I'm giving you here, you certainly could start down that path), but rather just a few of the easy things you can do tweak your theme just a bit. I'm going to talk about editing the look of your theme with CSS changes. CSS changes cover things like colors, text styles, link styles, and some of the layout aspects of your theme. When we have to change a few of the stylistic parts of the theme, we'll get into editing some of the PHP code that makes things happen. Neither of these sections are going to be thorough tutorials on CSS or PHP; that is well beyond the scope of this book. What I will do is demystify CSS and PHP so that you feel confident in knowing what to look for when you try to find that little bit of code to change to make your blog just perfect.

Always. Back. Up. Your. Theme. First. Before you start any of these customizations—which you will do on your local computer—after you download your theme, duplicate that folder and keep it set aside for safekeeping. It is supremely easy to mess up a theme. It happens to me all the time. At a certain point, you need to just stop, throw up your hands in defeat, and start over. This is why you need a clean backup copy. You've been warned.

The idea here, remember, is to focus on things that you're likely to want to do or encounter. Sure, I could write about adding a custom slideshow into your template that also changes colors depending on the category and the colors of the picture, but chances are that if you want that, you'll do what I do: Look for a plugin to do it and a theme that already supports those features. I prefer to spend my days writing, using, and teaching WordPress over coding plugins and themes. My guess is that you feel the same way, so let's get to the basics of CSS.

CSS

CSS stands for Cascading Style Sheet and was invented to define how a website looks from one file instead of in each individual file and occurrence of an object. For example, if I decided that I wanted all links to be purple with bold and underlining without CSS, I would define some of that at the beginning of the web page, but some of it (like bold) I'd have to do for every single link for every single page. If I changed my mind and wanted pink and italics, I'd have to do it all over again. The way CSS works is that one file tells web browsers how to display things, and within a given page, there is little or no style applied to common elements. For example, the purple, bold, and underlined link would look like this in the stylesheet:

```
a {
    color: purple;
    font-weight: bold;
    text-decoration: underline;
}
```

In the web page, the HTML would look like this:

```
<a href="http://usingwordpressbook.com/">This would be a link</a>
```

Because on the page there is no information about color or style, if I change the code in the stylesheet to this...

```
a {
    color: fuchsia;
    text-decoration: none;
    font-style: italic;
}
```

...all the links would become fuchsia, italicized, with no underline. One simple change in one file that all the pages of a website (or blog) use. Your stylesheet is generally called style.css, but that's just so we know what it is. You can call it thelook.css as long as you code into the website (or blog theme) to use that name. If you open the style.css file from any theme, you're bound to see code that looks like this (this is a section of the stylesheet for the default theme Twenty Ten):

```css
/*
LAYOUT: Two columns
DESCRIPTION: Two-column fixed layout with one sidebar right of content
*/

#container {
    float: left;
    margin: 0 -240px 0 0;
    width: 100%;
}

#content {
    margin: 0 280px 0 20px;
}

#primary,
#secondary {
    float: right;
    overflow: hidden;
    width: 220px;
}

#secondary {
    clear: right;
}

#footer {
    clear: both;
    width: 100%;
}

/*
LAYOUT: One column, no sidebar
DESCRIPTION: One centered column with no sidebar
*/

.onecolumn #content {
    margin: 0 auto;
    width: 640px;
}
```

```
/*
LAYOUT: Full width, no sidebar
DESCRIPTION: Full width content with no sidebar; used for attachment pages
*/

.single-attachment #content {
    margin: 0 auto;
    width: 900px;
}
```

There is structure to the information. Words preceded with a # are called IDs or identifiers and a "." are classes. The whole explanation of IDs versus classes often makes my head spin, but after a lot of reading (and even more mistakes), the best way to explain them is that classes are like barcodes, and IDs are like serial numbers. You can have the same barcode on a dozen TVs of the same make and model, but each of those have an individual (ID) serial number. This is how it works in practice; an ID such as #header is only going to be used once on a page, whereas something such as .entry is going to be used over and over again (lots of entries per page).

You're probably wondering at this moment why anyone in their right mind would want to edit CSS files. They look confusing, detailed, and fiddly. And you'd be right. I do a fair bit of work editing stylesheets for various clients (and myself), and honestly sometimes I wonder if it's worth it. Here is my advice to you: Dip your toe into CSS slowly. Sites like Dave Shea's CSS Zen Garden Resource Guide (http://www.mezzoblue.com/zengarden/resources/), Smashing Magazine (http://www.smashingmagazine.com/), Six Revisions (http://sixrevisions.com/category/tutorials/), and WPBeginner (http://www.wpbeginner.com/) all have a myriad of tutorials, code samples, and nifty tricks to learn. As I said previously, more and more themes are making it easier for you to tweak your theme without needing to know code, and I think this is a great thing. I teach full-day classes with that very goal: Create a website with WordPress and not know how to code. There are still a few more things that relate to CSS that you might like to know. One of those things is how colors are written in CSS.

What Are Color Hex Codes?

You've probably noticed that stylesheets don't often define a color with a name, but rather with a hexadecimal or HEX code like #73a0c5 (which is a blue color). Sure, names work, but they aren't specific. The "red" defined in the CSS definition might not be the red you want; you might want a lighter red or darker red or more orangey red. In the digital world, we often define a color as the percentage of red, green, and blue and specifically where 0 is none and 255 is 100%. White is all color, so 100% red or 255, 100%/255 green, and 100%/255 blue. Black is the opposite, so 0% for red, green, and blue. We usually just refer to the numbers as the RGB color.

Because we always give the numbers in that order, I can say I need something with RGB 31, 135, 69 (which is a dark green) and designers know exactly what I'm talking about. Hex codes come into play because it's easier to represent a color with a string of numbers and letters than three different numbers. Every number between 0 and 255 has a hexadecimal equivalent. For 0, it's 00 and for 255, it's ff, so green about is 1f8745. There are lots of resources online for converting colors from RGB to hex and for looking up a color and finding its hex number for web design.

As a shorthand, when you define black, red, green, and white, you can use #000 for black (because it's just six zeros), #fff for white, #f00 for red, #0f0 for green, and #00f for blue.

If you're looking for a cheat sheet for color codes, check out ColorJack (http://www.colorjack.com/sphere/), Color Scheme Designer (http://colorschemedesigner.com/), and Adobe's Kuler (http://kuler.adobe.com/)—not to mention these are great sites that can help you pick complementary color schemes.

It will take some fiddling to get the hang of what to edit and where, but you'll get it. Here are a few other things to keep in mind:

- You can use any basic text editor to edit stylesheets, but don't ever use a word processor such as Microsoft Word. Word breaks the code in the stylesheet.

- Browsers read stylesheets top down. So, you can override a setting from the top with a setting toward the bottom. When stylesheets don't seem to work, chances are that somewhere later in the stylesheet, the element you are styling has something redefining it. This is where a tool like Firebug (http://getfirebug.com/) is especially handy because you can see what parts of the stylesheet are doing what to any particular section of the page.

- There are lots of CSS tutorials online to help you learn the ropes of CSS. Sometimes the best way to learn is to take apart one of your sites, but not make any "real" changes; just use Firebug to see how things come together.

CSS can be maddening. Every browser and operating system renders CSS a little differently. Internet Explorer on Windows, especially IE6, is often the greatest frustration for designers worldwide. So don't lose heart when things start going off the rails.

Editing your theme's CSS might seem like a lot right now. Stylesheets are often pages long and hard to decipher. Keep at it, though—the results are worth it. When you can swap out a new header or custom background, all the headaches will be worth it.

PHP

Writing PHP scripts or custom functions is beyond the scope of this book. But I can give you a brief, practical look at a few places where you might need or want to edit your theme's PHP code to make a few subtle changes.

The first thing you need to know is that, like CSS stylesheets, you open PHP files in a text editor. As you've figured out by now, having a good text editor is essential when working with WordPress (any blog engine, really). Next, PHP is a scripting language, which means that you can see the code that makes a script work right there in the files and isn't compiled like Word or Firefox or Safari are. Like all scripting languages (and programming languages), there are rules, called syntax, that define how you write and express commands, variables, and so on.

It's important to know that a space between characters can matter, and there is a difference between a single quote (') and a double-quote ("). This is why when those of us who don't code in PHP all the time need to add new sections, we do a lot of copying and pasting. If we find an example that works, there is absolutely no benefit to retyping. Copy and paste helps to make sure that your new function will actually work.

There are two theme files that you'll find that you will update more than any other: header.php and footer.php. Header.php (99% of the time) is the PHP file that contains both the header graphic and also the top navigation. So, if you want to change how the top navigation looks or works, this is where to start looking. Same with making changes to the header area and the hidden parts of the page that search engines look for in the HTML head portion. The footer, in contrast, is where you find the things like putting your copyright info, other links, and at the end of the file, website tracking scripts for metrics. Editing those files will cover most of what you're going to want to do, but the part that you'll get the most out of here is how to add the new WordPress 3.0 menus to a theme that doesn't have them already.

 LET ME TRY IT

Adding Support for WordPress Menus into a Theme

For this Let Me Try It, you need to edit just two PHP files (functions.php and header.php) in a text editor. We use multicolor as the example here because it not only doesn't use the new WordPress menus, but it also looks rather nice, so keeping it wouldn't be a drag! You also need to be running WordPress 3.0 for this to work. If you're not sure which version you're running, go to your Dashboard; in the Right Now box, there is a line that says You Are Using WordPress.... If it doesn't say 3.0 (or higher), update to WordPress 3.0 first. (You can jump to Chapter 13, "Maintaining WordPress," if you'd like; I'll be here when you get back.)

1. Download multi-color from wordpress.org here: http://wordpress.org/extend/themes/multi-color. Unzip the file.

2. Using your FTP client, connect to your site, navigate to wp-content/themes/, and upload multicolor to your site.

3. Go to the administration area of your site and click Appearance. Activate multicolor.

4. Open the theme's folder on your computer (it should be called multicolor) and then open functions.php in your text editor. Start a new link right below `<?php` at the top of the file and put in this line:

```
add_theme_support('nav-menus');
```

It should look like Figure 7.13.

5. Save the file and close it. That line is all that's needed for the theme to load all the functions needed to support WordPress menus.

6. Click on Appearance and then Menus, and create a custom menu. Remember what you called it; we're going to need that for step 8.

7. Open header.php and look for the following:

```
<div class="menu">
    <ul>
        <?php if($options['mc_menu'] == 'pages') { ?><li
id="home"<?php if(!is_page()) {?> class="current_page_item"<?php
}?>>><a href="<?php bloginfo('home'); ?>"><?php _e('Home',
'multi-color'); ?></a></li> <?php echo re-
move_title_attribute(wp_list_pages('depth=3&title_li=&echo=0'));
?><?php } ?>
        <?php if($options['mc_menu'] == 'categories') { ?><li
id="home"<?php if(!is_page() && !is_category() ) {?>
class="current-cat"<?php }?>>><a href="<?php bloginfo('home');
?>"><?php _e('Home','multi-color'); ?></a></li> <?php echo re-
move_title_attribute(wp_list_categories('depth=3&title_li=&number=
10')); ?><?php } ?>
    </ul>
    <div class="clear"></div>
</div>
```

8. Select the two lines between `<ul>` and `</ul>` and delete them. In their place, put the following:

```
<?php wp_nav_menu( array('menu' => 'custom menu' )); ?>
```

I called my menu "custom menu." Replace that name with what you called your menu.

Figure 7.13 *Adding the menus function to the theme's functions.php*

9. Save and close header.php.

10. Back to your FTP client (reopen it if you have to); you're going to upload your new functions.php and header.php into multicolor.

11. Navigate to wp-content/themes/multi-color/ and drop in the new files. (Most FTP clients let you drag-and-drop files into the window to upload.) When you're asked if you want to replace (or overwrite) the old files with the new ones, the answer is Yes.

12. Go to your site's home page and refresh your browser. If everything worked, you'll see your new menu! (See Figure 7.14 for before and after views.)

It's a fair question to ask at this point whether learning PHP is even terribly important for working with themes. In most cases I've run into, it's not too important to know the ins and outs of PHP. Even when I've needed to paste in PHP code (note: paste), the instructions tell you what to look for and where the code goes. I have, however, run into a few times when I wanted to do something clever and not knowing PHP was an issue. Generally this was when I wanted to have layouts that would change depending on the category or tag or whatever. Lucky for you, WordPress theme support has evolved to a point where creating a tag- or

Figure 7.14   *Ta da! A new custom menu in place. The styling isn't perfect, but it works.*

category-specific layout is as simple as making sure you have the right filename. Maybe by the time the second of the edition of this book is written, themes will be even more advanced, and there will be even simpler ways to make complex layouts.

Custom Page Templates

When you create a Page in WordPress, it uses a template file all its own. The file is called page.php and doesn't look too different than other template pages. Here's the default Page template for Twenty Ten:

```php
<?php
/**
 * The template used to display all pages
 *
 * This is the template that displays all pages by default.
 * Please note that this is the wordpress construct of pages
 * and that other 'pages' on your wordpress site will use a
 * different template.
 *
```

```
 * @package WordPress
 * @subpackage Twenty Ten
 * @since 3.0.0
 */
?>

<?php get_header(); ?>

        <div id="container">
            <div id="content">

<?php the_post(); ?>

        <div id="post-<?php the_ID(); ?>" <?php post_class(); ?>>
            <?php if ( is_front_page() ) { ?>
                <h2 class="entry-title"><?php the_title(); ?></h2>
                <?php } else { ?>
                <h1 class="entry-title"><?php the_title(); ?></h1>
                <?php } ?>

        <div class="entry-content">
            <?php the_content(); ?>
 <?php wp_link_pages( array( 'before' => '<div class="page-link">' . __(
'Pages:', 'twentyten' ), 'after' => '</div>' ) ); ?>
 <?php edit_post_link( __( 'Edit', 'twentyten' ), '<span class="edit-
link">', '</span>' ); ?>
     </div><!-- .entry-content -->
    </div><!-- #post-<?php the_ID(); ?> -->

    <?php comments_template( '', true ); ?>

   </div><!-- #content -->
   </div><!-- #container -->

<?php get_sidebar(); ?>
<?php get_footer(); ?>
```

Twenty Ten has made the Page template simpler than previous versions. (Calls to The Loop are handled differently now.) Now, this is cool and all, but what if you want a special Page template that has no sidebars? You don't want all your Pages to lack sidebars, just one special Page (maybe two, but certainly not all of them). How do you pull this off? Page templates to the rescue! Within WordPress, it is easy to specify the template a particular Page uses (I'll talk about this more in Chapters 8, "Organizing the Content on Your Blog," and 9, "Creating and Managing Content with WordPress") and creating your own template is also easy.

LET ME TRY IT

Creating Your Own Page Templates

Remember, when we're talking about editing template files, we're editing the files using copies on your computer, not directly on the server. If you don't have a local copy of your template, use your FTP client to download a copy of your template from the server. It's in wp-content/themes/. Also, sorry WordPress.com users: This is another thing that you just can't do.

1. Start off with opening the page.php in your favorite text editor and put a line like this at the top:

```
<?php
/*
Template Name: No Sidebars
*/
?>
```

   This tells WordPress what the template's name is and how it should appear in the template menu.

2. Choose Save As from the File menu and save the file as no_sidebars.php. The filename isn't terribly important, but if I have a lot of Page templates, sometimes I make the filenames page-nosidebars.php or something similar to help me keep them straight.

3. Scroll down until you see `<?php get_sidebar(); ?>` and delete it. Save again. Now all you have to do is to upload this spiffy new file into your active theme's directory on the server. (If you were using Twenty Ten, the directory is called twentyten, by the way.) When you want to create a new Page, you choose No Sidebars from the Template menu on the right (see Figure 7.15).

You can get fancy with combinations of special pages that call and return certain blog posts (say, from one category or tag) or have other fun properties. I've used this trick when I created websites that needed different headers or sidebars for different pages. (Although in hindsight, I'm sure there was a smarter way to do it.)

There is a special case that doesn't require a special page template, but sometimes is a nice touch, and that is when you have a page as your home page and posts appear in another way. As I cover in more detail later in Chapter 10, "Creating Sites with WordPress," when you set your home page to a static page, you can create a page to display all your posts, just like it would have if you had a "normal" blog. Typically, I suggest creating a page with a title of Blog and no text in the body of the page. WordPress then knows that this page is special and when people visit it,

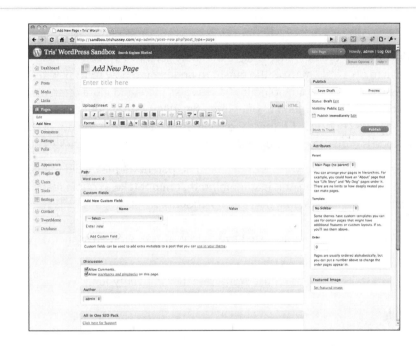

Figure 7.15   *Creating a new page with no sidebars*

it displays your posts as the content. Sometimes people create a special page template with wider columns or a different header for pages that are going to be post pages. You don't need to do this if your standard page template is okay (most of the time, I've found that it is just fine); it can just be an extra touch of coolness for your site.

Thus far, we've been working with "normal" themes—themes that the designers intended to be edited to some extent. The only problem is when your theme is updated because your custom code won't be in the updated theme. So, what do you do? You start getting into doing a lot of copying, pasting, and hoping that you marked all your changes with comments. (Yeah, like we all remember to do that.) The other option is to use a theme that has been designed with this situation in mind: a theme framework.

Using Theme Frameworks and Parent-Child Themes

Framework-based themes look boring at the outset, but that's because they are designed to be generic so that you can put your own style on them. The benefit of a framework is that the developer has spent a lot of time creating easy-to-implement functions that you can enable or disable as you need to. It's like taking a house plan that says only "master bathroom" and entering "add Jacuzzi tub, north-west corner" and it's there.

The downside of theme frameworks is that they can have a steep learning curve. You have to do a little more at the outset to understand how to work with it. For my time (and money), I am going for frameworks more and more often now in my own work because they tend to offer more flexibility, better options, and (often) better, cleaner code. Don't dismiss the benefits of nice, clean code out of hand. Clean code is easier to edit and tends to ensure your blog loads quickly.

The key to theme frameworks is understanding parent themes, child themes, and custom code. Believe me, this is something that might take a couple reads and a few examples to understand. Don't worry, though: I'm saying this because it took me a few run-throughs to really get it. To understand frameworks and the parent/child theme paradigm, you have to look at how WordPress themes work in general.

Figure 7.16 shows the files for the WordPress theme Twenty Ten.

Name	Date Modified	Size	Kind
404.php	Mar 29, 2010 3:03 PM	4 KB	PHP Document
archive.php	Mar 29, 2010 3:03 PM	4 KB	PHP Document
attachment.php	May 4, 2010 12:01 AM	8 KB	PHP Document
author.php	May 3, 2010 12:28 PM	4 KB	PHP Document
category.php	Mar 29, 2010 3:03 PM	4 KB	PHP Document
comments.php	May 4, 2010 12:01 AM	4 KB	PHP Document
editor-style-rtl.css	May 5, 2010 1:38 PM	4 KB	Style Sheet
editor-style.css	Feb 17, 2010 10:50 AM	4 KB	Style Sheet
footer.php	May 4, 2010 12:01 AM	4 KB	PHP Document
functions.php	May 5, 2010 8:04 PM	16 KB	PHP Document
header.php	May 4, 2010 12:01 AM	4 KB	PHP Document
images	May 6, 2010 2:00 PM	--	Folder
index.php	May 4, 2010 12:01 AM	4 KB	PHP Document
languages	May 6, 2010 2:00 PM	--	Folder
license.txt	Feb 7, 2010 8:16 AM	16 KB	TextW...ument
loop.php	May 4, 2010 12:01 AM	12 KB	PHP Document
onecolumn-page.php	Mar 29, 2010 3:03 PM	4 KB	PHP Document
page.php	Mar 29, 2010 3:03 PM	4 KB	PHP Document
rtl.css	May 3, 2010 12:17 PM	4 KB	Style Sheet
screenshot.png	Feb 22, 2010 6:23 PM	33 KB	Portab...image
search.php	Mar 29, 2010 3:03 PM	4 KB	PHP Document
sidebar-footer.php	Mar 29, 2010 3:03 PM	4 KB	PHP Document
sidebar.php	Mar 29, 2010 3:03 PM	4 KB	PHP Document
single.php	May 6, 2010 10:34 AM	4 KB	PHP Document
style.css	May 3, 2010 12:16 PM	25 KB	Style Sheet
tag.php	Mar 29, 2010 3:03 PM	4 KB	PHP Document

Figure 7.16 *The files for the Twenty Ten theme*

If you want to change how the footer looks, you edit footer.php. To change the header, edit header.php, and to change the sidebars, edit sidebar.php. Now if there is an update to this theme and you want to update it, you would have to do a lot of work to sync your changes with the updated files so that you don't lose any fixes or improvements. Now compare Twenty Ten's files with the framework core theme Thematic, as shown in Figure 7.17.

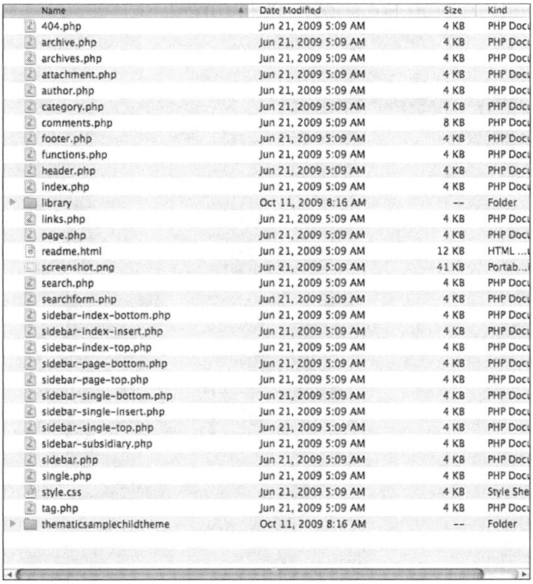

Name	Date Modified	Size	Kind
404.php	Jun 21, 2009 5:09 AM	4 KB	PHP Doc
archive.php	Jun 21, 2009 5:09 AM	4 KB	PHP Doc
archives.php	Jun 21, 2009 5:09 AM	4 KB	PHP Doc
attachment.php	Jun 21, 2009 5:09 AM	4 KB	PHP Doc
author.php	Jun 21, 2009 5:09 AM	4 KB	PHP Doc
category.php	Jun 21, 2009 5:09 AM	4 KB	PHP Doc
comments.php	Jun 21, 2009 5:09 AM	8 KB	PHP Doc
footer.php	Jun 21, 2009 5:09 AM	4 KB	PHP Doc
functions.php	Jun 21, 2009 5:09 AM	4 KB	PHP Doc
header.php	Jun 21, 2009 5:09 AM	4 KB	PHP Doc
index.php	Jun 21, 2009 5:09 AM	4 KB	PHP Doc
library	Oct 11, 2009 8:16 AM	--	Folder
links.php	Jun 21, 2009 5:09 AM	4 KB	PHP Doc
page.php	Jun 21, 2009 5:09 AM	4 KB	PHP Doc
readme.html	Jun 21, 2009 5:09 AM	12 KB	HTML ...
screenshot.png	Jun 21, 2009 5:09 AM	41 KB	Portab...
search.php	Jun 21, 2009 5:09 AM	4 KB	PHP Doc
searchform.php	Jun 21, 2009 5:09 AM	4 KB	PHP Doc
sidebar-index-bottom.php	Jun 21, 2009 5:09 AM	4 KB	PHP Doc
sidebar-index-insert.php	Jun 21, 2009 5:09 AM	4 KB	PHP Doc
sidebar-index-top.php	Jun 21, 2009 5:09 AM	4 KB	PHP Doc
sidebar-page-bottom.php	Jun 21, 2009 5:09 AM	4 KB	PHP Doc
sidebar-page-top.php	Jun 21, 2009 5:09 AM	4 KB	PHP Doc
sidebar-single-bottom.php	Jun 21, 2009 5:09 AM	4 KB	PHP Doc
sidebar-single-insert.php	Jun 21, 2009 5:09 AM	4 KB	PHP Doc
sidebar-single-top.php	Jun 21, 2009 5:09 AM	4 KB	PHP Doc
sidebar-subsidiary.php	Jun 21, 2009 5:09 AM	4 KB	PHP Doc
sidebar.php	Jun 21, 2009 5:09 AM	4 KB	PHP Doc
single.php	Jun 21, 2009 5:09 AM	4 KB	PHP Doc
style.css	Jun 21, 2009 5:09 AM	4 KB	Style She
tag.php	Jun 21, 2009 5:09 AM	4 KB	PHP Doc
thematicsamplechildtheme	Oct 11, 2009 8:16 AM	--	Folder

Figure 7.17 *File list for the parent-child framework Thematic*

There are many more files, but what is key here is the functions directory. Now look at Street, a child theme based on Thematic, which is shown in Figure 7.18.

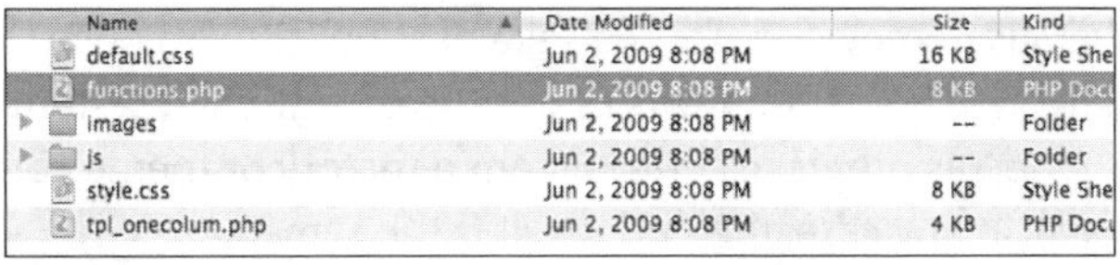

Name	Date Modified	Size	Kind
default.css	Jun 2, 2009 8:08 PM	16 KB	Style She
functions.php	Jun 2, 2009 8:08 PM	8 KB	PHP Doc
images	Jun 2, 2009 8:08 PM	--	Folder
js	Jun 2, 2009 8:08 PM	--	Folder
style.css	Jun 2, 2009 8:08 PM	8 KB	Style She
tpl_onecolum.php	Jun 2, 2009 8:08 PM	4 KB	PHP Doc

Figure 7.18 *File list for Street, a child theme of Thematic*

What happened to the files? The core files you need are stored in the Thematic directory. For Street to work, you need to upload both Thematic and Street. Without the files for Thematic, Street won't even be recognized as a working theme. Related to Thematic are the "true" frameworks: Carrington, Thesis, and Genesis. These don't create child themes but use special directories for your custom code. The only thing that is ever supposed to be in these frameworks are your customizations, which means that at upgrade time, you back up your custom directory, update the rest of the files, and put your custom directory back in place. The files for the Carrington blog are shown in Figure 7.19.

Name	Date Modified	Size	Kind
404.php	Aug 16, 2009 12:16 PM	4 KB	PHP Document
archive.php	Aug 16, 2009 12:16 PM	4 KB	PHP Document
attachment	Aug 17, 2009 9:33 PM	--	Folder
attachment.php	Aug 16, 2009 12:16 PM	4 KB	PHP Document
carrington-core	Aug 17, 2009 9:33 PM	--	Folder
comment	Aug 17, 2009 9:33 PM	--	Folder
comments	Aug 17, 2009 9:33 PM	--	Folder
comments.php	Aug 16, 2009 12:16 PM	4 KB	PHP Document
content	Aug 17, 2009 9:33 PM	--	Folder
css	Aug 17, 2009 9:33 PM	--	Folder
error	Aug 17, 2009 9:33 PM	--	Folder
excerpt	Aug 17, 2009 9:33 PM	--	Folder
footer	Aug 17, 2009 9:33 PM	--	Folder
footer.php	Aug 16, 2009 12:16 PM	4 KB	PHP Document
forms	Aug 17, 2009 9:33 PM	--	Folder
functions	Aug 17, 2009 9:33 PM	--	Folder
functions.php	Aug 16, 2009 12:16 PM	8 KB	PHP Document
header	Aug 17, 2009 9:33 PM	--	Folder
header.php	Aug 16, 2009 12:16 PM	4 KB	PHP Document
img	Aug 17, 2009 9:33 PM	--	Folder
index.php	Aug 16, 2009 12:16 PM	4 KB	PHP Document
js	Aug 17, 2009 9:33 PM	--	Folder
loop	Aug 17, 2009 9:33 PM	--	Folder
misc	Aug 17, 2009 9:33 PM	--	Folder
page.php	Aug 16, 2009 12:16 PM	4 KB	PHP Document
pages	Aug 17, 2009 9:33 PM	--	Folder
plugins	Aug 17, 2009 9:33 PM	--	Folder
posts	Aug 17, 2009 9:33 PM	--	Folder
README.txt	Aug 16, 2009 12:16 PM	8 KB	TextW...ument
screenshot.png	Aug 16, 2009 12:16 PM	16 KB	Portab...image
search.php	Aug 16, 2009 12:16 PM	4 KB	PHP Document
sidebar	Aug 17, 2009 9:33 PM	--	Folder
sidebar.php	Aug 16, 2009 12:16 PM	4 KB	PHP Document
single	Aug 17, 2009 9:33 PM	--	Folder
single.php	Aug 16, 2009 12:16 PM	4 KB	PHP Document
style.css	Aug 16, 2009 12:16 PM	4 KB	Style Sheet

Figure 7.19   *File list for the Carrington blog*

Although theme framework designers like having debates over semantics about parent-child versus frameworks, for the sake of simplicity, I'm going to call all these themes "frameworks." Some frameworks use the parent-child system to maintain custom code, whereas others use the custom directory or theme core directory (as Carrington does). In any case, the end result is the same.

Be forewarned that, despite what framework creators/designers say, stepping into theme frameworks is something that isn't for everyone. You have to be comfortable editing CSS files, working with PHP code examples, and doing a little fly-by-the-seat of your pants coding/testing.

If you're stepping into the world of theme frameworks, you're also stepping into a world where the basic text editor is just not going to cut it. It doesn't matter if you use Mac or Windows; you to need a programmer's text editor and a CSS editor to work with these themes and keep your sanity. A programmer's text editor (like TextWrangler for Mac or NotePad++ for Windows) is a tool that has extra features such as coloring the different parts of code so that you can read it more easily. The special features of a programmer's text editor make life easier for you when you edit PHP files.

CSS editors help you visualize what your changes will look like, and several of them have live previews that work like Firebug in Firefox, so you can see the changes you're making before you upload them. On the Mac, my favorite CSS editor is CSSEdit (not free), and on Windows, it's TopStyle (free and paid).

As a great little demonstration of parent-child themes and frameworks, let's make a new child theme for Twenty Ten. Twenty Ten was designed to be used like this: Instead of editing the theme itself (yes, I know we've been doing that in all the examples; stick with me for a minute), you create a child theme with all the cus-tomizations you might want. So, yes, in the preceding custom fields example, we would save the new single.php file into the directory with our new child theme and not Twenty Ten.

Not all themes are ready for the parent-child theming. The best way to find out is to look in the theme's description; if it says that it is designed to be a parent theme, then you're good to go. One of the most popular parent-child theme frameworks right now is the Thematic framework by Ian Stewart. Ian, as it happens, is the Theme Wrangler for Automatic (in charge of theme development for WordPress.com).

For this example, we create a new child theme using Google's free web fonts to give Twenty Ten a completely different look (as far as fonts go).

 LET ME TRY IT

Create Your Own Child Theme Based on Twenty Ten

1. Create a new folder on your computer for your theme. Let's call it mytwentyten.

2. If you have a CSS editor (such as CSS edit or TopStyle), open that and start a new file; otherwise, just open a text editor with a new file.

3. At the top of the file, put the following code, using your name and URL instead of mine:

```
/*
        Theme Name: My Twenty Ten
        Description: A Child Theme of Twenty Ten using the Google web-
ready fonts
        Theme URI: http://trishussey.com
         Author: Tris Hussey
         Author URI: http://trishussey.com
        Template: twentyten
        Version: 1.0
        */
```

   In this little block of text, the important parts are the Template and Theme Name lines; the rest is just extra. The Template line tells WordPress where to look for the core files (because this is the only file we're creating for this theme).

4. Save this file as style.css in your mytwentyten folder.

5. Next, put this line of code on a new line below that first block of text:

```
@import url(../twentyten/style.css);
```

   That line imports all the styles from Twenty Ten. This way, we don't have to define everything—just the things we want to change.

6. Next, go to the Google Font Directory and pick two fonts: one for your title and one for the body text. I'm going to use Reenie Beanie for my title and Cardo for my body text.

7. Click on the name of the first font you're going to use, and on the next page, click Get the Code.

8. Scroll down and click Font Variants and Advanced Techniques. Figure 7.20 shows what this looks like for Cardo.

9. Select and copy the line that starts with @import. This is the example for Cardo: @import url(http://fonts.googleapis.com/css?family=Cardo).

10. Paste that line below the other @import line in your style.css file, and save. This tells your browser to load that font with the stylesheet for your new theme. Pretty easy, huh?

11. Repeat this for your second font.

12. Using the local copy of Twenty Ten you have on your computer, open style.css from the twentyten folder.

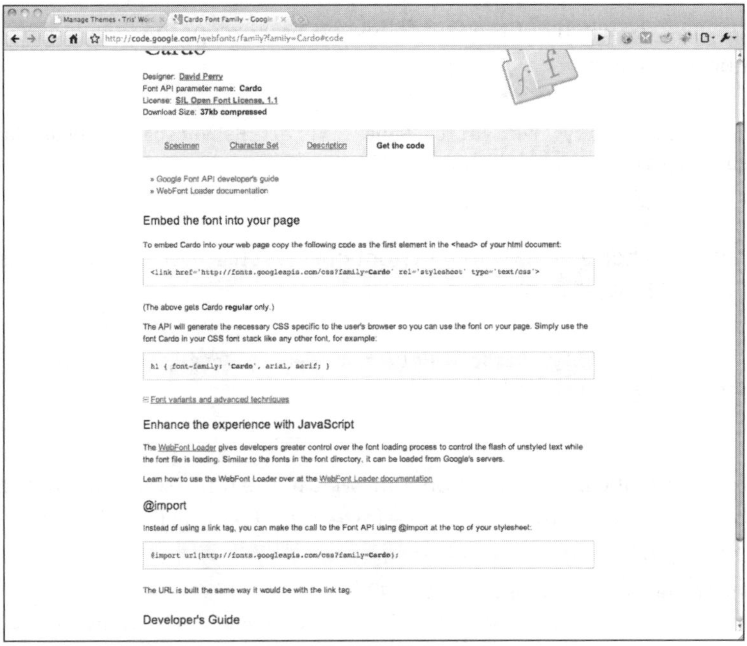

Figure 7.20   *The advanced techniques area for Cardo where you find the key @import line*

13. Scroll down until you see the section that starts with

```
/* =Fonts ------------------------------------------------------------
- */
```

and select that section stopping before

```
/* =Structure:
---------------------------------------------------------------- */
```

14. Copy that section of code, switch back to your stylesheet, and paste it in below your last @import line.

15. We are going to combine the CSS definition block that starts with body with the one below that starts h3#comments-title. First, delete the following text:

```
{
font-family: Georgia, "Bitstream Charter", serif;
}
```

Then put a comma after .pingback a.url and close up the space between .pingback a.url and h3#comments-title.

16. Find the line `#site-title` and delete it.

17. Now we to switch out the font for everything except the title and description. In the line

```
{
      font-family: "Helvetica Neue", Arial, Helvetica, "Nimbus Sans L",
sans-serif;
}
```

put your choice of body font in front of `Helvetica Neue`. In my case, using Cardo, it looks like this:

```
{
      font-family: Cardo, "Helvetica Neue", Arial, Helvetica, "Nimbus
Sans L", sans-serif;
}
```

18. To set the title and description font, we use the font-family line from the body but use our title font choice instead of the body font. On a new line, put the following:

```
#site-description, #site-title {
font-family: "Reenie Beanie", "Helvetica Neue", Arial, Helvetica,
"Nimbus Sans L", sans-serif;
}
```

19. Save style.css and close it.

20. Open your FTP client and connect to your site.

21. Navigate to wp-content/themes/ and upload your mytwentyten folder.

22. Go to your site Administration area, and click on Appearance. You should see something like Figure 7.21.

23. Click Preview below the name of My Twenty Ten. If it looks right to you, click Activate.

24. Go to the home page of your site, refresh your browser, and see your handiwork! Figure 7.22 shows (from left to right) the original Twenty Ten, my version of My Twenty Ten from this Let Me Try It, and a version of Twenty Ten I created that I'm using called Twenty Ten dot Five.

A few things you might be wondering....

What happened to my custom header image I set with Twenty Ten?

Because you use a new theme, even though it's a child of Twenty Ten, it's new, so it resets the header image (and background) to the defaults.

Figure 7.21   *Manage themes with the new My Twenty Ten ready to be activated*

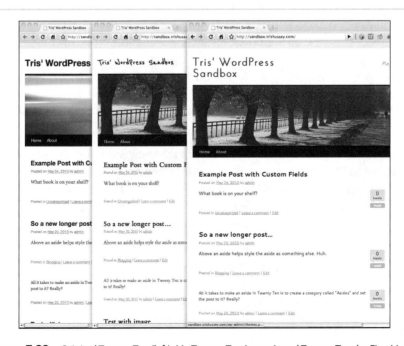

Figure 7.22   *Original Twenty Ten (left), My Twenty Ten (center), and Twenty Ten dot Five (right)*

Why is there just a big white box instead of a picture about My Twenty Ten?

If you put a PNG image called screenshot.png, that image will be there. Typically you use what a site looks like using the theme, but really it can be anything.

Why did we keep all the other font names in the theme? Isn't one *enough?*

One font is generally enough, but those extra fonts are backups. Why? First, not all browsers support importing fonts like that (older versions of current browsers in general); if the fonts can't be imported, you want the page to "fail gracefully." Next, if for some reason Google's servers are slow or the fonts don't load, you want the other fonts to take their place. Finally, it's good practice to define fonts like that. You have a few specific fonts (for example, Helvetica, Arial, and so on) followed by the general font type (sans serif).

Now that you have this child theme working, if you want to make the change in the single.php file, instead of replacing the file in the twentyten directory, you just add it to your mytwentyten folder. WordPress reads the single.php file (and any other theme files) in that folder before it looks for them in the parent theme.

Commercially Supported Themes

Throughout this chapter, I've been discussing themes that are free and available through WordPress.org, but it won't take you long to learn that there is a whole world of themes that are "commercially supported." These are themes that either a) you pay to download or b) you pay for some measure of support or "members only" services. There is an important distinction within the world of commercially supported themes: Many themes that you buy restrict how you can use the theme. For example, you might buy the theme but only be able to use it on one site, even if the second site is one of your own sites. The theme authors listed on WordPress.org at http://wordpress.org/extend/themes/commercial/ release the themes to you under the same GPL license as WordPress.

There are a lot of great themes here. Some of the ones you might like to check out are the StudioPress themes from Brian Gardner (I own a developer's license to all the StudioPress themes), Woo Themes (they contributed some of the code for the new WordPress Menus system), Graph Paper Press, and Pagelines. All these themes are commercially supported in some way, shape, or form but retain the GPL license.

One of the more popular commercially supported themes is Chris Pearson's Thesis, which is not released with a GPL license. I also own a developer's license for Thesis, but the terms of the license are that I can only use it on my own sites, unless I pay an extra fee per site. Thesis is a powerful Theme framework that many high-profile websites use, and there is little question that using it gives you a solid foundation on which to build sites.

There are complicated issues around commercially supported themes and the GPL license—so complicated that this is what the following Tell Me More audio segment is all about.

 TELL ME MORE   Media 7.4—Are Premium Themes Worth It?
Vancouver-based WordPress expert and theme developer Catherine Winters joins me for a discussion about commercially supported (premium) themes.
Access this audio recording through your registered Web Edition at
my.safaribooksonline.com/9780132182836/media

Theme Best Practices

All this talk about themes might have raised more questions for you than answers. You can do this or that, but don't forget about these other cool things! You must be wondering by now, "Is there anything that I can use as a guideline?" It's hard to have guidelines when you combine personal taste and technology, but in this final section of the chapter, I'm going to tell you what I think are "best practices" for themes. These ideas come from not only years as a blogger, but also 15 years as a web developer.

Columns

Personally I'm a fan of the three-column layout with a wider column for content on the left and two narrower sidebar columns on the right. I like my content column to be at least 450-pixels wide (right now, my blog is set to 620 pixels) and the sidebars about 220 pixels each. This means that if you have your screen set to 1024x768 pixels, you can see the entire blog and sidebars with your browser at full screen. Think that sounds crazy? I don't think so. The data that I see on my site is that most of my visitors have screen resolutions bigger than that; most of my visitors have widescreen monitors. How do I know this? My webstats tell me. It's a calculated risk, given my audience. I might not be 100% right, but I think 480 pixels for content gives a nice size for both text and images. I like two sidebars so I can offer more information without having people scroll forever. Because I only have only one ad at the top of my sidebar, it isn't ads I want visitors to see. I have search boxes, other information, links to posts, and all sorts of social media goodies I want people to check out. I want to run out of sidebar before running out of content on the home page. If I decided to go to two columns, I would only make the content area wider and not the sidebar (maybe to 240 pixels), because I like more room for content.

Early on in web design, the left column was for navigation because we knew that what was on the left would definitely be on people's screens. The farther to the right we went, the less sure we were. This idea stuck with us in early blog designs until we learned that our sites would be indexed more efficiently if we had sidebars on the right so that search bots would hit content first, not sidebar. Today, with better CSS layouts, SEO isn't the reason we do it. I think we're doing it for A) style and B) to maximize reading efficiency on a page. With words going left to right across the pages, I want people's eyes to return to my content and not get distracted by the sidebars. At least that's the theory.

Your decision about the number of columns should be based on what kind of content you are going to present. If your content would look better with a wider content area, I'd go for two columns or one column with content at the top and an extra-large footer at the bottom for sidebar content (the "Giant Web 2.0 footer").

Backgrounds

I've had some ugly web page backgrounds in the last 15 years. Really ugly. My background at the moment? White. White background with black text. The key when you pick a background is thinking about both how the site looks and how readable it is.

Personally, I don't like dark backgrounds. Too often, designers don't have enough contrast between elements, and it's easy to get lost. If you use a background image, I suggest you ensure that the image doesn't distract from reading. For example, if you have a giant neon flower taking up the top-left quarter of the page and the flower stays there as you scroll, that will become distracting. However, make it smaller or less intense, and it might look great. No, there aren't set rules, but I think we've all seen enough ugly websites and MySpace pages to know what makes you want to claw your eyes out.

Last word on backgrounds: Make sure that the background still looks right regardless of the size of the visitor's screen. I've had more than a few "oops" moments when a background repeated on large screens or on a small screen something that was supposed to be off to the side as blocked text. I'm seeing a trend toward more solid color backgrounds and more subtlety, which isn't just easy to design for, it's a lot easier to test, too.

Widgets

Earlier in the chapter, I talked about widgets and reminded you (several times) that less is more. There isn't a set number of widgets that you shouldn't exceed, but having so many widgets that your pages takes a minute to load is bad. When my blog starts looking or acting wonky, widgets are some of the first things that I start yanking to see if that fixes things. Also, rushing to add the latest widget could open up a security hole in your blog. The widget might not let hackers into your server, but it could deliver spyware and nasties to your visitors. Google will find out about this, and your visitors can be greeted with a This Site Has Malware warning. You don't want that to happen, so use a bit of caution when adding a ton of quiz, test, and other interesting (and fun) widgets.

On my blog, I check the widgets about once a month to see if I still want or need them on the sidebar. I might take one off or just move them around. Make this a habit of yours so that you cannot only keep your blog looking fresh, but also interesting, relevant, and speedy.

Headers and Footers

Because by this point, we've covered themes from top to bottom, it's time to talk about headers and footers. Your blog header is what people see first when they come to your blog. You know what they say about first impressions, right? If you have a large image (say more than 300 to 400 pixels high) as your header image, visitors will have to scroll down just to see content. Keep your headers neat, clean, and professional. Yes, your header and footer are good places for ads, but use these with caution. If you think a header ad will work for you, try it. If it isn't driving clicks and bringing in money, pull it off the header and put it somewhere else.

Although many sites are opting for giant footers that take the place of many sidebar elements, I don't think that's a good idea. I don't want people to have to scroll to the bottom of the page to see recent posts or comments. I have a small footer where I have a copyright statement and a few other links. My gut tells me that this is the right call.

WordPress.com Notes

Throughout this chapter, I avoided talking about WordPress.com as far as themes go. The obvious reason is that on WordPress.com, you are limited to the themes they offer, you can't edit the core files, and you can edit only the CSS if you pay extra. Will this change in the future? I don't think so, but if a really good and stable parent-child theme system is developed just for WordPress.com to let people edit their CSS and create custom functions appears, maybe it will change.

The limitations around themes (and plugins) on WordPress.com is one of the main reasons that I don't usually recommend it for professional or business blogs. It's a great platform for personal blogs, and I recommend it over other free blogging services without hesitation, but some of the limitations might prevent a company from truly leveraging WordPress to their best advantage.

No matter how awesome your blog looks, it's content that draws people in. This chapter is about organizing your content to make sense.

8

Organizing the Content on Your Blog

Wow, lots of geeky stuff so far. I don't blame you if your head is spinning a bit. This chapter is completely different, however—it is about how to organize your content on your site. In Chapter 9, "Creating and Managing Content with WordPress," I talk about writing and how to use the Post, Page, and Image editors in detail, but this chapter focuses on how the different content types work together (and how they don't!) to become a great site.

At first, you might think this is pretty esoteric stuff, but what I've learned (the hard way, as always) is that if you don't take some time to *think* about how you want to set up things, you'll be smacking yourself in the head later. Even if you just want "a simple blog," just knowing how to use Posts, Pages, Categories, Tags, and your Blogroll can make things so much easier for you—and easier for your readers to find the content that they want to read.

Understanding Posts Versus Pages

In WordPress, there are two large classes of content: Posts and Pages. Posts are what you think of as blog posts. They can have categories and tags assigned to them and are the content type that you think about when you're reading a blog. Posts are also the only content type sent out in the RSS feed for the site; Pages do not. Pages are the parts of the site like "About me" or "Contact us"—pieces of content that are more static and informational. Here is the key difference between Posts and Pages: Posts are meant to be connected to other posts via categories and tags; Pages are intended to stand alone and be independent of other pieces of content.

When I capitalize *Post* or *Page*, I'm talking about the content type; when the words are lowercase, I'm talking about an individual piece of content.

Posts

Posts are the lifeblood of a blog. The Post content type is what almost all blogs are built upon and generally represent the lion's share of content on a blog. For example, my personal blog has 2,700+ posts and only 5 pages. (And some of those pages aren't even in use and could be deleted without people noticing.)

When you think about a post, think about it as part of a larger web of content on your blog. Say you have a cooking blog, and you're talking about making a seafood stew. When you write a post, you'd want to make sure people can find that post in several ways. Chances are that you'd have a category called "Recipes" and maybe subcategories for stews and seafood. Maybe in the post you talk about how to pick and buy a good stew pot, so the post might also fall under the category of cookware. Your post talks about several aspects, or categories, of cooking. If readers are looking for information on how to buy cookware, clicking on the Cookware category would bring them to all the posts that talk about cookware. Even if a post isn't *all about* cookware, that's okay—if part of it *is* about cookware, then it's about cookware.

In addition to categories, Posts can have tags assigned to them. I get into the nuances of categories versus tags later in the chapter, but for right now, think of them as search terms or keywords. Maybe for your seafood stew, you put in haddock and lobster (if you do, please invite me to dinner), but you don't really talk a lot about those ingredients, so you include the *tags* haddock, lobster, fish, and probably a few others. When someone clicks on the haddock tag at the end (or top, depending on your theme) of your post, she will get a list of all the posts that have been tagged with haddock.

Tags and categories aren't just for *readers*; they are for *search engines* as well. Tags and categories help the search engines put your posts and entire blog into a context of all the other content on your blog and blogs across the Internet. People who know how to tag and categorize effectively do rank higher in search engines compared to people who don't. Tags are specific, whereas categories are general. If you created categories for everything (and I was guilty of this), you will wind up with categories with maybe one or two posts assigned to them. Chances are that if you think about it, you can condense those categories into larger bins, and maybe change those categories to tags.

Categories and tags are the biggest differences between Posts and Pages. Pages can't have categories or tags associated with them. They are independent of other content within your blog. The other important difference is that only Posts are pushed out via RSS or through to Twitter (for most of the Twitter tools out there).

This means you can publish a page and hide it in plain sight. For example, if I need to do a screencast for a friend or client, I'll often embed that screencast into a *Page* so that the rest of the world doesn't immediately find out about it.. If the content isn't secret, having the page public isn't a problem. Sometimes it's just nice of have something that can be sent to people and to figure that the chances of others finding it are pretty low.

Pages

As you've gathered by now, Pages are a completely different content type than Posts. It's a strange thing, but if you look at the big picture, it works. Pages are designed for "static" content and to be, essentially, independent of other pieces of content on your site. Not that you can't link a post to a page, or vice versa—it's that because there is no system like tags and categories for Pages, they are those kinds of content that are important, but you don't often change, update, or look at.

The best examples of the use of the Page content type are the About and Contact pages. I have an "About Tris" page on my site because it's essential to let people know a little more about me and what the site is all about. Likewise, my contact page is a simple form that lets people email me easily. Both of these pages need to exist outside the Post framework that is not only tied to content but also *time*. If I made a "contact me" post, that post would quickly be lost among all the other posts I write. This special nature of Pages is why Pages are usually the default for navigation. They are like section chunks of the site, sort of.

You create a Page, and a link to it goes on the navbar (usually unless you specifically exclude it), so no matter what—no matter how old that Page gets—it's still right there for people to find. I might update my About page a few times a year, but I write posts almost daily. After my contact form is up and working, the chances of me touching it are pretty slim, but it's on the navbar nonetheless.

There is another special property of the Page; it can include a call to The Loop to have blog posts as well as static content displayed at the same time. The most common use of this is creating a page for blog posts when you have a static front page for your site. That functionality is central to using WordPress to build "regular websites," which I cover in detail in Chapter 10, "Creating Sites with WordPress."

Pages, however, have one more feature that you can use to organize content: child pages. The interesting thing about child pages is that although they behave like Pages, they have a lot in common with subcategories. I'll talk about both these ways to organize content when I'm done talking about their parents.

Post or Page: How to Choose

If this discussion of Posts versus Pages has left you more confused than anything, don't worry—deciding between something being a Post or Page isn't always obvious. The key to deciding which content type is right depends on a couple of factors: time and organization.

First, looking at time: The question you ask yourself is whether the content is independent of time when it is posted and how it relates to similar content matters. Let's take a musician releasing albums and promoting concerts. There are several ways to organize listing concert tour dates. First, I'd create a Page that lists all the tour dates as they are finalized, but I'd also have a series of Posts with a category like "Touring" to let readers know when a new date is added. A Post with details of the concert is then linked to the Page with *all* the information in one place, but someone can also look at the category archive to see updates from the road and other interesting information. Releasing a new album is the same; you might have a Page called "Discography" but a category like "In the Studio" talking about recording, producing, and releasing your latest masterwork.

In those examples, you see that *time* is important to both concert announcements and releasing a new album. You not only want readers to find out about the new coolness through RSS, but you also want fans to read them in *(reverse) chronological order*. Reading about a past tour date before one coming up doesn't help your fan. If your fans are waiting with bated breath for your next release, and have subscribed to the category feed In the Studio, you want them to read about a song release when it happens. The second part is organization: the archives. If you write a post about each album released, readers can check your discography, but also looking in the archives gives them an album-by-album description; you can add the ever-popular "Buy Now" links to those posts as well. Pages? They don't work as well for that.

Similarly, your biography, CV, contact page, media page, and similar content, make terrible posts. They are easy to get lost in the shuffle—not to mention you want them to stand alone. You *want* people to see those right off and click on them. They are important, individual pieces of content.

Here's a rule of thumb: If the content "never gets old," it probably belongs on a Page. If it's part of lots of content that you want people to see all at once with one click (and no work on your part), it's a Post.

And if you guess wrong and change your mind, that's cool, too.

Organize Your Posts with Categories

Categories are an integral part of organizing your Posts. When I'm talking about Posts, talking about Categories just come naturally. All Posts are in a Category. Period. It's a rule of WordPress. When you install WordPress for the first time or create a new WordPress.com blog, there is a category created (with the unimaginative name of "Uncategorized"); if you don't assign a category to a post, the post goes into Uncategorized. Yes, you can rename "Uncategorized" to something else or define a new default category. In fact, that is one of the first things I do with a new site. Regardless, all Posts are always put into at least one category.

As discussed previously, when you think of categories, think big buckets. Think of how you would group things together in a large scale, or macro, way—like Recipes, How to, Reviews, Poetry, or things that lots of posts would fall into. As a rule of thumb, I aim for 10–15 categories max on my blogs. (You'll probably notice that I often don't follow my own advice and have way too many categories.) More than that, I think you might be categorizing too much and maybe either need to pull some categories together or make them *subcategories* of a larger group (more on that in a moment). Don't worry: You don't have to decide what all your categories will be right away. You can create a new category as you write a post and edit categories through the Categories section of the administration area. I often add categories on-the-fly, especially when I'm branching out into a new content area.

You might be thinking: "Okay, grouping posts into categories is all well and good, but what does it actually get me?" Well, categories have some pretty darn cool tricks up their sleeves. For example, one of the categories on my site is "Books"—if you want to see everything I've written about my books, you just need to go to the category archive page (http://trishussey.com/category/books/) and you get everything in one place. To make it easier for you to find that archive, you don't have to browse for a post about books; you can click "Books" in the navbar.

Okay, what if you do like everything I write about my books, but that's all you want to read of my content? As much as I'd be disappointed (not that I'd know if you did or didn't), all you'd have to do is enter http://trishussey.com/category/books/feed/ and you get the *automatically generated* RSS feed for that category. Imagine what this lets you do; you can offer readers niche content, and all you have to do is create the category and assign a post to it.

Of course, remember that you can have special template pages for a specific category—your readers can not only read and subscribe to only the content they want, they can also feel like they were at a *completely different site* depending on the category. This clever trick gives you tremendous flexibility in branding, marketing, and even just running a multi-author blog. Each author could have his own distinct look, and all it takes is one simple category template per author.

Categories sound pretty cool and are a great way to organize things, but what about if you have that author set up and each author wants a category for each of *his* topics? Ah, this is where *subcategories* come into play; as I alluded to previously, subcategories are great ways to further organize content (not that they don't have their own quirks, of course).

Using Child Pages the Right Way

Pages can have child pages; categories can have subcategories. You wouldn't think that these would have a lot in common, but actually they do. Let's get into child pages first because, of the two subclasses, these are the easiest to wrap your head around.

Child pages are an interesting part of the Page content type. Child pages are connected to their parents in hierarchy (for example, for navigation), but not such that if you create child pages from a parent, the children automatically appear on the parent page. So, child pages are great for organizing content, especially for your navbar, and putting the pages into some sort of context but not for creating indices of related content. You can edit your Page template(s) so that you have a list of the child pages under the current page, but you have to edit to do it. Should this be an automatic function in WordPress? Probably not—the function to make the list is already within the code, ready for you to use, and you just have to code to use it. There are plugins that give you easier access to these functions, but again, you need to edit templates to make use of them. Just think of child pages like teenagers: They might be related to their parents, but they don't like to acknowledge their existence.

Using Subcategories Effectively

For the most part, subcategories behave like categories. If you go to www. trishussey.com/category/books/using-wordpress/, you'll come to all the posts related to this book (and WordPress in general); putting feed/ at the end of the URL will give you the feed for the subcategories. If you have Categories in your navbar (like on my site), the subcategories can appear as drop-down menus just like child pages do. The interesting thing about subcategories is, like child pages, there isn't an automatic connection to the parent. In fact, it's *harder* to code to reveal the parent-child relationship for categories (at least as far as the code examples I found go).

Continuing with the Books category example, if I put a post in the Using WordPress category, but not in the Books category (because that isn't automatic), that post *won't appear in the Books category archive page*. To change that, you have to change how the archives are coded to check if there are any subcategories of that category and then make sure those are included in the listing. If at this point you're shaking your head, you're not alone; I'm right there with you. I wish template designers would code that into all archive pages to do that check, or at least give you the option to include subcategories.

In any case, even though this is a little frustrating, using child pages and subcategories is a powerful and simple way to give your content both context *and* structure. The URLs for the kids and subs show the hierarchy, so search engines pick that up. Themes with drop-down navigation give you a way to get more content into your navbar without taking up more horizontal space (which is at a premium). So, don't toss them out with the bathwater. Just know the limitations *before* you're designing a site around a particular function that you think should be there, but isn't.

 LET ME TRY IT

Creating Categories and Subcategories and Assigning Them to Posts

Part 1: Creating the Category or Subcategory:

1. In your administration area, click the Posts button and then the Categories link. Figure 8.1 displays.

2. To add a new Category, just enter the name you want in the Name field. The name can contain spaces and even the ampersand character (&), so **Stories & Such** is just fine. I leave the Slug field blank most of the time.

3. (optional) If you'd like to add a description to your Category, do it now. Most themes don't use the Description box, so most often it's left empty. The new default theme Twenty Ten *does* use Category descriptions, so if you're using Twenty Ten you might want to use the Description field.

4. Click Add New Category.

Figure 8.1   *The Category Management and Editing page*

5. If you want your new Category to be a Subcategory of an existing Category, choose a Category from the Parent menu.

Part 2: Assigning Categories to Posts:

1. Click the Posts button and then the Add New item *or* use the New Post button in the top menu bar to get to a new post window. The Add New Post screen displays, as shown in Figure 8.2.

2. To assign a category or categories to a post, click the check boxes next to the category name in the Categories box on the right side of the screen. If you click the Most Used tab link you see a list only of the categories you use most often.

3. If you want to create a new Category or Subcategory, click the Add New Category link below the list of Categories, enter the name of the new Category, select if it will be a Subcategory, and click the Add New Category button.

4. Publish your post as normal.

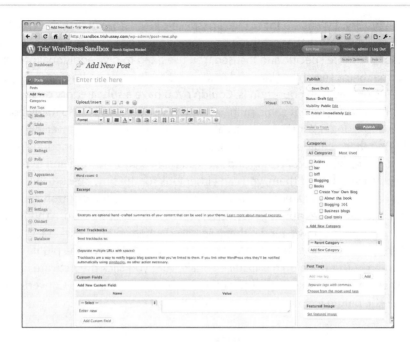

Figure 8.2 *The Add New Post screen. Note the Categories are on the right side. The add new category area is already clicked open. (It is closed by default.)*

Connect Your Posts Together with Tags

The last of the content-classifying tools are tags. Tags aren't unique to WordPress; they were "invented" and put into popular use by David Sifry of Technorati. At first, we all called them Technorati tags" and when you included them in your post, you were actually connecting your post to all the other posts on the *Internet* using that tag. If you clicked the tag link, you were whisked away to Technorati.com and saw all the related posts from all the other bloggers. At the time, this was *awesome*; you could get a huge amount of traffic to your blog and particular posts just from "tag traffic." Sadly, Technorati collapsed under its own weight and has been pushed to the fringes of the Blogosphere for a couple years now. In the meantime, the people building blog engines figured out that maybe it wasn't a great idea to send all your traffic away to another website. Maybe having an *internal* system of tags would be better—a system where when you clicked on a tag link, you saw all the posts on *that* blog that were related. That is the way things are now. WordPress 2.3 Dexter brought native tag support to WordPress in September 2007. This marked the turning of a tagging tide that would eventually reduce Technorati's influence to its sideline status that it has now.

Enough history.... What are tags? Tags are specific keywords you use to describe a post. If you remember that categories are larger-scale, big bucket kinds of collectors, tags are more specific and focused. You use a tag to give additional context to a post that helps search engines and readers place the content into a more specific place. The obvious next question is: Couldn't you have a subcategory do the same thing? Yes, exactly, and at some point when you've used a tag for so many posts, you have to wonder if it should be a category (or subcategory). Conversely, you might find that a category has so few posts in it, you might think about deleting it. For just this reason, WordPress includes the handy category-to-tag and tag-to-category converters. To find them, you can either look for the tiny, obscure link at the bottom of the tags or categories pages, or better, click the Tools button and then Import. The categories and tags converter will be right there. Because this function isn't often used, it's now a plugin that is installed when you first click the Categories and Tags Converter link on the Import screen. (Figure 8.3 shows the plugin installation screen.) After the plugin is installed, make sure you click the Activate Plugin link. Then return to Tools, Import to get to the Categories and Tags Converter. Don't worry—the plugin installation is a one-time thing.

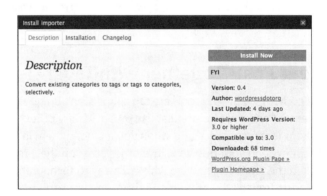

Figure 8.3   *The first time you click the Categories and Tags Converter you are asked to install the plugin for it.*

Figure 8.4 show the Categories and Tags Converter (in this case, the Categories to Tags screen).

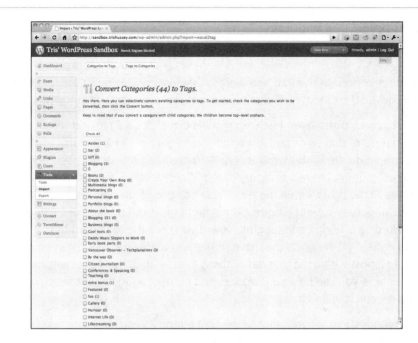

Figure 8.4 *The Categories and Tags Converter*

Now when you move a category to a tag, you still have to delete the category if you don't want it any longer. When you convert a tag to a category, however, it's just done. In WordPress, a category and a tag can overlap (and do taxonomically), so don't worry when you see the little "*" saying that the category is also a tag.

 **LET ME TRY IT**

Converting a Category to a Tag

Let's say you have a few too many categories and before you merge them into larger categories, you want to turn them into tags. That's what we do here:

1. Click Tools, Import and then Category and Tags Converter. If, as in the earlier section, this is the first time you've clicked the link, you are asked to install the new plugin.

2. Check the box or boxes of the Categories you'd like to convert to tags.

3. Click Convert Categories to Tags.

4. You should get a nice confirmation message that it worked and you're done.

One rather important thing to note here is that just converting a Category to a Tag *doesn't* delete the Category: You still have to do that manually (if you wish).

As you tag your posts, over time your readers can click on a tag and see all the posts that share that same tag. Although you might not think that this is what a reader might do, think about it this way. You're reading one of my posts about WordPress plugins. I have a category called "WordPress," so if you click the category, you'll see all the posts within the WordPress category. However, not *all* of my posts in that category are about plugins. Some might be about themes, or security, or other WordPress things, and plugins. Now, if you click the *tag* "WordPress Plugins," you go right to all the posts that have something to do with WordPress plugins. I don't tag a post with a tag that has nothing to do with it; that's counterproductive. By using tags, you can help your readers find more of your content faster without having to search to find it.

Like categories, you set your tags in the Post editor. As you use more tags, WordPress keeps track of them and can suggest tags based on your most common tags. There is no engine to analyze your content to make real suggestions of tags, but listing your most popular ones gives you a chance to make sure you use the same tags consistently. If you need to manage your tags, like deleting or renaming them (fixing a typo, for example), you do that just like categories under the Post button in the content block.

Managing all your tags works just like managing Categories. The two screens are nearly identical. If you click Post Tags under the Posts button in the administration area of your site, you see what I mean. The only difference is that tags cannot have subtags associated with them (see Figure 8.5).

Custom Post Types and Custom Taxonomies

WordPress 2.9 introduced custom post types and custom taxonomies and WordPress 3.0 has expanded on this powerful functionality and made it even more powerful. Let's start with the easier of the two custom content types to understand: custom taxonomies.

The first thing to understand is that with *custom taxonomies* is that you're just building on system of tags and categories (which are the built-in taxonomies). Categories and Tags are great, but what if you want to organize a recipe site in a way that readers could see what kind of dish it was but not have to clutter up your category list with a lot of extra information? You could have categories for stews, or

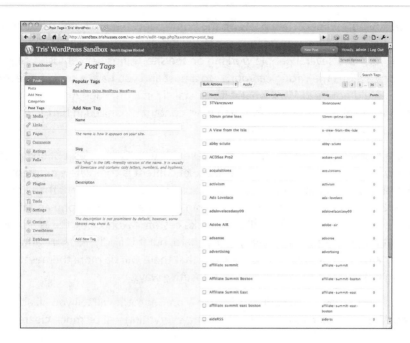

Figure 8.5   *The Post Tags manager/editor*

ingredients, and so on, but what if you wanted to include an easy reference to cooking time or complexity? Sure you could type that into every post, but if there were something like a category you could set, then you could just check off that the cooking time was short and complexity was easy. Then your template could manage all this for you and, better yet, you could easily create special templates for your taxonomies.

Yes, the same thing can be done with categories, but this way you eliminate clutter. You are breaking up how you organize your content so you can have Categories for what the post is about and a custom taxonomy for what is in the post itself.

Creating custom taxonomies is a simple matter of pasting some code into your theme's functions file and then some code into your theme to display the new taxonomies. However, this is easier said than done. For this reason, what you find is that more themes are going to offer custom taxonomies prebuilt for you or more plugins like Simple Taxonomies (http://yoast.com/wordpress/simple-taxonomies/) will be used. Sure people can code their own taxonomies, but there are also still people who code HTML by hand, too.

From custom taxonomies, we move smoothly into *custom post types*. Like custom taxonomies, custom post types are all about organization. Say you're creating a site where you only want certain posts on the home page. Generally you'd accomplish this by having only certain categories appear there. This works, but often, especially if you have several people working on the site, things get confused. Maybe someone assigns the wrong categories to a post and you have a post in a section that it should not be in. Well, what if it's crystal clear: Front Page Articles as an option with Posts and Pages? You then have content organized in better ways so you can tap into them more easily.

As with custom taxonomies, you can achieve this with Categories, but again what we're talking about is saying that this piece of content is completely different than other pieces of content and we want to manage it in a way different than Posts or Pages. Custom post types are defined within a theme's functions.php and then called by the theme's template files. Also like custom taxonomies, this is a coding job that is far from a piece of cake; it's not hard, but it is fiddly. As more and more themes are coded for WordPress 3, I know that there will be more themes that have custom post types set up and used in innovative ways.

Custom post types are so cool, this Tell Me More segment will tell you all about them. After you listen to the audio segment, everything will be much clearer.

 TELL ME MORE   **Media 8.1—Using Custom Post Types in the Real World**
Access this audio recording through your registered Web Edition at
my.safaribooksonline.com/9780132182836/media

Adding a Blogroll of Links to Your Blog

Not long ago, having a blogroll, maintaining your blogroll, and deciding who was on your blogroll (and who *wasn't)* was a big hairy deal to people. Your blogroll, then and now, is just a link to sites you like. Yeah, that's it. Most folks put their blogroll in their sidebars and list their friends, influencers, and other cool stuff. When I started blogging in 2004, being listed on a popular blog's blogroll was a *huge* deal. Back then, blogrolls, almost even more than who you linked to in a post, were how you found new blogs to read. Blogrolls also became one of those "here are my friends, and if you're not on this list, I don't think you're important" kinds of things. Visiting someone's blog—a person who you *thought* was your friend—and seeing your name absent from their blogroll was a slight. A public slight.

Then we got over ourselves.

What happens is that people make their blogroll off the top of their heads and sometimes forget to add people. Often people don't go back and check their blogrolls to update them with all the *new* blogs they found and like. This is why I don't maintain a blogroll of friends anymore. Frankly, I know way too many amazing people, and if I tried to include links to all their blogs, it would be a mile long, and I'd *still* forget someone. (And that person would be offended.) My blogroll consists of links to the other places you can find my stuff online. I don't even try to maintain a list of "Great Vancouver Bloggers" (who elected me the arbiter of greatness?) or "Must-read WordPress blogs." If I develop a site for a tradeshow or event client, for example, the "blogroll" is often links to sponsors and speakers. The blogroll is a great way to make it easy for people to find out more about the people and companies associated with an event. Blogrolls are great for something like an organization where you want to provide links to members' sites (maybe just board members, if it's a large organization). In both of those examples, the process of grouping the links together is made easier with—you guessed it—categories.

Using Link Categories

Blogrolls have their own set of categories, but they work the same as Post categories. Link categories just put a bit of organization into your list of links. As a bonus feature, when you put the Blogroll/Links widget into the sidebar, you can have all of the links displayed and organized by category. Unlike Post categories (yes, you can have subcategories as well), there isn't a feed for your links, and your blogroll doesn't have its own unique URL, unless your theme supports an automatic Links page. A Links page works just like the special Blog page we've already touched on. If your theme supports it, you create the page and publish it; that page should have a list of all your links, by category. Whether this works for you depends on your theme.

 SHOW ME   Media 8.2—Creating Link Categories

Just how do you keep all your links straight? Link categories! It takes just a minute to have a well-organized blogroll.

Access this video file through your registered Web Edition at
my.safaribooksonline.com/9780132182836/media

9

All sites need to have content. This chapter covers not only how to manage the content, but also how to create great content.

Creating and Managing Content with WordPress

It doesn't matter how secure your WordPress install is, or how cool your plugins are, or how awesome your theme is—if you don't have content, you don't really have a site or a blog. This chapter is all about content. One of the best things about all blogging engines (WordPress, Drupal, MovableType/TypePad, Blogger) is that if you can use Hotmail, Gmail, or Yahoo! Mail, you can write and post with ease. It doesn't matter how skilled you think you are (or aren't) with computers, WordPress makes posting a breeze.

In this chapter, I'm going to cover the mechanics of the standard Post/Page editor (which are essentially identical, save a couple small differences), the image editor, adding multimedia to your blog and managing comments, and then spend some time on how to write good blog posts. I think you'll find a lot of the editor tools to be self-explanatory, but I will give you a few tricks here and there along the way.

Hands On with the Editors

One of the best things about the editor built into WordPress is that it is based on a standard editor framework called TinyMCE. TinyMCE is the de facto standard for visual, web-based editors for tools like WordPress (and many others). So, once you learn and understand the editor in WordPress, you're pretty much set for anything the Web might throw at you! The other smart thing about the visual editor in WordPress is that it is identical between Posts and Pages, with the exception that on the Posts editor, you have a categories and tags section; in the Pages editor, you have the Parent-child and Page template section. The editors are *so* similar, it's pretty easy to get confused and accidentally make a Post a Page or a Page a Post because you don't realize you're in the wrong section!

Components of the Visual Editor

Let's get down to business with the *visual* part of the editor for starters (see Figure 9.1). Visual refers to it being WYSIWYG (What You See Is What You Get); therefore, you don't need to know the HTML codes for bold, links, inserting pictures, and so forth. The editor handles all that for you. The long rectangular area at the top is where you put the title to your post or page. The posting/editing area is right below, and you use it to type or paste your text just like you would with web-based email.

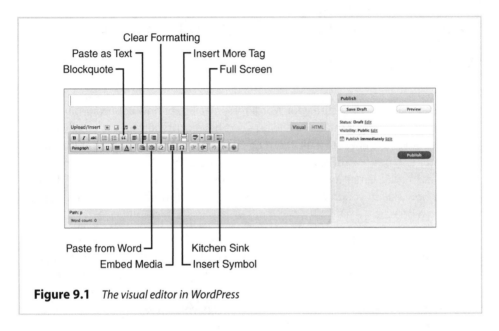

Clear Formatting
Paste as Text
Insert More Tag
Blockquote
Full Screen

Paste from Word
Kitchen Sink
Embed Media
Insert Symbol

Figure 9.1   *The visual editor in WordPress*

The first thing I'm going to *strongly* recommend is that you click the button on the top row that's all the way to the right. The button is called (I kid you not) the Kitchen Sink button, and it displays the second row of buttons you see in Figure 9.1. I click it to get access to the most powerful button in the whole editor: Paste from Word. What this does is let you copy text from Word, paste it into a special window, and have the text appear (with formatting intact but missing extra code that comes from Word). The button to the left is Paste as Text, which does, essentially, the same thing, but you lose all the formatting in the text you're copying. That button is handy if you are copying and pasting text from a website into your post.

The buttons should be fairly self-explanatory from just about any word processor you've run into lately. There are a few interesting ones that you might wonder about, so I'll talk about these now. The Blockquote button indents the selected text. Within your stylesheet, a blockquote is not only indented, but treated as special text that will set it off from the surrounding text. Blockquote is intended for quotes, not indenting.

The Insert More Tag button puts a special marker in the text so that when your post is on the home page or an archive page, there is a Click to Read More or similar link on which readers have to click to continue. It's a nice way to save space and entice readers to stay around and read.

The Full Screen button puts the editing window, and just the editing window, full screen in your browser window, which is nice when you want to have more room to write and fewer distractions.

The Clear Formatting button is a saving grace if you forget to use the Paste from Word or Paste as Text buttons. Clear Formatting removes any formatting from the selected text, which is especially important if you copied and pasted text from another site that has a different font, colors, or font size. Nine times out of ten, when people ask me why their post looks funny, they copied and pasted from another site. A quick click on clear formatting usually does the trick.

Use the Embed Media button to paste a link to a YouTube video or the embed codes from another site to have the movie appear in your post. It's a pretty simple and spiffy tool.

One of the new features in WordPress 2.9 is that you can now just paste the URL from sites like YouTube and Flickr into your post and the media will automatically be included in the post just like if you used the embed media button. To pull off this magic, WordPress is tapping into the new multimedia standard called oEmbed, which is now supported by most of your favorite multimedia sharing sites.

The last button to cover, at least for the visual editor, is the Insert Symbol button. Use this button to put in characters like & and ≤ or > or curly quotes. Most of us don't remember the HTML entity codes for these and more obscure symbols, so the button is rather handy.

Icon	Name	Description
B	Bold	Bold/unbold selected text
I	Italic	Italicize/unitalicize selected text
ABC	Strikethrough	Strikethrough/unstrikethrough selected text

If you happen to know how to type those symbols on your keyboard, WordPress will do its best to swap in the right entity. Double-check after you post because you might not get what you were thinking and might have to go back and edit it.

I could drone on about what each of the buttons do in nauseating detail, but honestly you don't need it. Bold, italics, underline, bulleted, and numbered lists all work exactly how you'd expect. Bear in mind that because you're theme is driven by a stylesheet, WordPress tries to keep you from mucking that up. Changing the font (from Arial to Verdana) or the size (from 12 to 14 point) is something that you should manage within your stylesheet. So, if you want to always have the font be Verdana or have certain sections be Times New Roman, you should make changes in your stylesheet. Okay, this seems a little nit picky and "geeky, just because I said so," but it is really to save you work in the long run and to make sure all your posts look great. When any work has a mishmash of fonts and font sizes without any rhyme or reason, it's rather distracting. So, if you want to break the rules once and a while, you can edit the text in HTML mode and add some local style classes, but don't say I didn't warn you.

Components of the HTML Editor

If you're a brave soul who prefers to edit in HTML instead of using the visual editor, click the HTML tab (see Figure 9.2).

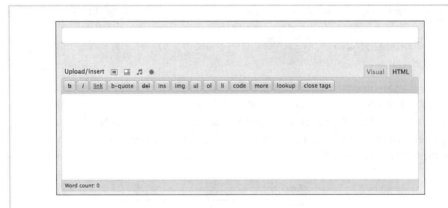

Figure 9.2 *The HTML editor in WordPress*

Even if your preference is to use the visual editor, sometimes you need to flip into HTML mode to fix something that looks strange, paste in some special code, or edit an HTML tag. One of the handier buttons is the Close Tags button, which will find errors in your HTML and fix them for you, at least as best as WordPress and TinyMCE can figure out. If you are working in HTML mode and happen to leave an "open" HTML tag, TinyMCE closes the tags for you if you switch to visual mode. It has to do this for the post to be displayed correctly in the visual editor.

When you run into troubles with the formatting in a post, HTML mode is often the only thing to fix it. Remember, you'll be seeing your post in HTML, with all its geeky, code-rich glory revealed, so be careful about what you're deleting and leaving behind. You don't want to make things worse!

The little gray buttons above the main toolbar are the multimedia buttons, which I'll describe in more detail later in the chapter (Adding Media to Your Blog Posts).

The last section of the posting area that I think you should know about is the Publish panel on the top right, which is shown in Figure 9.3. In the figure, all the sections of the panel are open. When they are closed, you use the Edit link to open them.

Figure 9.3   *Publish panel when editing posts or pages*

The Status pull-down is set to Draft by default and can be set to Pending Review before you publish the post. After you publish a post, you can switch the post back to Draft or Pending Review if you want to pull the post from the site. Pending Review is the default setting for contributors when they are done.

The Visibility section lets you make a post Public, Private (logged-in users only), Password Protected (public, but you have to have the password to few it), and Public, but Sticky. A "sticky" post means that, no matter what, the post stays as the first post, even if there are newer posts. The newer posts will start below the "sticky" post. Sticky posts are great for announcements or something else you'd like people to see every time they come to the site for a period of time. Most of the time, you'll want a post to be visible to the public, but sometimes you don't.

Speaking of time, the Publish section lets you set the publishing date of the post either to post in the future or post in the past. Future-posting is pretty obvious—sometimes you want a post to be live *after* a certain period of time—but back dating posts? Isn't that cheating? No, sometimes you just have to do it to fix a chronology. Because posts are arranged by *time*, the only way to really set an order for them is through changing dates. Often when I am setting up sites with a lot of content, I need to reshuffle things into a more logical order. The only way to do it is with the date function.

Post Editor in WordPress

Now it's time to switch gears and talk about the differences between the editor when you're writing a *Post* versus a *Page*. Let's look at the Post version of the editor first (see Figure 9.4).

Figure 9.4   *Post tags and Categories panels in the Post version of the editor*

The Post version of the editor has an area for Post Tags and Categories. Clicking the Choose from the Most Used Tags in Post Tags link gives you a tag cloud, where the bigger the word is, the more often you use the tag (see Figure 9.5). When you're adding tags, you can add them one by one or list them separated with commas, such as: blogging, blog editors, WordPress, WordPress tips. Yes, you can have two-word tags. In fact, your tags can have as many words as you want, but in practice, I'd stick with three at most.

Figure 9.5 *Looking at the most common tags I use in my posts within the Post Editor*

In the Categories panel, clicking the + Add New Category link expands the panel to enable you to not only create the new category, but also decide if it is going to be a sub-category or a top-level (parent) category (see Figure 9.6).

Using the Page Editor to Create Static Content

For Pages, there is only one additional panel in the editor: Attributes (see Figure 9.7). In the top section, you can decide if the Page you're creating is going to be the child of an existing page or not. That's followed by which Page Template you'd like to use. Finally, you get to Order, and this one needs a little explaining.

By default, pages are ordered in a navbar by "menu order," which is what the number in the box represents. If all the pages have menu order 0, they are ordered alphabetically. Here's where you can have some fun. If you set the menu order of a group of pages to 0 and another group to 1, in a navbar all the 0 pages would come first (alphabetically) and then all the 1s (again alphabetically). So, for posts all you can do is mess with *time* to change the order of Posts; with Pages, however, time doesn't matter, so you change the menu order to put the pages in an order you'd prefer. Now *that's* slick.

Figure 9.6   *Expanding the Category box to add a new Category within the Post editor*

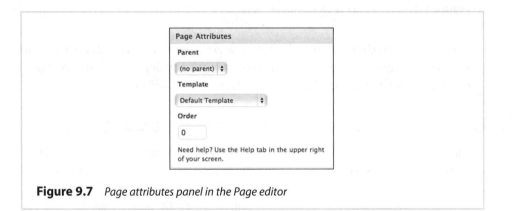

Figure 9.7   *Page attributes panel in the Page editor*

I think the simplicity of the fact that WordPress doesn't clutter up either posts or page-editing areas with a lot of extras is nice. It lets you focus on writing. Keeping both of the editing areas essentially the same might seem confusing at first, but what it should remind you is that the important thing is just creating content. Just writing because you love your topic.

SHOW ME   **Media 9.1—Post and Page Editors**

Access this video file through your registered Web Edition at
my.safaribooksonline.com/9780132182836/media

Hands On with the New Image Editor in Detail

How often have you uploaded an image to your blog only to realize not only is it too big, but also if you cropped it a little, it would look a whole lot better? Probably often enough that having the new image editor will be something you might use a good bit. (It was introduced in WordPress 2.9.)

 LET ME TRY IT

Using the WordPress Image Editor

1. First click the Media button to see your Media Library.

2. Then hover your mouse over the image you'd like to edit, and click the Edit link (see Figure 9.8).

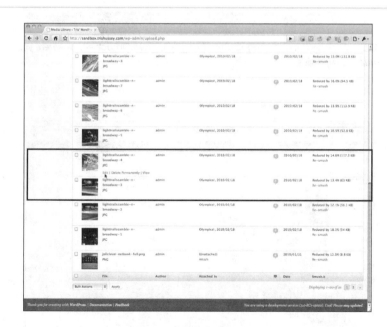

Figure 9.8   *Hovering your mouse over an image in your media library reveals the Edit link.*

3. This brings you *not* to the Image Editor, but to something more like the image properties editor (see Figure 9.9). To edit the image, click the Edit Image button, and then you'll be in the editor (see Figure 9.10).

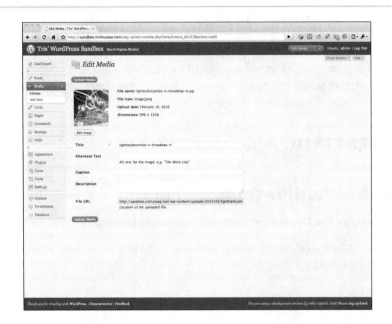

Figure 9.9   *Clicking the Edit Image button brings you to the image editor where you can see the image's properties.*

Figure 9.10   *The WordPress image editor*

The first thing to know right away is that the image editor is *not* a painting and drawing tool. You can't change an image's colors or add text or draw on it. This is basic image manipulation: cropping, scaling, rotating, and flipping. Before you say "That's it?!?!," remember that WordPress is designed to work with, well, words, and adding this to the arsenal is pretty darn cool.

Are There Great Online Image Editors?

If you don't already have an image-editing program, you can find some great options online. Adobe has a free version of Photoshop at Photoshop.com. Picnik.com is a great free photo editor that I've used a great deal. To top it all off, a site and company called Aviary.com has probably the richest set of online image, and now audio, editing tools around. If you can't do it with one of Aviary's tools, you probably can't do it at all.

With any online tool, you'll have to upload an existing image to edit it. Picnik assumes that you have an image to work with, whereas Photoshop and Aviary enable you to create something from scratch. Aviary even has a screen-capture tool if you need to take a great screenshot of your amazing blog for posterity!

Once you're done editing the image online, you'll need to save it back to your drive, and then upload up to WordPress to use it. Will WordPress at some point make a plugin or some other tool to make this process easier? Maybe—you never know. There are some pretty amazing WordPress developers out there.

The basics of rotating and flipping are self-explanatory, and if you need to go back, there are Undo, Redo buttons for you. The interesting parts come with cropping and scaling. Let's start with cropping, because although they are very cool, some features aren't immediately obvious.

 LET ME TRY IT

Cropping an Image

1. Open the Image Editor as described in the previous Let Me Try It.

2. In the Aspect ratio boxes, enter 1 in both of the (ratio of 1:1).

3. Hold down the Shift key while selecting part of the image to have that ratio applied. If you have already selected part of the image, putting a ratio into the boxes will apply the ratio to the current selection (say 2:1, 4:3, and so on).

If you click the Help link, you get some handy (and important) tips like these keyboard shortcuts:

- **Arrow**: Move by 10px
- **Shift + arrow**: Move by 1px
- **Ctrl + arrow**: Resize by 10px
- **Ctrl + Shift + arrow**: Resize by 1px
- **Shift + drag**: Lock aspect ratio

Another cool feature of the image editor is Scale Image, which enables you to *proportionately* scale your image to the size you need. The warning about not making it bigger than the current size is nice, but what I think is *more* important is that the scaling is automatically proportional, and you can't change that. This means you can't make the image bigger or smaller and have the image look stretched or squished.

When you're done scaling, cropping, flipping, and turning the image, make sure to save it. Now, note the box that says Thumbnail Settings; when you save the changes, you can have them reflected *only* in the thumbnail, all sizes, or all except for thumbnail. Figure 9.11 shows all the Image editor options, including cropping, scaling, and which sizes to apply the changes to.

Figure 9.11   *The Image Editor showing all the options opened*

Unfortunately, the image editor doesn't include a Save As or Create New and Save option. This means that if you want to have a "regular" version and a flipped version, you have to upload the same image twice, but only edit one of them. No, it isn't a huge deal, but it would certainly save time if we didn't have to have that step in the first place.

SHOW ME   Media 9.2—WordPress Image Editor
Access this video file through your registered Web Edition at
my.safaribooksonline.com/9780132182836/media

Adding Media to Your Blog and Posts

Blogs are made for multimedia. Except for including images, including other multimedia hasn't always been easy for blogging engines, WordPress included. Lucky for us, developers have listened, and now on most blogging engines, you can put almost anything you can imagine into a post. This section isn't going to get into the *creation* of media, rather the *curation* and display of multimedia on your blog in various ways. The focus will be how to not only embed media into your posts, but also how to deal with audio and video files (which tend to be rather large, to say the least). We're going to start off easy with images.

Let's Talk Copyright

This is a bit of a touchy subject, but it's important to talk about it now before you get in trouble. To clear up any confusion you may have, just because you find a picture, video, or song online *does not* give you the right to use it on your site. Artists post images all the time with no intention that someone will use their pictures without their permission. Many sites, like ones who offer images of celebrities, can be pretty harsh on people who are caught using their images without their permission. In this case, "harsh" means a large fine and potentially having your site taken down.

You see, even if I don't put "Copyright 2010, Tris Hussey, All Rights Reserved" on an image, video, or something I wrote, it is covered and protected by copyright law. The easiest way to avoid trouble? Ask first. Most of the time, if I'm asked if someone can use one of my pictures for themselves, I'll say yes. If it's a company who wants it as part of a promotional campaign, sure, I might ask for some money—that's only fair.

In the U.S., there is a law called the Digital Millennium Copyright Act, or DMCA for short, which protects the rights of artists and others from their works being used without their permission online. Before you wave your hand like it won't matter much to you, know that your site can be shut down if you violate copyright laws. The Electronic Frontier Foundation has a page that covers DMCA in detail: http://www.eff.org/issues/dmca.

Adding Images

There's a reason the cliché "a picture tells a thousand words" still stands—because it's still true. Of all the media types you can add to your blog and posts, images are by far the easiest and maybe the most rewarding. Most of the time, you are going to upload images from your local computer, but sometimes you'll want to insert images from elsewhere. Either way, the process is simple.

When you insert an image into your post that you haven't uploaded to your server, but is somewhere else on the Internet, this is called "hotlinking." By and large, hotlinking is *strongly* discouraged; however, a few sites like Flickr don't mind if you hotlink. (In fact, Flickr encourages it.) As a rule of thumb, unless you are given code to copy from a site or told to "use the image from our servers," download the image you are going to use and then upload to your own server.

 LET ME TRY IT

Inserting an Image into Your Post

1. Start a new Post or Page—your choice—it works the same with either content type.

2. Click the nondescript gray button (see Figure 9.12; I think it's supposed to look like a picture in a frame), and you get the window shown in Figure 9.13.

3. The default that comes up first is Upload from Your Computer; if you click the From URL tab, you get what is shown in Figure 9.14.

If you have already uploaded the image you want to use, so clicking Media Library gives you a list of all the files you've already uploaded (see Figure 9.15). After you find the image you want to use, click the Show link to the right of the image.

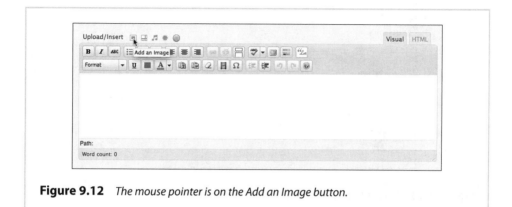

Figure 9.12 *The mouse pointer is on the Add an Image button.*

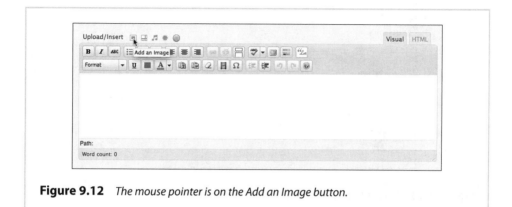

Figure 9.13 *The Add Media Files dialog*

4. Coming back to uploading an image from your computer, let's click that Select Files button and get some images in there! As you might gather from the fact that the button says Select *Files* and not Select *File*, you can upload more than one image at one time. And that's exactly what I'm going to do (see Figure 9.16).

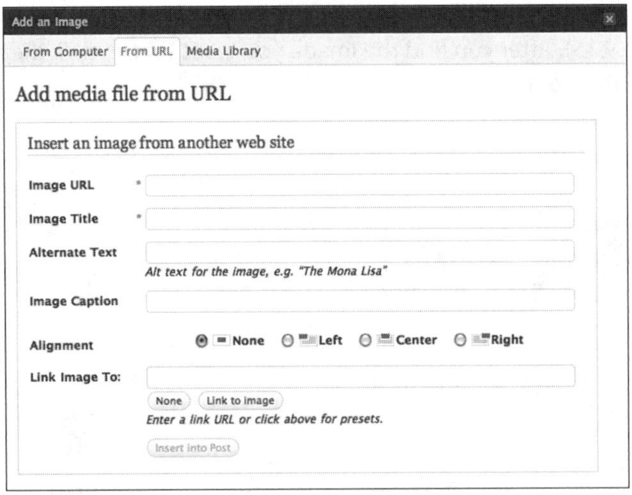

Figure 9.14 *Inserting an image from a URL (that is, from another website)*

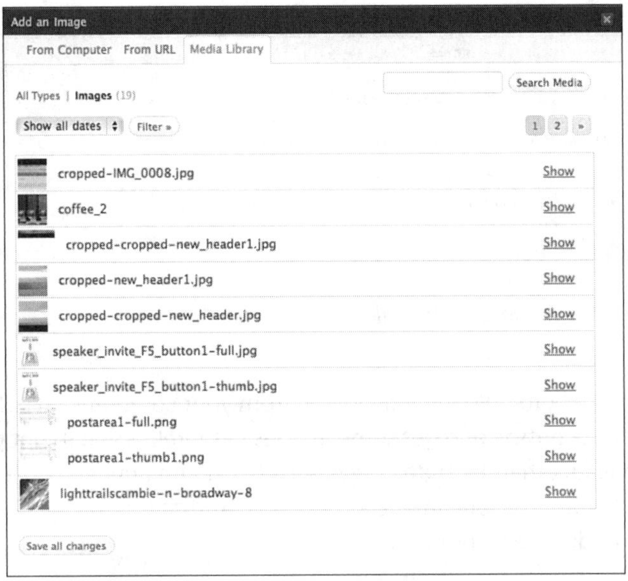

Figure 9.15 *Getting an image from your existing media library*

Figure 9.16 *Selecting multiple files to upload*

5. When you click Select Files, the standard Open dialog box opens. If you only need to upload one file, just click to select it and the click Select or Open to start uploading. If you'd like to upload more than one file at once, Ctrl+click (Windows) or Command+click (Mac) the files you want to upload, then click Select or Open. There is a "gotcha" to this uploader. The default uploader uses Adobe's Flash player, and while it works for almost everyone, sometimes it doesn't. If the Flash uploader doesn't work for you, and you have to use the Browser uploader, then you can only upload one file at a time. After, the files are uploaded you get what is shown in Figure 9.17.

6. At this point, it's easy to get confused as to what to do. If you want to put one of those images right into your post, click the Show link and then look (carefully) for the Insert into Post button, which can be hard to spot (see Figure 9.18).

7. Before clicking Insert into Post, you can edit the Title, Alternate Text, Caption, and Description. What I really want to focus on is the alignment (how text does or doesn't wrap about the image) and the (rough) size (you can adjust the size later as well). For this example, I'm going to pick the medium size, wrapping left. Then click Insert into Post.

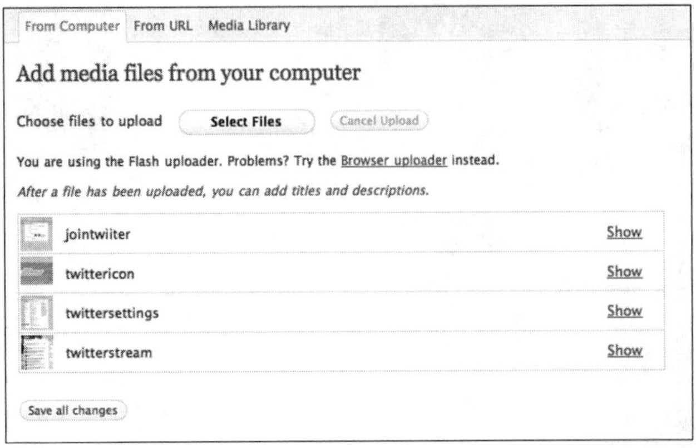

From Computer
From URL
Media Library
Add media files from your computer
Choose files to upload
Select Files
Cancel Upload
You are using the Flash uploader. Problems? Try the Browser uploader instead.
After a file has been uploaded, you can add titles and descriptions.
jointwiiter
Show
twittericon
Show
twittersettings
Show
twitterstream
Show
Save all changes

Figure 9.17 *Images uploaded!*

You are using the Flash uploader. Problems? Try the Browser uploader instead.
After a file has been uploaded, you can add titles and descriptions.
jointwiiter
Show
twittericon
Show
twittersettings
Show
twitterstream
Hide
File name: twitterstream.png
File type: image/png
Upload date: January 24, 2010
Dimensions: 500 × 360
Edit Image
Title
twitterstream
Alternate text
Alt text for the image, e.g. "The Mona Lisa"
Caption
Description
Link URL
http://trishussey.com/wp-content/uploads/twitterstream.png
None
File URL
Post URL
Enter a link URL or click above for presets.
Alignment
None
Left
Center
Right
Size
Thumbnail (150 × 150)
Medium (300 × 216)
Large
Full size (500 × 360)
Insert into Post
Delete
Save all changes

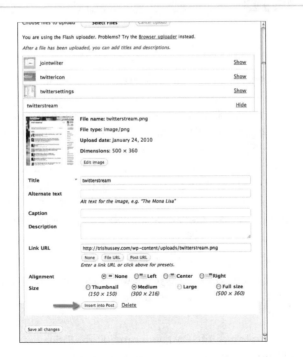

Figure 9.18 *Inserting an image into a post*

8. The result isn't quite what I wanted, so I'm going to edit the image proper-
    ties—not scaling or cropping—by clicking on the image and then clicking
    on the mountain button (see Figure 9.19).

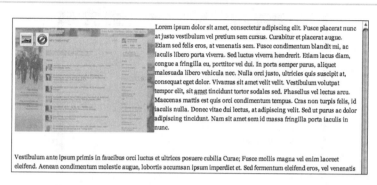

Figure 9.19 *Click the edit image properties button within the image, which is the mountain button.*

You get to this screen first (see Figure 9.20).

Figure 9.20 *Default screen of the Edit Image Properties dialog box*

What I actually want is on the "Advanced Settings" tab, so that I can add 10 pixels of space around the image and reduce the size to 90% of the original (see Figure 9.21).

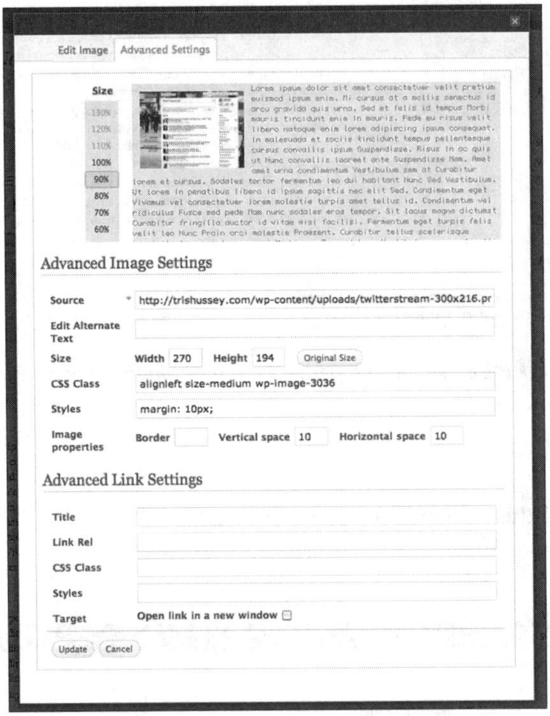

Figure 9.21 *Advanced image settings*

9. Click the Advanced Settings tab.

10. Move the percent slider down (or up), I chose 90% for this example.

11. Enter 10 in the Vertical and Horizontal Space boxes.

12. After clicking the Update button, you return to the editor. Now the image is a bit smaller, and there is a nice amount of padding on the sides of the image (see Figure 9.22).

That covers both adding an image to a post, and how you tweak the settings of any image that you insert into a post.

You might have noticed that the WordPress developers have reused a lot of the same interfaces for several different, but related, tasks. Adding new themes is very

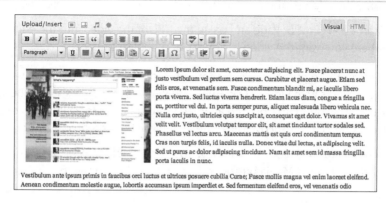

Figure 9.22 *Image properties edited and looking much better now*

much like the process of adding new plugins. You've seen in this chapter that the editing areas for Posts and Pages are essentially identical (as far as the writing part goes). In fact, if you click the remaining gray buttons along that line, video, audio, and just plain old media, you'll find that the interfaces are all the same. You learn one, you've learned them all.

The important distinction about adding types of media other than images is that all they do is insert *a link to the file*. So, pointing to a YouTube movie through this tool won't embed it for you to play in your post; it just makes a link to it. Now, if you want to embed a video to watch and display in your post, that's a horse of a different color.

Embedding Video

We love our Internet video, don't we? Between animals doing silly things (or interesting things) and people becoming overnight video success stories (for a day or two, at least), one of the things people *most* want to do on their blog is post videos. Not long ago, I would have given you a pretty complex series of steps involving copying embed codes, switching to HTML mode, and publishing. Now all you need to do for a simple video embed is copy the URL and paste it into your post. That's it. Let me show you how it works with a Let Me Try It.

 **LET ME TRY IT**

Inserting a YouTube Video into Your Post or Page

1. Go to YouTube, pick a video you'd like to embed into a Post or Page.

2. Copy the address of the video from the address bar of your browser.

3. Start a new Post or Page and paste the URL of the video into the editing area where you want the video to appear, and publish the post.

This all works through the magic of oEmbed, and in addition to working with YouTube, it works with Viddler, Qik, Hulu, and Vimeo. For pictures, Flickr supports oEmbed as well, but unlike placing an image through the Media Library/Loader, you don't have any control over how the image will be presented in your post.

What if you want more control over how your video looks in your post? That's when our friend, the Embed Media button (refer to Figure 9.1), comes in.

 LET ME TRY IT

Using the Embed Media Button to Embed a Video into a Post or Page

1. You still only need the URL from YouTube (just like the previous Let Me Try It). However, instead of pasting it into the post, you click the Embed Media button, paste the URL into the File/URL box,

2. Hit the Tab key (that kicks the process into gear to get the size filled in for you). If you need to change the size, click the Constrain Proportions box and then make the video larger or smaller (I'm betting smaller) (see Figure 9.23).

3. The Advanced tab has a lot of tweaks to the embedding process, but most of the time aren't needed at all. Yes, you can play with the alignment and several other parameters, but only in pretty rare times have I had to mess with those (and often, the messing turned into deleting and starting over).

4. When you click Insert, you're going to see a yellow box the same size that the video will be when you post. Don't worry—this is normal. Having the video playing while you're editing would create headaches for both you and the WordPress engine, so they wait to display it for real until you publish the Post or Page and view it on your site.

That, believe it or not, is the entirety of what you need to know about adding a video into your post.

"Wait, hold the phone. What if I don't want my video on YouTube! What if I want it on my own server! What then?"

Darn, I was hoping you wouldn't have thought of that. Okay, there is a little more to the whole video thing if you want to host the video yourself. First, you're probably

Figure 9.23 *I've pasted in the YouTube URL, and now I'm adjusting the dimensions of the video to better fit in my post.*

not going to be able to use the media uploader within WordPress. Almost all hosts have PHP set not to allow uploads that large through the Web, so you're going to have to upload via FTP. I upload all my videos and podcasts to my uploads directory. This way, the URL to the media is easy to remember: trishussey.com/wp-content/uploads/. All I have to do is have the filename handy. Although there are lots of ways to embed videos using various plugins, try using the Embed Media I described earlier. If you're uploading something like a QuickTime movie (.mov), you'll have to type in the dimensions yourself (no matter how many times you hit tab—trust me, I tried). How the video will look can be hit or miss depending on how you created it, but that's how you do it. Of the video plugins to use, Viper's Video Quicktags is the one to choose and download (http://wordpress.org/extend/plugins/vipers-video-quicktags/). Alex "Viper007Bond" Bond is one of those gifted plugin developers that Automattic hired to be able to do more awesome things for the community. You can't go wrong with his plugins.

 SHOW ME   Media 9.3—Embedding Videos and Images into Your Posts or Pages

Access this video file through your registered Web Edition at
my.safaribooksonline.com/9780132182836/media

Embedding Podcasts

You might think that putting a simple MP3 file into a blog post for people to listen to would be a simple and easy thing to do. Oddly enough, embedding an MP3 file for a podcast is the only thing in this section that requires a plugin to work effectively. Good thing that there is a great plugin to embed your podcasts—Blubrry PowerPress from blubrry.com. You can see the Blubrry PowerPress Settings page in Figure 9.24.

Figure 9.24 *Blubrry PowerPress settings*

 LET ME TRY IT

Installing and Using the Blurbrry PowerPress Plugin for Podcasts

This Let Me Try It assumes that you already have the MP3 file created for your podcast.

1. Download the plugin from WordPress.org (http://wordpress.org/extend/plugins/powerpress/) or through the administration area of your site and install it.

2. Activate the plugin.

3. Go to the settings and set your uploads directory (see Figure 9.24) and click Save Settings.

4. Start a new Post or Page and scroll to the bottom of the window until you see the Podcast area (see Figure 9.25).

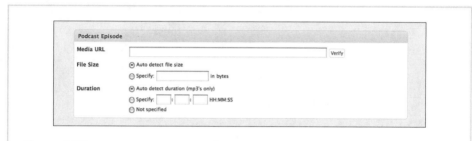

Figure 9.25   *PowerPress podcast entry area in the Post or Page editor*

5. All you need to do is paste in the URL to the MP3 into the Media URL box and click Verify. The default is for both the file size and duration to be automatically determined.

6. Now write the post and hit Publish. PowerPress takes care of the rest. Depending on your preferences, the player will be at the beginning or end of the post. No matter where it is...it's there!

   I've had great success with PowerPress for MP3s, but not as much for my own videos I've uploaded. I don't blame the plugin, however; I think I just didn't have my movie optimized for the area it was being put in.

As you can you can tell, adding multimedia to your WordPress blog is very simple and straightforward. When I'm teaching classes on WordPress and get to the part about embedding movies, there is a collective "that's it?" when I'm done. Yeah, that's it. It's easy.

TELL ME MORE   Media 9.4—Tris' Secret Tips and Tricks in the Editors

Access this audio recording through your registered Web Edition at
my.safaribooksonline.com/9780132182836/media

10

By the end of this chapter, you will be able to create several different types of websites using WordPress and know how to convert an existing site to WordPress.

Creating Sites with WordPress

If I had divided the book into parts, this would be Part II and is where the rubber hits the road. We have a domain or domains and a host. We've installed and tweaked WordPress. We've chosen a few themes to play with and have started to flesh out our site with content. So, I think it would be safe to call Part I of this book "Building the Foundation." Everything is in place to start getting down to business.

As you've gathered by now, WordPress is a *very* flexible publishing system. There are probably more ways to use WordPress than there are *users* of WordPress. Okay, that might be exaggerating just a little; but in truth, I've seen a lot of people use WordPress in some pretty amazing ways. In my time using WordPress, I've set up blogs (of course), websites (and I teach a very popular class to do this), collaboration systems, and even store fronts; and those are just the beginning. In this chapter, we're going to talk about using WordPress to build blogs and websites, how to convert an existing website to use WordPress, and use WordPress as a content management system (CMS). We'll then push into some new territory by using WordPress for project management and team collaboration, and then get into how you can use WordPress in Multisite mode and a set of plugins called BuddyPress to make your own social network. In the *very* short time that WordPress has been around (a mere 7 years in 2010), it has leapfrogged over many blogging engines, even ones with commercial support, to become a powerful tool. WordPress' success is a testament to the devotion and skill of the WordPress community, and I see no reason its popularity and usefulness is going to change anytime in the future.

WordPress as a Blog

WordPress started as a blogging engine and nothing in this chapter is going try to suggest that WordPress has lost sight of its bloggy beginnings. I would hazard to say that with the release of WordPress 3.0, WordPress' strength as a blog engine is even *stronger* than it has ever been. The reason for this is obvious—the appeal of blogging hasn't lessened in the past years, but grown and multiplied. *The New York Times*, CNN, *People*, and other high-profile websites use WordPress to power their sites, which speaks to the power, flexibility, and stability of WordPress.

If you've worked through the preceding chapters of the book, you are ready to blog away to your heart's content. As you develop your blog, one thing to consider is that you don't need to have *all* your content on your home page. There are lots of themes that enable you to have "featured" posts that draw from only one category. Although my blog's home page is a catch-all for all my posts, I have worked on several blogs where that isn't the case. Having only certain categories of posts appear on the home page is a good way to highlight particular content, while also having additional content people can delve deeper into within the site. At several points in my time as a blogger, I would post seven or more posts *in a day*, which is great from a content-perspective. But if you figure that, by default, the homepage only displays the 10 most recent posts, there is a lot of content falling off the front page. To counter that, you can have categories such as "Featured" or "What's Hot" as the only categories displayed on the home page, which enables you to put the posts that you think deserve the most attention on the home page. Another popular option, and one I particularly like, is to use a magazine-style theme, where you have several smaller sections on your home page and each section displays posts from a different category.

You might be wondering if blogs organized in these ways even qualify as "blogs." Absolutely, they are. There are no rules saying a blog must look like this or that. The number-one rule of blogging is writing with passion about the things you love. How you present those posts are up to you. Don't let convention or "tradition" (which is more than a tad ironic because most blogs are less than 10 years old, including my own) dictate how you want your readers to read your posts. Maybe you write about fashion, movies, and restaurants and want to have men's fashion, women's fashion, movie reviews, and restaurant reviews all get equal billing. That's hard to do when you just have one column of content, and all your posts go there.

Here is what you should know about using WordPress as a blog—write what you want to write about and make your blog reflect you, and you'll be far ahead of anyone following "convention."

WordPress as a Website

Here's a challenge for you. Make a website that looks great, is well-organized, easy to update, and attracts search engines like bees to honey. How long do you think that would take you? When I built sites using static HTML files and images, it could take a few *weeks* to get the look right and all the structural elements in place (blank pages ready for content). Today, I build "regular" websites using WordPress, and the answer to that question can be as little as a day or two. Even if the "look" (aka theme) isn't perfect in a day or two, you can start adding content to the site immediately.

This wasn't possible before. Adding content to HTML pages before the look was complete would only lead to having to rework the content and the page later.

It wasn't long after WordPress started to become popular that people wanted to make a Page the home page instead of the "normal" blog (or Posts). At first, making a Page the home page and still having Posts somewhere else took a couple plugins and a few tweaks to the .htaccess file that weren't for the faint of heart. With the launch of WordPress 2.1 in January 2007 (code named "Ella"), these features for constructing a blog this way were built into the WordPress core; users had to make only a few clicks in the "Reading" section of the Settings to get going. (Refer to Chapters 3, "Getting Around WordPress," and 4, "Configuring WordPress to Work Its Best," for more about settings.)

Why is using WordPress to build a website not only easy, but also practical, time-saving, and better for the long run? Well, I've already told you that the development time when you use WordPress to build your site is a fraction of what it would be if you built a site with static HTML pages. You probably know that faster isn't always better, but faster and *more efficient* is better. The first efficiency you gain by using WordPress to build a website is that because your *content* isn't connected to the *theme*, if you need to update the theme for any reason, you don't have to worry about your content being affected. Posts, Pages, Categories, and Tags aren't affected at all when you update a theme. In development terms, this means that you can be adding content while the theme is being tweaked to your liking. No waiting for the final look to be approved and polished—just start writing and posting. Speaking of writing and posting, you've seen how easy the WordPress editors are to use. If you've used any web-based email program, you're set to start editing and posting content. If you're working with a team of people, this means little to no training is needed for them to get to speed. If it's just you, you don't have to learn arcane interfaces or procedures to update a page. You edit your content, simply and straightforwardly.

When the site is up, and you're updating content frequently, you can quickly see that your search engine traffic is substantial quickly. Sometimes within a month, you can be in the top 10 sites for your key search terms. Why? Because blogging engines, and WordPress especially, are tuned out-of-the-box to be structured the way search engines *want* sites to be. You have good, simple HTML with an RSS feed of all the latest content. All the posts and pages are linked together. Now combine that with categories, tags, and a couple of SEO plugins, and you don't have to worry about SEO if you write, post, and publish on a regular basis. You are well on your way to being found on search engines for the terms that match your niche. Ready to set up a site now?

 **LET ME TRY IT**

Creating a Website with WordPress: Having a Static Page as Your Homepage

1. Create a Page with a title of "Blog" or "News" or whatever you're going to call your posts. (By default, you already have the About Page, which will do fine as a home page [assuming you edit it], but you need one more Page for things to go smoothly out-of-the-box.) You can change the name of the page later, if you want. Don't put anything in the body of the Page and click Publish.

2. Go to the Reading section of Settings. At the top is the section determining what your home page will be. Click the A Static Page radio button and then choose About (or whichever Page you want as the home page) for the Front page and Blog (or whatever you called it) for the Posts page.

3. Click Save Changes and...that's it. Your former WordPress-powered blog is now a WordPress-powered website (see Figure 10.1).

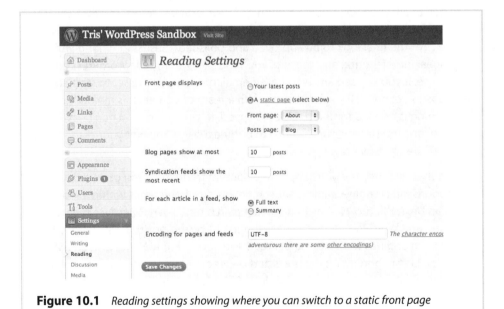

Figure 10.1   *Reading settings showing where you can switch to a static front page*

 SHOW ME   Media 10.1—Creating a Website with WordPress
Access this video file through your registered Web Edition at
my.safaribooksonline.com/9780132182836/media

From here on, it's just putting content together and getting your theme right. Some of the decisions you want to think about are whether you are going to use Pages for your Navigation or Post Categories or both. How many levels deep are you going to want to go?

However, don't worry if you make some missteps getting things ready. WordPress is very forgiving about those kinds of things. Yes, after you launch and people are using the site, when you change URLs around or delete Pages to make them Posts, you might cause a few 404 Not Found errors, but before that—don't worry. If you've followed my steps and advice for setting up WordPress in general, you're set. The settings I went through in Chapter 4 are the basic, core settings you should use, regardless of whether you are using WordPress as a blog or a website.

Many WordPress themes are more blog-centric than site-centric, so I've found myself having to do more theme editing when I'm working with WordPress-based websites than when I work with blogs. Most of the time, all that needs to be changed is excluding the Page ID that is also the home page from the navigation. Doing this makes sure you don't have two seemingly different links (say, Home and About) that go to the same Page (refer to Chapter 7, "All About Themes"). If you are going to stay with page-based navigation (which is probably the easiest), remember that when you create parent and child Pages, both the child *and* parent Pages should have meaningful content. You might chuckle, but I made this mistake making a site. I made a page for a top-level heading and two child pages. The child pages looked great and had content. I forgot to put any content in the parent (because I always navigated straight to a child page), but clicking on the parent page link was the *first* thing my boss did when I showed him the new site. Oops.

If you want to be more creative with your navigation, don't forget to take advantage of setting the menu order of pages that you'd like to group together. I've done this as a faux-grouping to put similar pages into context or to order pages the way I wanted them (instead of alphabetically). Just remember in WordPress page ordering that zero is the *highest* number, and all Pages with the same number are then sorted alphabetically (all the 0s, then all the 1s, then 2s, and so on). The next level of creativity is using *category-based* navigation with your page-based navigation. You can use a simple line of PHP code to list the categories you have set for the site:

```
<?php wp_list_categories(); ?>
```

To get a more detailed list of categories, ordered by name, up to three levels deep, *and* a link to the category's RSS feed, which would be a spiffy looking navigation menu for a site, use this line of code:

```
<?php wp_list_categories('orderby=name&depth=3&feed=RSS'); ?>
```

When you're building a website based on WordPress, don't think that you have to have only static Pages as your content. Using Posts for news releases, product listings, events, and other *time-sensitive* data is great, not to mention that having a whole section that is a standard blog is a great way to get the most out of your website. Remember, a website based on WordPress is as follows:

- Basic CMS

- Designed for multimedia

- Designed for different types of content

- Tuned for search engines from the start

- Easy to learn how to update

If you're concerned about WordPress becoming old hat or the technologies becoming obsolete, don't be. Not only is WordPress open-source with strong community support, the parts that make it run (PHP and MySQL) are also open-sourced with strong community support. Finding people who know PHP and MySQL isn't hard; it's a core part of most IT curricula now, and several other common CMS systems such as Drupal and Joomla are based on the same core technologies. The last, and most important, factor is that the WordPress community is built upon the philosophy that *you* own your data, not the platform. If you need, or want, to switch from WordPress, the export files are written in standard XML that any system can parse and pull out your data.

All this advice is all well and good if you don't have a site already, but what if you have a site built on HTML files (URLs that end with home.html or about.html or products.html)? What can you do then? Are you out of luck? Hardly. You just have to do a little more planning and work to get the site transferred smoothly.

Converting a Website to WordPress

Moving an existing website to WordPress isn't very hard, but there are some things you need to consider before you undertake this little project. The most important thing is that if your site has been around for any length of time, there are links to your site on the Internet. You don't want to "break" those links by changing the URLs of the existing pages, at least not without a way for people to find or be redirected to the new ones (Google especially). The next thing to consider is scale. How big *is* the website that you are planning to move? (Geeks call it "porting.") The bigger the website, the more links and URLs you're going to have to manage and redirect. Redirecting links and URLs doesn't even address moving the *content* (which luckily is often just a case of copy and paste), which can be tedious and time consuming to say the least.

Asking yourself, "Wait, why did I say I wanted to do this again?" is appropriate. It isn't a quick, easy, or painless process. The process takes time, planning, and effort. When you're finished, however, you have future-proofed your website. When you complete the process of porting all your content into WordPress, you can export your content to a single XML file any time you want. This can be a fail-safe backup, or for publishing or to move again. Because XML is an industry-standard for transferring information, especially large amounts of text and structured content, you can relax in knowing that your content is easier to work with and archive. When your site is tied into a traditional HTML-based website, your content isn't easily pulled into one transportable document. There is a tremendous amount of inertia to move or change anything with the site, even moving or adding a section. Making a structural change to an HTML-based website can mean changing hundreds, maybe thousands of files, which isn't fun. Adding a new section to a WordPress-based site is as easy as adding a new parent/top-level page or category and putting in the content. The rest of the site will take care of itself.

Now, let's get to the "how" you're going to do it.

Without a doubt, the first, and most important, priority is keeping your current live site up and running without interruption (except for the moment of the switch, which should only be a moment). Sure you want to have the old site gone and the new one up, but it can't happen overnight. It doesn't matter how much coffee you pour into a team of WordPress developers—flipping over a site in a few hours just isn't a practical target. Depending on the size of your site, plan for between a week and a month to move your site to WordPress. Most of that time will be spent tweaking your theme and copying content. If you have lots of content and want lots of changes to a theme, the process is going to take longer. If you don't have a lot of content and are happy with a theme as it is except for minor changes, the process might be shorter. Again, the important thing is planning. You have to plan how everything will happen. Surprises and "oops" aren't welcome additions to creating a new WordPress-powered website.

I'm going to outline some *basic, high-level* steps for moving a site to WordPress. I can't account for all contingencies or situations here in this book, but I'm going to try to hit the big items.

 **LET ME TRY IT**

Moving a "Static" Website to WordPress

1. Make a backup of your current website *off your server*. The simplest thing to do is to use your FTP client and download the entire

public_html/www/web/htdocs folder to your local computer or external hard drive.

2. Pick a date when you will freeze content changes on the old site and stick to it, and make sure others stick to it as well. One of the most frustrating things when I'm porting a site is when I've checked off a page from my to-be-moved list and then someone changes the content on that page. Even if you're doing this all yourself, make sure you don't keep changing content on the old site.

3. Install WordPress. If you're like me and want to install WordPress in the root directory of the site, not a subdirectory like /wordpress/, be *absolutely positive* that none of the files or directories in your current site have the same name as WordPress files.

   If you prefer to install WordPress in a subdirectory, you will have two parallel sites that are running independently. You can work on your theme edits to your heart's content and no one will be the wiser. (I call it hiding in plain sight.) You can also add content the site, but when you're done, you'll have to change the setting for the address of the site from *yourdomain. com/ wordpress/* to just *yourdomain.com* and make sure that the new content is pointing to the right URLs. (For example, old about.html points to the new About Page, and so on.) No, it's not hard, just *fiddly*, and there is a big of a leap of faith when you make the switch.

   A method described by David Cooley of CyberCoded (http://www. cybercoded.net/convert-static-html-site-to-wordpress-easily/) has you install WordPress at the root of your old site and then *copy* your index.html file (or whatever the filename of your original site's homepage is) to the new theme you are using (just copy the file itself to wp-content/themes/ *your-theme/*) and call it home.php.

4. Now, create Pages for all the pages in your existing site. So if you have a page named products.html on your current site, create a Page called Products.

5. Copy and paste the content from the old html-based pages to the new WordPress pages, and if you use the Paste from Word button, your formatting should remain intact. You might have to re-insert your images into the new pages, but that isn't a huge hurdle. What you're doing is making a mirror of the site until you're ready to flip over.

One more thing to make this all come together is setting your permalink structure to %permalink%.html *after* you've finished pasting all your content over. (This makes sure you don't have conflicts with the html versions.) To use .html on *Pages*, you'll need a plugin called ".html on pages" to enable you to do the same for Pages as you have for Posts (available from the WordPress plugin repository at: http://wordpress.org/extend/plugins/html-on-pages/).

6. Copy the content from your old html home page and create a new Page for it to paste the content into. I'd set up WordPress to use that Page as the homepage with the Use Static Page option I talked about previously (a lot easier than editing more template files, I think). Now delete the home.php file from the theme directory and rename all the old html files from your site by adding "old_" so your new WordPress site will be live!

The one thing about any of these approaches is that tweaking your theme in transition isn't terribly easy. It's hard to see what things will look like when it's all said and done. Yes, as you're working with the WordPress pages, you can have a good idea what an individual Page or Post (or Archive of Posts) will look like, but it's going to be a small leap of faith for the final product. My "secret" for this is to either use or buy a theme that you really like with minimal tweaks *or* install WordPress on your laptop or desktop computer, work on the theme there, and then when you're done, upload those files. Working off a local copy isn't hard and can save you a lot of headaches if you want to have an elaborate theme. There is another way, though.

Think of the theme that you make the switch with as a transition theme. As you've seen in the various Show Me screencast examples, changing themes in WordPress is easy; if you're converting a site to WordPress, it's the converting process that is the hardest and worst part of the whole thing. So, get your site moved. Get all the content sorted out, links checked, and all that. Then use a plugin like Theme Test Drive (http://wordpress.org/extend/plugins/theme-test-drive/), which serves one theme to the admin user and another to everyone else, to work on an improved theme. Switching back and forth between old and new themes is painless and can be done so quickly; most visitors would never notice. This approach enables you to worry more about moving content and making sure you aren't breaking old links in the process versus how the new site will look. Of course, you want your site to look great, but there are hundreds of great themes that you can use in the interim while you work on a new killer theme.

In the end, moving your site to WordPress will be one of the best things you've done for your Internet presence. Just don't stress out about it.

WordPress as a CMS

This section is a little odd because WordPress *already is* a content management system (CMS), but what I'm talking about here is *expanding* WordPress' capabilities beyond a few basic content types (mostly Posts and Pages) to include types that you'd find in more standard CMS systems such as employee records and profiles. There are two ways to approach the fact that WordPress has limited content types. One is to use custom fields to give you more data per Post or Page to work with; the other is to develop plugins to allow you to build more data structures into the database that you can *then* put into special Pages. Confused yet?

Using WordPress as an *über*-power CMS is something that is a little beyond us mere mortals. One of the hottest plugins to really kick start the "WordPress as a CMS" movement has been Pods CMS. Having tried the plugins, and gone through the tutorials, I can safely tell you that this plugin is only for people who have exhausted using custom fields and other "simple" tricks like tweaking Post and Page templates.

Here is the trick to using WordPress as a CMS—just use it as a CMS. The idea of a CMS is to allow authors to easily contribute and edit content to the sections that they are responsible for, but not be able to muck about in areas they shouldn't. The one area where WordPress lacks in the whole CMS arena is in approvals processes and only allowing people to post to certain categories. Certainly not Earth shattering, by any stretch of the imagination, it just means that as a moderator you need to pay a little closer attention to what people publish (or when you give approval to publish). My guess is that over the next few months the CMS-related functions will start to improve in WordPress. WordPress 3.0 has significantly improved on previous versions' capabilities for custom post types and custom taxonomies (two parts key to improving WordPress as a CMS). I'd wager that in short order there will be CMS Themes and CMS plugins to help us mere mortals work with custom post types and custom taxonomies more easily.

Beyond Blogs: Other Uses for WordPress

Up until now, all the examples of using WordPress have been content-driven. Blogs, websites, and CMS systems are all about delivering content to people so that they can *read* it. Pretty much doing what websites have been doing since they started in 1991. (Yes, it's only been 20 years since the web was born; the Internet, however, is 40 years old.) In this section, I'm going to show you examples of some of my favorite uses for WordPress: Project Management, Team Collaboration, and Online Communities. These examples focus more on tricks, tools, and plugins that can help you leverage WordPress as a *communications* tool versus just a *publishing* tool. One of the challenges of using WordPress like this is that there are few out-of-the-box, instant solutions to pull off any of these uses. You have to use plugins, themes, and more than a little creativity to pull it off. What's the pay off? When it works, it *really* works well.

Project Management and Collaboration

Project management and collaboration, at least doing them online using the web, are pet interests of mine. I've been a telecommuter working from home for almost all of the last ten years, so you figure out pretty darn fast how to keep a project on the rails and the lines of communication open when you might have only email, phone, instant messaging, and the web as your communications tools. Project management and collaboration overlap a great deal with each other because they have one important (critical) thing in common: communication. Well-run projects and teams *always* know what is going on from the big picture to the smallest detail. How does WordPress help with this? Aren't you just pushing this whole "WordPress is awesome" thing just a bit too far?

If you step back and look at what WordPress is all about, publishing and communication, you can see the beauty in using WordPress like this. Here you have a system where you can publish an update that is immediately available and can be discussed. You publish something, and the team members can get an email there is something new or via RSS or even via Twitter. (That's a really cool one, I think.) No, using WordPress to do this won't generate 3D flying Gantt charts and administer electric shocks through the keyboard if someone misses a deadline. (Wouldn't that be interesting to watch?) What it *can* do is let people share information, updates, tasks, and documents and have discussion *asynchronously* and with little to no training.

I'm working on the electric shock thing.

Project Management

Using WordPress for project management is really pushing things to the edge. Oddly enough, it's not because WordPress can't *handle* being used as a project management tool; it's that there aren't many plugins to help you in the process. The critical part of any project is keeping everyone on track and on time with their tasks. Neither WordPress nor any of the plugins I found are going to help you with that. I wasn't able to find snazzy gadgets for Gantt charts or those fun tools of the PM trade either. What is left is what WordPress is great at: content.

When you're setting up a WordPress install (can't really call it a "blog," can we?) for project management, the first question to ask is whether the site is for the team, clients, or both. On a site for just the team, frank and open discussion about the project are essential. On a client-facing site, some of the frankness and honesty needs to be tempered and toned down a notch or three. Regardless of client or team, chances are pretty good that you don't want other folks snooping around your site, so you need a way to keep the Huns at bay but still keep it easy for the permitted few to get in. I've found an excellent plugin called Registered Users Only (http://www.viper007bond.com/wordpress-plugins/registered-users-only/), which simply blocks anyone and everyone, except people with accounts (even a sub-scriber level is enough), from seeing any part of the site. I often pair it with a plugin called Private Files (http://jameslow.com/2008/01/28/private-files/) to make sure clever people don't try to sneak a peek at uploaded files as well. With those two simple plugins, you have a nice, closed-off extranet for you and whomever you want.

It is exactly this setup that I used with my editors and I while writing this book (see Figure 10.2). When chapters, videos, or podcasts were finished, I would upload them to my Editors extranet and email the team. The files were all zipped and ready to be downloaded. For a larger project (not that writing this book hasn't been a large project), you might upload the overall project plan as a Page so people have a reference. Team members can be listed on another page for easy access to contact information. If you're using other sites like Basecamp.com or LiquidPlanner.com for your project, have those as links in the sidebar for reference. Updates from various parts of the team can be posts with comment to discuss issues and questions.

Like all tools, it doesn't matter how cool it is—if people don't use it, the point is moot. I wish I had an easy answer for that problem, and if you have one, do let me know, but one thing I have found recently that has worked for projects and class-room collaboration is a very special theme called P2 from the folks at Automattic (see Figure 10.3).

P2 morphs WordPress and Twitter together into a theme designed for people to just use it *without ever going to the dashboard*. Post right from the home page. Leave a comment. Jump to a section that is more relevant to you. New items have a subtle yellow color until you scroll by it. Content is organized by tags not cate-gories, but each tag has its own RSS feed so team members can even focus on the part of the project they are most interested in. I've put this at the end of the project management section, and before I talk about collaboration, because it is the P2 theme that I've found to be *very* successful at helping collaboration as well. For some great insight on how P2 works, Matt Mullenweg's post about how P2 changed Automattic is well worth the time: http://ma.tt/2009/05/how-p2-changed-automattic/.

Using WordPress Book Editors Site
Private Blog for the editors of Using WordPress

Status Update   Blog Post   Quote   Link

Hi, Tris. Whatcha up to?   Upload/Insert

Tag it   Post it

Recent Updates   Toggle Comment Threads | Keyboard Shortcuts

Tris Hussey 11:09 am on February 1, 2010   Permalink | Reply | Edit
Tags: book files (6), Videos (4)

Video segments for Chapters 8 & 9

Here are the video segments for Chapters 8 & 9...
Chapter 8-9 video (465 MB zip file)

Tris Hussey 11:30 am on January 31, 2010   Permalink | Reply | Edit
Tags: Videos (4)

Video segments for Chapters 6 & 7

Here are the screencast-showme segments for Chapters 6 & 7. I did 4 for each ... Let me know what you think
about the style and such. I recorded the audio separately from the screencast so we can tweak if needed.
Chap 6-7 video

Tris Hussey 10:26 pm on January 25, 2010   Permalink | Reply | Edit
Tags: book files (6), chapters (3), Figures (2)

Chapters and figures for Chaps 6-9

Files for Chapters and figures for Chaps 6-9
6344ch6-ch9

Search for: Search

Recent Posts

Video segments for Chapters 8 & 9
Video segments for Chapters 6 & 7
Chapters and figures for Chaps 6-9
Podcasts for Chaps 2 and 4
Video Segments for chapters 4 & 5

Recent tags

Videos (4)   RSS
book files (6)   RSS
Figures (2)   RSS
chapters (3)   RSS
audio files (1)   RSS
chapter 4 (1)   RSS
chapter 2 (1)   RSS
images (1)   RSS
text (1)   RSS
All Updates RSS

Recent comments

Meta

Site Admin
Log out
Entries RSS
Comments RSS
WordPress.org

Figure 10.2   *The extranet that I made for my editors and I to exchange content and comment on the project*

Collaboration

Online team collaboration sites...well, there are lots of them. Some are better than others, and I've used my fair share of the good, bad, and the "please just put it out of its misery" collaboration sites over the years. One of the success factors (or failure points) of a collaboration tool is how easy it is for people to use and adopt into their daily routine. Because "collaboration tools" cover a *huge* gamut of use cases and needs, I'm going to pick one use case to focus on, and I hope that this example will help inspire and guide you in using WordPress for collaboration in other ways.

 SHOW ME   **Media 10.2—Using WordPress As a Collaboration Tool**
Access this video file through your registered Web Edition at
my.safaribooksonline.com/9780132182836/media

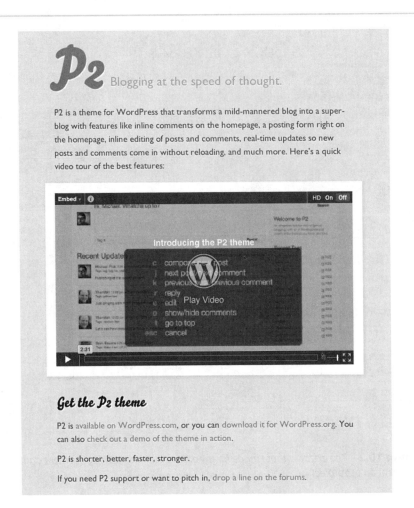

Figure 10.3   *The P2 theme from Automattic for painless discussion and collaboration*

I'm in the tech industry, in case you hadn't guessed by now, but I also occasionally teach classes at a few local universities here in the Vancouver area. One of the hard parts about teaching is getting the class to participate and engage. I thought about hooking up a car battery to their chairs, but that idea didn't go over so well with the administration, so I started a private class blog instead. My class blogs are based on the same model as I described for the site I have with my editors; the class blogs are closed off to the outside world and use the P2 theme to collaborate. I *don't* use it for sending out homework and mundane class related stuff; I use it to help my students learn more about the tech world. For example, for a seminar class called "Trendsetters," the idea is to talk about what's next and what's new and challenge the students to look at the world a little differently. As part of class, each student needs to contribute just one post a week with a bit of interesting news or information from the tech world or even something that just inspires them.

In a previous class, I tried a different blogging platform that I *thought* would be easy enough for people to contribute, but for busy students, even a little bit of hindrance is too much. Using P2, each student just logs in, types their little bit at the top, and they're done. Over time and with practice, I think my students (I often teach the same students from the same program) will start using it to share and collaborate more. This is just one example of how to use WordPress for collaboration.

How about working on sections of a document? A Post can be a section, and through group editing, you can revise it over time. WordPress now tracks all the changes in case you needed to roll back to a previous version.

I wouldn't recommend using WordPress for formal approvals processes, unless you can have a special plugin developed to help you manage it; however, for almost any other collaborative effort, WordPress is a strong option to consider. Like you, I was a bit of a skeptic until I read how the Automattic team took P2's predecessor theme, Prologue, and transformed it into P2, and how they collaborate with each other. Automattic is a virtual company. The employees are, literally, spread out around the world. To keep all the wheels in motion with WordPress.com and the development of WordPress and other company business, they used to use IM and good old IRC (Internet Relay Chat). Those two methods *are* great, and I've used them to work with virtual teams as well, but they have a *huge* drawback: time. If you've left your computer (I've heard people do this) and come back to a long IM chat that started, or continued, without you, catching up can take a few minutes. There might be a lot of chatter that doesn't really matter, and it's easy to miss the important "Okay, we've agreed the meeting is at 2 PM, downtown..." message. The folks at Automattic were having the same problem. So, with IM, IRC, and email, it got a little insane (I gather). Then came P2, and it changed *everything*. Now people could jump back to the site and new stuff (posts or comments) were yellow. If someone needed to catch up on *just* a particular conversation to topic (think tags for this), they would just jump to that section. Time became less important because the time it took to catch up was shorter. Sure there might be idle chatter going on in some threads, but the critical information stands out.

This is all well and good, but it does a fat lot of good if you can't get people to use it. That is the topic for another book I think, but the only advice I can give is *taking away* other less efficient forms of communication can help. Unless you're the boss, in which case you can just say so.

Creating Communities with WordPress

Today our Internet world is dominated by social networks and communities. Facebook is one of the highest-trafficked sites in the world with *millions* of members worldwide. We form groups with services like Ning or affinities through LinkedIn, but what if you want something all your own? What if you want a community with your own unique twist? What if you wanted to do it with WordPress?

One way to go about it is to just make a multi-author site and customize the theme to give each author a special template look. (This is now possible with recent versions of WordPress.) However, that becomes more like a publication than a community. And there is no way to allow for features like friends, messaging, wall posts...that is, until BuddyPress came along.

BuddyPress was a huge innovation for WordPress. It isn't a fork or branch or flavor of WordPress; it's a set of plugins that sits on top of WordPress. What BuddyPress does is to create all the features that you need to build your own social network. Oh, and it's free, too. Andy Peatling developed these plugins so well, Automattic hired him to develop for them full time. As WP innovations go, BuddyPress is right up there with the revolutionary changes like static front pages. BuddyPress expands how WordPress can be used into a *whole new level*.

At BuddyPress' core is WordPress running in multisite mode, so each user can have their own blog and even have multiple authors on the blog. Like WordPress.com, there is a limited set of themes offered, and plugins are managed centrally at the server level. What is completely new, different, and revolutionary is the layer *above* that: the community layer. Each user has their own profile area where they can post status messages, consolidate blog posts, manage friends, and send messages. Essentially, just like any other social network you can join. BuddyPress also offers forums and groups that operate separately from each other and blogs—yes, exactly as you'd think it would. One of the problems with WordPress multisite mode has been the challenge in creating aggregated stream from a single user and all users. WordPress.com implemented a system of systemwide tags, so you could read everything about a topic across *all* of WordPress.com. BuddyPress took that a step further with entire activity streams encompassing everything that goes on the site—forum posts, groups, blog posts, new members—all if it can be poured into the activity stream.

 SHOW ME   Media 10.3—Using BuddyPress to Make Your Own Social Network

Access this video file through your registered Web Edition at
my.safaribooksonline.com/9780132182836/media

At this point, you might be thinking, "Awesome! Sign me up! I want one; where do I go?" The easy answer to that is after installing WordPress, you need to go to BuddyPress.org to download and install those plugins. The system requirements for the whole thing are the same as for WordPress, but with a twist. BuddyPress can work with WordPress 3.0 in both "regular" and multisite mode, but remember, running WordPress in multisite mode isn't for novice users.

So, if this final bit of this chapter has you chomping at the bit to make your own social network with BuddyPress—believe me, the more I read about it, the more I'm trying to find a good project on which to try it out—the first thing is to start reading both the WordPress and BuddyPress forums. Then, if you think you can manage the install, give it a shot. If you run into trouble, hit the forums again. If all else fails, there are WP gurus everywhere; reach out through Twitter, Forums, and local WordPress groups, and I'm sure you can find someone to help you.

In this chapter, tune your WordPress-based website for search engines with the right settings, plugins, and content.

11

Tuning WordPress for Search Engines

If I were the cheeky sort (well, you know by now that I *am* that sort), I would just say:

"WordPress is already tuned for search engines. End of chapter."

However, that isn't what you bought the book for, and in all truth, that's not 100% true. With a default install and using the settings I've outlined earlier, WordPress is about 90% there, as far as search engines go. With a couple of SEO plugins (or SEO-aware themes), you can get to about 95%; to get to 100% (or at least 99%), you need to also adapt how you *write* your content. This chapter is all about tackling that last 10% you need to tune your site for search engines.

If you're thinking, "Wait, if I'm 90% there before I really do anything, that's pretty darn good, isn't it?," you're exactly correct. You can see why WordPress-based sites (and blog engine-based sites, in general) do better with search engines than "regular" sites any day, any time.

Here's a real-life example that will open your eyes. One of my client's had a well-established website, but not a lot of traffic. Searching Google for its product name didn't have it in the top-five results, and what you did find wasn't terribly great either. So, to help promote its app, I helped build a small, WordPress-powered site. It was mostly how-to videos for the product and not much else. Even without adding content regularly, the WordPress site leapt to the top of Google for not only the name, but other key terms as well—in the space of a couple months. If it had used the site more regularly and posted content, the time span would have been cut down to a month. Now it is working diligently on the site, so I expect that its topic-domination of Google will only continue.

In this chapter, I talk about the exact same plugins, tools, techniques, and writing styles as I used for that client. These are techniques that I've honed over many years of working with websites and blogs and having discussions with friends at Google. I do not, and will not, suggest or encourage anything that is even the slightest bit into a "gray area" of SEO. I will be telling you *exactly* what Google wants you to do—no magic, no tricks.

So, let's get on with the fun, shall we?

The WordPress SEO Checklist: The Must Dos for Every Kind of Site

Although a lot of SEO with WordPress is easy, invisible, and painless; it's worth just stepping through a few reminders to make sure that the *key* things are in place before we get to tuning things up.

Here's our WordPress SEO checklist:

1. Make sure your blog title is descriptive and identifiable as your blog.

2. Make sure you have changed the tagline from "Just Another WordPress Blog" to a description of what your blog is about.

3. Install and activate Google XML Sitemaps and All in One SEO Pack plugins.

4. Set your permalinks to something that includes **%postname%**; I like **/%year%/%monthnum%/%postname%/.** (even though I have my blog at something different—we all have to learn from our mistakes.)

5. Create categories for what you will be talking about on your blog or site. Remember, these are *general* topics; specifics are best as *tags*.

6. Edit your About page. Make sure it's either about you, or just delete it. Remember that *all* content on your site will be indexed.

7. Delete the first default post and comment.

8. Change the name of the default category from "Uncategorized" to something more descriptive about your site.

 SHOW ME   Media 11.1—The Core Settings for WordPress and SEO
Access this video file through your registered Web Edition at
my.safaribooksonline.com/9780132182836/media

There's not much to the list, is there? When you get through step 8, you've hit that 95% mark. You might be wondering about steps 1 and 2: "What does 'descriptive' mean?" Your blog name should be a short and catchy name. Mine is TrisHussey.com—well, at least that's what goes in the *blog name* section. I'll talk more about advanced names in the next section. My tagline is "Social Media News,

WordPress Info, and Opinion from Tris Hussey, Author of Create Your Own Blog and Using WordPress." which while rather long, is full of the keywords I want Google to index my site with. Your tagline is a very important part of your site's metadata—info that search engines use to put your site into context with all the other millions and millions of sites out there on the Internet. My tagline includes everything that I want to be indexed with. Am I number one in Google for "create your own blog" or "using wordpress?" Nope, but not for want of trying. Those phrases are so entrenched in other posts, pages, and sites that winning the Google war on those terms is going to be a long battle. However, my *name* is associated strongly with those terms not only through the tagline, but also categories, post titles, tags, links in posts, and the text of my posts. As you will learn throughout this chapter, there is no one magic bullet or panacea for good SEO; good SEO relies on a number of factors to be successful.

Let's work on number three from the preceding list and tune Google XML Sitemaps and All in One SEO Pack, as well as talk about the new SEO-aware themes that are now more common than ever.

Using SEO Plugins and SEO-Tuned Themes

Let's tick off the easiest part first: configuring Google XML Sitemaps. The default settings are great unless you *really* want to tweak the weighting the sitemap gives particular types of content or *exclude* some pages or categories. Don't bother worrying about getting a Yahoo API ID, because Yahoo will be using Microsoft's Bing search engine in the near future. This is the beauty of this plugin—you don't *need* to do anything when it's running for it to start helping your site tremendously (see Figure 11.1).

What the settings do, as I've talked about before, is to create a sitemap of all the content within your site—not just recent content, *all* content—and then let Google, et al know when there are updates. What Google does then is use the sitemap as an index to find and catalog the new content and put it into context with the *rest* of the content on the site. The sitemap also tells the search engines how often certain content is updated: the home page, daily; posts, hourly; archives, monthly, yearly. With an xml-based sitemap at the ready, Google knows where all your content is, when it was last updated, and how often Google needs to come back to check for more. You're handing all of this to Google on a silver platter in *exactly* the format Google wants (see Figure 11.2). Yeah, that's why it's one of my core, must-install plugins.

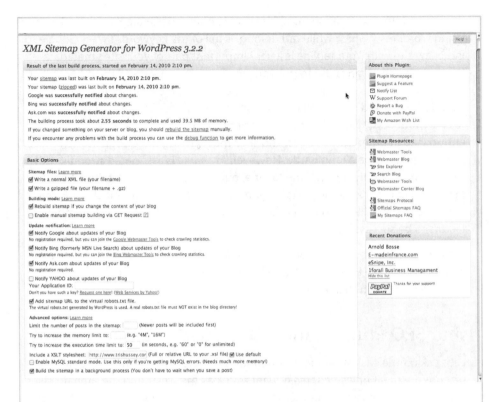

Figure 11.1 *A portion of the default settings for Google XML Sitemaps from my own blog. The bottom of the page are settings and defaults you rarely need to change.*

All in One SEO Pack needs a little more configuration, but really just at the top. I've experimented with different settings, and I think the default settings are just fine for most sites. All you need to do is fill in the home page title, description, and keywords at the top of the screen, save, and you're done. Those three boxes let you have a special metadata for *your home page only* that you can use to give search engines more detail about your site when the home page is indexed. I use the home page title to combine my blog title and tagline together, but only on the home page. I used the description and keywords essentially in the same way, making sure that I include the key ones for me.

```
sitemap.xml    (no symbol selected)
<?xml version="1.0" encoding="UTF-8"?><?xml-stylesheet type="text/xsl"
href="http://trishussey.com/wp-content/plugins/google-sitemap-generator/sitemap.
xsl"?><!-- generator="wordpress/2.9.1" -->
<!-- sitemap-generator-url="http://www.arnebrachhold.de"
sitemap-generator-version="3.2.2" -->
<!-- generated-on="February 14, 2010 2:10 pm" -->
<urlset xmlns:xsi="http://www.w3.org/2001/XMLSchema-instance"
xsi:schemaLocation="http://www.sitemaps.org/schemas/sitemap/0.9
http://www.sitemaps.org/schemas/sitemap/0.9/sitemap.xsd"
xmlns="http://www.sitemaps.org/schemas/sitemap/0.9">    <url>
        <loc>http://trishussey.com/</loc>
        <lastmod>2010-02-14T22:09:21+00:00</lastmod>
        <changefreq>daily</changefreq>
        <priority>1.0</priority>
    </url>
    <url>

        <loc>http://trishussey.com/2010/02/14/would-anyone-other-than-silent-bob
        -just-gotten-the-silent-treatment/</loc>
        <lastmod>2010-02-14T22:09:21+00:00</lastmod>
        <changefreq>hourly</changefreq>
        <priority>0.6</priority>
    </url>
    <url>

        <loc>http://trishussey.com/2010/02/13/a-few-thoughts-on-olympic-protests
        /</loc>
        <lastmod>2010-02-13T21:23:44+00:00</lastmod>
        <changefreq>hourly</changefreq>
        <priority>0.6</priority>
    </url>
    <url>

        <loc>http://trishussey.com/2010/02/12/taking-my-own-troubleshooting-
        advice/</loc>
        <lastmod>2010-02-12T22:38:12+00:00</lastmod>
        <changefreq>hourly</changefreq>
        <priority>0.6</priority>
    </url>
    <url>

        <loc>http://trishussey.com/2010/02/12/do-you-use-wordpress-galleries-i-
        want-to-know/</loc>
        <lastmod>2010-02-12T22:13:25+00:00</lastmod>
        <changefreq>hourly</changefreq>
        <priority>0.6</priority>
    </url>
    <url>

        <loc>http://trishussey.com/2010/02/12/microsoft-and-rim-together-would-
        be-great-for-the-iphone-and-nexus-one/</loc>
```

Figure 11.2 *A portion of the sitemap for my blog. See, no person would ever want to read that!*

What? Google Doesn't Look at the Description or Keywords?

We all had quite a shock in late 2009 when we learned that not only had Google stopped indexing the keywords and site description in weighing sites, but they stopped in 2003! Yep, all that careful meta keyword work and crafting meta descriptions was for naught as far as Google was concerned. Yahoo! kept including that metadata until 2009, and then stopped. So, A) why bother filling them in and B) why did they stop in the first place?

I'm going to hit "B" first, which will help "A" make more sense. What happened was that as the Web became enormously popular, SEO "experts" decided that stuffing the meta keyword and description fields with the same keywords over and over, using competitor names, and all sorts of "SEO from the Dark Side" tricks was a dandy idea. They did this so often that Google realized that the amount of junk data overwhelmed the amount of *good* data they were pulling in. So to try to keep the search results fair, relevant, and spam-free, keywords and descriptions were taken out of the ranking equation. I think Google still indexes the data and might use it in some fashion, maybe for whitelisted sites, but that's only a gut feeling. This brings us to the answer to "A": I still create a nice, short description and about 10–15 relevant keywords for my blogs because I think the data is still being used, or will be used in the future.

I think that if you play by the "rules" and use both Google's and Microsoft's webmaster tools, that the keywords and descriptions help your site. If nothing else, they can't hurt. As an example, here is the description and keywords for my site:

Description: Tris Hussey, writer, teacher, blogger, photographer. Author of *Create Your Own Blog* and *Using WordPress*.

Keywords: Tris Hussey, teacher, speaker, WordPress, Social Media, Vancouver, author, *Create Your Own Blog*, *Using WordPress*.

Short, sweet, and maybe due for a tweak, but *not* spammy and *all* relevant to the site.

Farther down the page, the only check boxes I like to check are to add categories as keywords as well as tags. My categories are often just as important as my tags for searching, so I want them in there, too. Anything else? Nope. That's it. All the other settings are just fine. Figure 11.3 shows all the settings I use for my site.

As much as I love All in One SEO, more and more WordPress themes are adding those features right into the theme itself. If your theme offers those features, go ahead and use them if they cover all the bases that All in One SEO does. Having one less plugin installed and activated is a good thing for keeping your blog trim and running fast. How do you know if your theme supports this for you? Just look for theme options either under Appearance or as a button of its own. If your theme has SEO support, compare it against what the plugin does. If you see the same things covered in both, go with the theme route. I believe that means less server overhead for you and less processing that has to be done when your post is displayed or posted. Is there a replacement for Google XML Sitemaps? Nope, sitemaps are a totally different animal, but like these key SEO steps, they are *essential* to good SEO.

With these core configuration steps done, now you need to master Google's Webmaster tools and see just what Google knows about your site and even what it thinks about it.

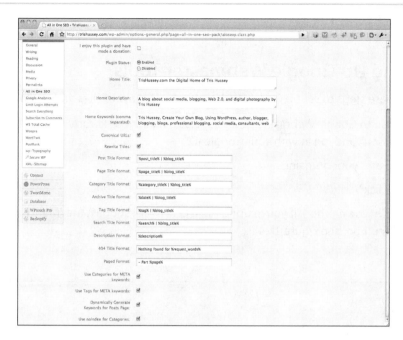

Figure 11.3   *My All in One SEO Pack settings*

SHOW ME   Media 11.2—Using All in One SEO and Theme-Specific SEO Options

Access this video file through your registered Web Edition at
my.safaribooksonline.com/9780132182836/media

Mastering Google Webmaster Tools

Google's Webmaster tools (https://www.google.com/webmasters/tools/) are some of the easiest things you can use to learn more about your site than you ever really wanted to know in the first place! If you want to know how Google has indexed your site, and with which keywords, and if you have bad links or other problems, that's the place to be. The first step is verifying that you are the holder of your domain. Google makes this easy for you by giving you the option of adding some code into the header of your site or uploading an HTML file.

If you're using a theme like Thesis that enables you to easily add code into the header, go that route (I think Google likes it better); if not, the HTML file route is fine. Here's how to do it....

LET ME TRY IT

Setting Up Google Webmaster Tools

Use these steps to set up Google Webmaster tools for your sites and domains:

1. Go to Google Webmaster tools at https://www.google.com/webmasters/ tools/ and log in with your Google ID.

2. Enter your domain(s).

3. Click Verify.

4. Choose method. If you're using All in One SEO, I suggest the "Meta tag" method (see Figure 11.4).

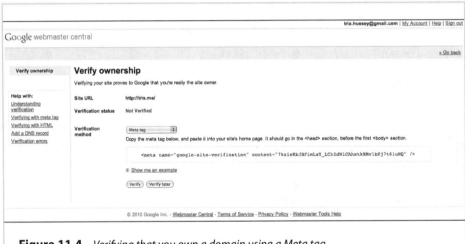

Figure 11.4   *Verifying that you own a domain using a Meta tag*

5. Copy the "<meta name=…>" line and paste it into the Additional Home Headers box in All in One SEO options on your blog's administration area and click Update Options to save the update (see Figure 11.5).

6. If you're not using All in One SEO and your theme supports adding extra headers use that instead (still using meta tag verification). If all else fails, you can use Google Integration Toolkit (http://wordpress.org/extend/plug-ins/google-integration-toolkit/) or All in One Webmaster (http://wordpress.org/extend/plugins/all-in-one-webmaster/).

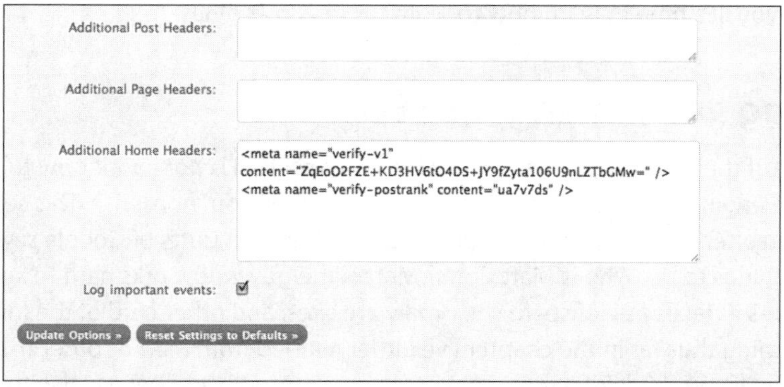

Additional Post Headers:	
Additional Page Headers:	

Additional Home Headers:	`<meta name="verify-v1"`
	`content="ZqEoO2FZE+KD3HV6tO4DS+JY9fZyta106U9nLZTbGMw=" />`
	`<meta name="verify-postrank" content="ua7v7ds" />`

Log important events:	☑

Update Options »   Reset Settings to Defaults »

Figure 11.5   *Where to paste the Meta tag in All in One SEO to verify with Google that you own the domain*

7. Click Verify.

8. Sit back in awe of what Google already knows about your site.

If you've done this step *after* everything previously described in this chapter, Google *should have* already found your sitemap. Otherwise, you can tell Google where it is located, which will be http://www.*yourdomain.com*/sitemap.xml. If your site is fairly new or doesn't have a lot of content, don't worry if there isn't much data there. Show Me Media 11.3 provides an example of what the data looks like for my site.

SHOW ME   Media 11.3—Setting Up and Verifying Your Site with Google Webmaster Tools
Access this video file through your registered Web Edition at
my.safaribooksonline.com/9780132182836/media

As you can see, my site isn't perfect. I have some 404 not found errors to fix, and I'd like to be indexed with a few more keywords, but all in all, it's not bad. Over time, you'll be able to know more and more about your site and how Google perceives it. Now you can see why I think meta descriptions and keywords are important. I think Google is using them, if nothing else, to help people looking at search results understand which sites talk about what. I think the metadata is used for *context*.

We've covered a lot of mechanics so far in this chapter—stuff that once you set it up, pretty much runs itself. The reality is, though, that plugins, themes, permalinks, and settings are only the bit that's going to get you to the 95% mark; the last 5% is up to you. It's time to learn how to write for search engines.

Writing and Linking for SEO

Right off the top, I'm going to tell you that this section is *not* about how to trick search engines or "the secrets that Google won't tell you" nonsense. This section is written after long years of work *and* reading what Matt Cutts of Google says are the right things to do. Who is Matt Cutts? Matt is the guy who works hard to keep Google's indexes free of spam sites, malware sites, and other crud of the Internet. Everything thus far in the chapter I've either learned from Matt or other trusted sources. If you think for a moment you can trick Google and get away with it for long, you are sadly mistaken.

So, how do you write for search engines? Easy—be descriptive with your writing. If you're writing about a woodworking project, talk about tools, plans, projects, kinds of wood, any terms that make sense, and variations of all of the above. Write as you normally would, but instead of always using the same term for something, if there is an alternative term, use that, too.

Look at it like this. How many times have you gone to rent a movie and can't find it because you don't know how that store has classified the movie you want? Oh sure, there are movies that are clearly comedies or horror or sci-fi, but what about the sci-fi action flicks? Or comedic dramas? Or horror spoofs (or horror movies so bad that they *become* comedies)? So you wander the store trying to find it yourself until you break down and ask. The person working there brings you to a section you wouldn't have thought to look in. The movie wasn't *classified* how you thought it should be, so you couldn't find it. Now look at what you're writing in the same light. Are there other ways someone might say something or call something? Sure, sometimes there is just one way to say something, but when I write about SEO, I also make sure I have search engine optimization in the post as well. Not everyone searches for SEO.

I started right into your *post* without talking about your *title*, which is fine because often the best titles don't come until *after* you've written the post. With titles, you don't have nearly as much space to play with as in your post, but you can still be concise and descriptive. You can use things like "Top 5 ways to fix WordPress SEO problems" or "Choosing the right birdhouse pattern to build at home with your kids." You know by looking at that title what you think the post should be about. Not only that, you see that the titles contain keywords that also match with the post. Nice, huh? Sneaky? Not so much—just simply being descriptive.

While we're being descriptive, let's talk about links. Way, way too often, I see posts with lines like this: "...and for more information, click *here*." The word "here" is the link, but what does that tell you? More information about what? How about this: "...download a PDF of more information about our birdhouse plans..." I'm betting you know *exactly* what you're getting—and not only that, so does Google. This is what you want to be going for: *descriptive link text*. Click here doesn't help or tell anyone anything. Being descriptive doesn't stop with links; it works for images, too. You know that "alt" or "alternative text" box you often see when adding an image? Yeah, that space is for you to describe what the image is. Yes, this is not always easy, and I will admit that I don't do this often enough myself (tsk, tsk). However, not only does it help Google understand what that image is and what context it has within the Post or Page, but also if your site is visited by someone who is blind and is using a text-to-speech browser, the visitor will at least get some idea of what else is on the page.

The final part of the SEO-content equation is your tags. We've talked about tags before but not in a search engine context. Remember to think of tags as keywords and recall the movie rental example where you might classify something as x, but someone else as y. Cover your bases and have x, y, z, and any other letter that makes sense to have as your tags without going completely crazy, on it. In fact, don't go crazy with any of these points. Google's algorithms are sophisticated enough to separate *real* natural language and contrived language. Don't be fake; be authentic. If you do everything described in this section, you'll hit the rest of the 100%. Now all it takes is hard work—writing and linking to start crawling up the Google rankings.

Avoiding the Dark Side of SEO and Getting into Trouble with Google

Throughout this chapter, I've alluded to staying away from the Dark Side of SEO. Lots of well-meaning people have been taken in by SEO "experts" who essentially sold them down the river and got them removed from Google's index in the process. Believe me, getting removed from Google's index is a *huge* deal. Search engine traffic often makes up 50% of a site's total traffic, so imagine half your traffic going away over night. That's exactly what happens when Google de-lists you. Here are things to avoid:

1. Anyone who tells you that he will create mirror sites or has thousands of sites that will link to yours. Google knows if a link is relevant to the content, lots of back links from link farms is bad—really bad.

2. Putting text the same color as the background of your page so it is invisible to people, but search engines will read it. Generally, people do this to increase the number of times keywords are used on their site. Google doesn't look kindly on this either.

3. If you make a duplicate of your site, with a different URL, but all the other content the same. Bad news: Google will penalize *both* URLs. Having different URLs point to the same site (or sections of a site) is okay. For example, usingwordpressbook.com points to trishussey.com/category/books/using-wordpress/, and that is okay.

4. Stuffing your keyword and description fields with the same few words over and over. This is one of the reasons Google stopped indexing keywords in the first place. It got to be too much work to get the wheat from the chaff. One thing is clear, though: Doing this will put Google on notice that you might not be on the up and up.

5. Anyone who promises that you'll be on the top of Google rankings within a month, and you don't have to write any additional content, use better tags, or anything like that...big flashing red light warning there. Yes, it is possible to rocket up to the top 10 of Google on a keyword, but it takes *work*. You need to write about that topic, link to other sources on that topic (and have them naturally link back to you), and use good keywords in your titles and content. There is no magic bullet.

If you do fall prey to a SEO scam, all hope is not lost. Google will let you back in after you've cleaned up whatever mess the SEO people made in the first place. You might have to go through your templates with a fine-tooth comb to find cruft (otherwise known as crud) hanging out in the corners and try to block some sites from linking to you (or at least don't link back to them), but eventually Google will let you back. It happens often enough to innocent people that Google can be pretty forgiving, but you do have to make amends.

Just remember the old advice: If it sounds too good to be true, it probably is.

WordPress.com Notes

If you're using WordPress.com, don't worry—you're not left out in the search engine world. Some of my colleagues feel that WordPress.com blogs are *better suited* for SEO than those of us who do DIY. I'm not about to get into that discussion, but I will tell you this. By default, all WordPress.com blogs have an XML sitemap made for them, have the right kinds of permalinks, and more and more of the themes are more SEO-aware. Pretty much all you have to worry about is picking descriptive category names and writing good content. That seems to be a fair deal, I think.

This chapter covers how to use the built-in media manager in WordPress and other sites to manage all your multimedia effectively.

12

Managing Multimedia with WordPress

Blogs and multimedia go together like peanut butter and jelly. One of the challenges with multimedia is *managing* it. Not only are the files rather large, video files especially, but also each type of file has its own quirks that make it even *more* fun to deal with. (Note the sarcasm in this introduction.) Sometimes I wonder, as I'm trying to get a podcast to upload, a video to embed, or a hi-res picture show lo-res on the blog but link to the hi-res, if just having a completely image-free, text-only blog might be a good idea.

Just taking pictures as an example, I've been a photographer since I was *nine*. Yes, nine years old. Some of my friends don't recognize me unless I have a camera stuck to my face. Okay, that's stretching it, but I have (right now) over 14,000 pictures uploaded. That's only from the last, oh, six or seven years. That's only the ones I *upload*; I have gigabytes of photos that I have archived. How many of those are in WordPress? Not many. Why? Well, because I like using Flickr for photos. In the same vein, I like using YouTube for video. Podcasts, well, those I host myself. As you can see, you might *think* this is an easy, cut-and-dried chapter (Ha! Fooled you!), but really it isn't. Managing your multimedia with WordPress has to be in balance with all the *other* ways to manage your pictures, videos, podcasts, and even files.

Organizing Your Pictures, Videos, and Files in WordPress

As you can gather from the introduction to the chapter, I don't advocate managing *all* your pictures within your WordPress install. This doesn't mean that I don't have hundreds of pictures stored in WordPress; I just don't use it for *all* my media. There are a couple barriers to managing all your media within WordPress. One is the upload limit. For *most* servers, you can't upload a file through WordPress that's more than about 2MB-7MB. By the way, these days that's not much. If I don't resize my pictures I shoot with my digital camera, a 2MB picture is pretty average. Video and audio files? Yeah, those are huge, too. Oh, I can just FTP the files up, right?

Exactly, and that's what I end up doing a lot of the time, but there's a hitch—when you upload via FTP, WordPress doesn't know about the files, and it's difficult to get it to account for them. (That would be the second barrier.)

Drat. This is one of the downsides to trying to manage *all* your media from within WordPress. So, don't. Within WordPress, I have images that I've used in blog posts—screenshots, product images, and so on—a few PDF files, and a smattering of audio files (only if they are under 2MB). The remainder of my multimedia is managed on YouTube and Flickr (and for documents, Scribd and SlideShare), but first let's talk about doing all this within WordPress.

Like all things in tech, to keep from becoming *completely* frustrated by something, you need to understand its limitations. We've established that keeping *all* your media in WordPress isn't going to work. Fine. Now, let's move on. Griping aside, when you do keep media in WP, you get the benefit of calling the media from any-where within WP. If you are working with images, having the image stored locally lets WordPress make its own optimized copies of it, in addition to whatever magic your theme might have up its sleeve. Many themes have a built-in thumb-nailing tool and image caching. If Flickr or YouTube have a hiccup, and believe me *they do*, your video or picture is going to have one of those nice broken image icons on it. When YouTube has "issues," your blog will slow to a crawl while it tries in vain to get the stupid player to load. So, see, there is a benefit to having key media on your site.

As you've seen in previous chapters, you get to your media library by clicking the Media button in the Content block. It doesn't matter if you load through the Post/Page editor (or even if you tell it you're going to upload a picture and then choose video); the end result is the same. The file will be there, and you'll have a chance to make sure the name, description, and other key data are filled out to your liking.

Interestingly enough, one piece of data that's *missing* from the media info is tags. There isn't any way to categorize your media beyond it being an image, a video, an audio file, or other media. Being able to group similar items together—like screen-shots, WordPress podcasts, or photos—would be helpful as you get to the point, like I am, where there are hundreds of pieces of media uploaded and no easy way to find what's already there. It doesn't take long before your media library is going to fill up with a lot of images, files, and audio segments (those less than 2MB, that is). Search, I'm afraid to say, is only going to get you so far because it is dependent on you knowing the filename (or part of it at least). I don't know about you, but when I'm uploading images for a post, coherent, consistent file-naming conven-tions isn't on the top of my to-do list. (Clearly, I'm chastising myself a bit here.)

One of the choices in the preferences that you might have missed is whether to organize your media by year and month or just put it all together. The default is year and month, and is under Media. Currently I'm going for the all-in-one place method, which has the benefit that if I'm *looking* for media, I can use search tools within my FTP client or on the server more easily. The downside is that I have hundreds of files and the listing is a little chaotic. For that reason, I recommend you use the month-year folder system. Yes, it does get a little tedious to navigate through all the folders sometimes, but you can more easily tie media to a post (because you'll know *when* it was published).

Managing media from within WordPress is going to be more of a matter of uploading what you need, when you need it, rather than looking for past media files to use. This brings us to the next quandary: What do you do with/about media that's *larger* than 2MB, but you want to host on your own server? There are no easy answers here either, but at least you *do* have some more options. When I'm uploading podcasts, I *generally* upload them to a show-specific directory—like my "WordPress One-Minute Podcast" would go into a wp1min folder within uploads on the server. Do I *have* to put the files in uploads? No, certainly not, but it is a central location, and if I put the files there consistently, at least I have *that* going for me when I'm looking for a file or typing a URL. Unfortunately, WordPress doesn't allow you to scan the uploads directory and locate files *not* in the media library and *add* them. This would be rather handy for those of us who wind up uploading files on a semi-regular basis. Because there isn't an easy scan-for-all-new-media function, the best you can do *is* the faux organization of creating folders for the media you upload on a regular basis. Because managing larger media files within WordPress isn't the best thing in the world, you need to look at the alternative options you have. The best part of these alternatives is that if you set them up correctly, you get an additional boost within the search engines for your site *and* your media.

Alternatives to Using WordPress for Managing Media Online

With the notable exception of podcasts, the free or nearly free alternative places to upload and manage your media will cover all the remaining media you might want to upload. Because, for the most part, these are stand-alone sites where you have a personal profile and corner to showcase your media, you have another touchpoint with search engines that is *extremely* helpful if sharing media has any place in your larger social media/Internet presence. We're going to look at Flickr.com for pictures, YouTube for video, SlideShare for presentations, and Scribd for other document files. There are many other media-sharing sites for all of these categories, but for the sake of simplicity, I'm going to look at these three as the "best in class" within their niche.

I started this section by saying "with the notable exception of podcasts" because in that particular case, if you have a server already (that is, you did a DIY install of WordPress), all the podcast services will only cost you additional money for little benefit over hosting your files yourself. If you're using WordPress.com, I recommend choosing the space upgrade and using *its* servers over paying someone else for the same privilege. When podcasting first started, there were several podcast hosts, and the reason for using them was that both server space and bandwidth were rather expensive. You could quickly fill up your server space allocation in a few months, and if your podcast "hit it big," you could tap out your bandwidth for the month in a couple days. Server offerings changed with the times and video blogging became the rage (I know there are still lots of podcasts out there), and the podcast hosts faded away. There are a few left now, but the free options are sparse and the paid options don't offer you much more than you can do yourself. On the other hand, there are at least half-a-dozen places to host your videos for free (granted, usually only about 10 minutes max), and the pay options offer things like conversion and mobile versions that *are* worth the money. Let's step back for a moment and talk about *my* favorite media: pictures.

Managing Pictures

Sharing pictures over the Internet continues to be one of the most popular things people do online. It doesn't matter if it's Snapfish, Picasa, Facebook, or, my favorite, Flickr; they all have the same goal—put your digital photos online so you can share them with friends and use them in other websites. Flickr is available in regular and Pro versions. The Pro level is about $25/year and gives you unlimited uploads and unlimited sets of pictures. The "non" Pro version caps you at five sets, and there is a monthly upload cap. I recommend going right for the Pro level. Once when uploading pictures for a client to their new Flickr account, I maxed out the upload limit in just a few minutes. Granted, I was uploading a lot of pictures, but no more than what you might have from a weekend trip or a day of sightseeing. Flickr is owned by Yahoo! and you reach it at Flickr.com (see Figure 12.1).

Armed with a Flickr account, you can now have high-resolution pictures available (and backed up, by the way), but still be able to embed smaller versions within your posts. I frequently put a picture or two from an event within the post and then embed a Flash-based slideshow of all the pictures from that event at the end of the post. As we learned in the Chapter 9 Show Me video about embedding videos and images, Flickr is one of the sites participating in the oEmbed protocol, so you can easily put images into your post with a quick copy and paste. I think oEmbed is great for a single image to be displayed on its own, but for more flexibility, I like to use the pre-made code for embedding pictures into your post.

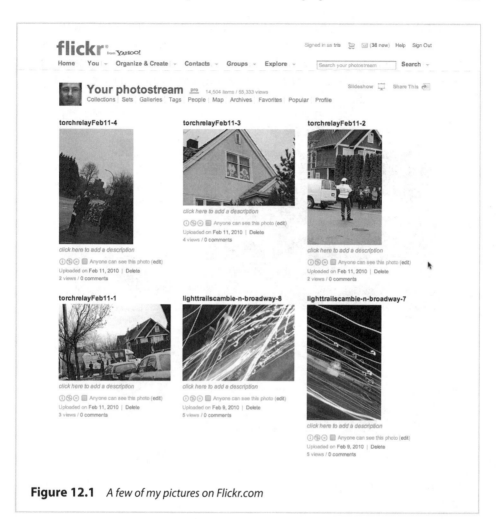

Figure 12.1   *A few of my pictures on Flickr.com*

Like most of the Web 2.0 world, Flickr uses tags to describe images. Your tags not only connect your photos to each other, but also to all the other public pictures on Flickr. I made the note about this being public because you can have private pictures, and because Flickr has a social networking component to it, you can have pictures visible only to friends or family. I'm sure you're wondering (because it's the next logical question people ask), if you put something on Flickr, can't someone just steal it and use it for their own stuff? Yes, they can, but I have three defenses for this. First, Flickr enables you to set a Creative Commons License for your pictures (see Figure 12.2). Mine is noncommercial, with attribution, and no derivative works, without permission. That is made clear on the site, but I don't stop there. I also embed my copyright into the image file's information and finally I watermark all my images with my name and copyright. Is search any better on Flickr than on WordPress? Well, yes and no—yes, in that you can search for tags as well as a file-name, but again if you don't provide the data, you can't search for the data. In this case, I don't need to chastise myself; I obsessively tag images on Flickr.

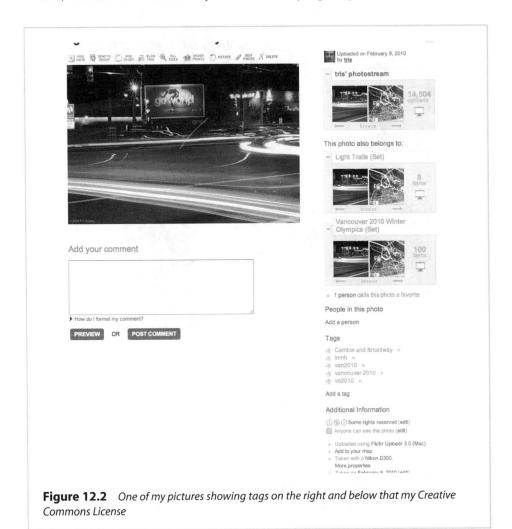

Figure 12.2 *One of my pictures showing tags on the right and below that my Creative Commons License*

I started using Flickr soon after I started blogging, primarily because it was the cool thing to do. Yes, it might not have been the *best* reason in the world, but Flickr was a Vancouver-based company before it was acquired by Yahoo!, and all the photographers I knew in the city used it (and still do). What Flickr has done for me is given me another place to publish my images in a way that is incredibly findable, embeddable into not only my blog but other people's blogs, and served as a blog platform-independent storage area for my images. Any post that I embed a Flickr image in will be the same regardless of how many times I move servers. The image isn't stored on my server, but Yahoo!'s search engine reach combined with easy portability is why I stick with Flickr. Sure, moving 14,000+ pictures would be a pain (and take a long, long time), but it isn't that inertia that keeps me using Flickr—it's the benefits that it gives me. There are several other photo-sharing sites out there, and of the ones that integrate well into WordPress, only SmugMug comes close to matching Flickr. SmugMug is geared toward professional photographers who are also interested in selling their work. Flickr is more of a hobbyist website (with a large professional community as well).

Managing Video

Before we switch gears to YouTube, it is worth noting that with a Flickr Pro account, you can upload up to 90 seconds of HD-quality video to your account. Flickr video is *not* intended to replace YouTube; rather, it's intended for more slideshow-like applications.

If you want to upload videos somewhere besides your own server, YouTube is the 300-pound gorilla of video. Yes, YouTube is filled with a lot of skateboarding animals and silly videos, but it is also filled with great video blogs and content from well-respected companies. Why would a well-respected company choose YouTube? Because if you want to get attention for your video, you need to be where the people are, and the people are on YouTube. YouTube, owned by Google, enables you to upload video that is up to 10 minutes in length and up to 2GB in size. That might not *seem* like a lot, but 2GB of video might take several hours to upload over all but the most powerful Internet connections. Uploading video segments for this book (and when I upload, I usually upload several chapters' worth at once) was a process of starting the upload before I went to bed and letting it run all night. Like Flickr, you use YouTube for the extra punch it gives you with search engines. You have a profile page and channel page that you can use to promote your primary site. You can see my YouTube Channel in Figure 12.3.

Like Flickr, YouTube uses oEmbed, so posting a video is now as easy as copy and paste. If you want to upload larger videos (or videos that are longer in duration), you can use pay sites like Vimeo and Viddler for that privilege. Yes, both Vimeo and Viddler have free options as well, but their real benefit is being able to pay for larger file sizes, longer videos, and more automatic video format conversions. Of course, you can also have videos on your own server and play them from there—there's no reason why not—and if you want some videos to be private or to sell access to them, that's a good way to go. Just remember that you are dipping into your bandwidth and server space allocation, not to mention it's easier to embed a video from YouTube than it is from your own server.

Figure 12.3   *My YouTube Channel on YouTube with a few of my videos*

SHOW ME   Media 12.1—Using YouTube and Flickr for Managing Media

Access this video file through your registered Web Edition at
my.safaribooksonline.com/9780132182836/media

Working with Downloadable Files in WordPress

The world isn't limited to pictures, videos, or MP3 files. There are PDFs, PowerPoint presentations, zip archives, and myriad other file formats that you might want to include in your blog. Although we're used to downloading files from "regular" websites, downloading from a blog seems odd somehow. Let me assure you that it isn't weird or strange at all. Although you don't usually lump downloadable files in with "multimedia," these files are increasingly becoming more media than file; however, that's not to say dealing with a PDF file and its kin doesn't have its own issues. To manage files with WordPress, there are a couple ways to go about it, of course, both by yourself and through a service.

Let's take the example of a presentation you gave that you'd like to share with your blog audience. If you don't want people to download it or embed it in their own sites without giving you full credit, you can use SlideShare. If you gave a great talk and the audience is clamoring for you to post it online, what are you going to do with it? Well, most of the time you'd just upload the file to your site and link to it. Simple, easy, and straightforward, but also rather limited. What if you didn't want people to download it, but still want to share it? Or allow users to embed the presentation on their own sites but make sure you get full credit for it? That's exactly what SlideShare does, and it's one of my favorite ways to share PowerPoint presentations. For all the reasons that you post pictures on Flickr or videos on YouTube, you post presentations on SlideShare. Because SlideShare is free, easy, and secure (for keeping track of your presentations) it's the go-to place for putting your PowerPoint slides online for the world to enjoy. Figure 12.4 shows my SlideShare profile area. If you've written a great whitepaper or other document, a service called Scribd.com is your best bet. Scribd.com focuses on sharing more than just presentations; you can share any kind of document. Unlike SlideShare, on Scribd you can also have the option for people to *purchase* your document. I use Scribd (as you can see in the Show Me video) to share longer, nonpresentation types of documents. As a speaker and teacher, I'm always asked if my notes and presentations will be online. By using Scribd and SlideShare, I can put my documents online for people to enjoy and still track how the documents are shared.

SlideShare and Scribd.com bridge the gap between the usual "just toss it up there" approach and emailing out a copy of the presentation to people who want it. Both of those methods have their own issues of control and ownership, and neither gives you a lot of help in the search engine department. Because you can set the permissions on SlideShare and Scribd, you are saying, "Yes, I want to share what I know, but I don't want people to outright steal it." This step is meaningful, and especially important for documents and presentations.

If you've dipped your toe into software or creating your own WordPress theme or plugin, you might want to have people easily download your creation so that they can use it. Within WordPress, assuming that you aren't over the 2MB limit, you can upload using the media manager just like any other file. You can have it inserted into a post with a click, just like anything else. If the file is more than 2MB, you use FTP and link to it as usual. If you'd like to manage things a little more professionally, you can think about using Google Code or GitHub to store your file and source code. GitHub (http://github.com/) and Google Code (http://code.google.com/) are both designed to enable you to work on code-related projects collaboratively, but those are both subjects of other books.

Figure 12.4 *My SlideShare profile with some of my presentations*

Is there a "best" way to manage files? What's wrong with just having everything on my own server? Nothing actually, and I have a mix for all the preceding content types. What you have to think about is what you want to do with the files and how you want them shared (or not), and then you can choose the best method for your purposes.

SHOW ME   Media 12.2—Using SlideShare.com and Scribd.com for Uploading and Managing Files for Your Site
Access this video file through your registered Web Edition at
my.safaribooksonline.com/9780132182836/media

Using WordPress Photo Galleries

It was hard to decide if this section is better in Chapter 9, "Creating and Managing Content with WordPress," or here, but keeping with the theme of how to deal with pictures and such, I decided it works best here. Now if I wanted to make sure this is my last book for this publisher, I'd write this section as thus:

WordPress galleries—just don't.

However, because I enjoy my job as a writer, I'm going to elaborate a little more. At this point (WordPress 3.0), galleries aren't the strongest feature in WordPress. The idea is that you can easily embed a gallery of pictures with the simple, short code [gallery], and you're off to the races. The trick is, however, that you have to *upload* the images for them to be attached to the post to have them for galleries. Pictures you've already uploaded? Yeah, it doesn't work that way; those pictures can't be put into *new* galleries. Here how galleries work now....

 LET ME TRY IT

Putting a Gallery into a Post

1. Start a post.

2. Click the Add Media button and upload two or more images.

3. Click the Gallery tab, and you see the options for the gallery.

4. When you have the options set, click Insert Gallery, and you're done.

 SHOW ME   Media 12.3—Inserting WordPress Galleries in Your Posts
Access this video file through your registered Web Edition at
my.safaribooksonline.com/9780132182836/media

As you can see, like Flash media and other embedded items, there is a placeholder for the gallery. You can still adjust the options when you've inserted the gallery, and beyond that there isn't much more about galleries to cover. This is a gap that I hope WordPress bridges in future versions. It would make sense to mark existing images as part of a gallery for a new post. In the meantime, you can use a variety of gallery plugins, like NextGEN gallery (which is one of the more popular ones), or use Flickr's slideshow feature to embed into your post.

Because putting galleries into posts is something a lot of bloggers want to do, let's compare working with WordPress galleries with using NextGEN galleries for showing off your pictures (and expanding on your story with images).

LET ME TRY IT

Using NextGEN Galleries

Here's how to use NextGEN Gallery to insert image galleries into posts and pages:

1. Download, install, and activate NextGEN Gallery through your Plugins page in the administration area or WordPress.org (http://wordpress.org/extend/plugins/nextgen-gallery/).

2. Click the Gallery button in the sidebar to get to the NextGEN Gallery Preferences (see Figure 12.5).

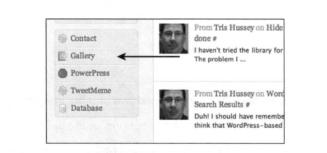

Figure 12.5   *Gallery button to open the NextGEN gallery overview*

3. (Optional) If you would like to have Flash-based slideshows, go to http://www.longtailvideo.com/players/jw-image-rotator/ and download JW Image Rotator.

    a. Unzip the JW image Rotator archive and upload the folder to your wp-content/uploads/ directory on your server.

    b. Click Options under the Gallery button, and then click Slideshow in the Options area.

    c. Put the URL to the slideshow files in the Path to Imagerotator (URL): box. For my sandbox the URL looks like this: http://sandbox.trishussey.com/wp-content/uploads/imagerotator/imagerotator.swf (see Figure 12.6).

    d. Click Save Changes at the bottom of the screen.

4. Click Add Gallery/Images and create a new, empty gallery. The name can have letters, numbers, "_" or "-", but cannot have spaces in it, so something like "my_new_gallery" is okay, but "my new gallery" is not.

Figure 12.6 *Putting the URL to the Imagerotator into the Options*

5. Click Upload Images.

6. Click Browse to select the images from your computer to use and then select the name of your gallery from the Choose Gallery pull-down menu. Click Upload Images (see Figure 12.7).

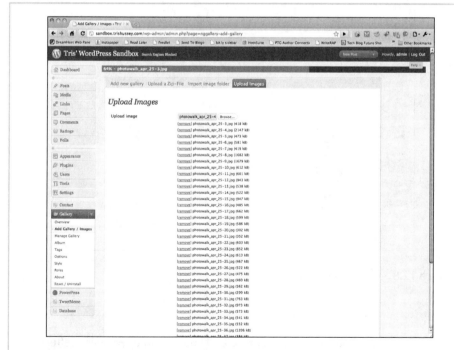

Figure 12.7 *Uploading images into a gallery*

After the upload completes the new gallery is ready to be put into a Post or a Page.

At this point you can have NextGEN gallery create a page for you or insert the gallery into a post or page yourself. Option 1 shows auto-creating a Page; in Option 2, we insert the gallery into a Post.

7. (Option 1) Click Manage Gallery in the sidebar.

    a. Click the name of the new gallery you created.

    b. Edit the title if you want. (This will be the page's title.)

    c. Decide if it is a parent or child page, and click Add Page (see Figure 12.8).

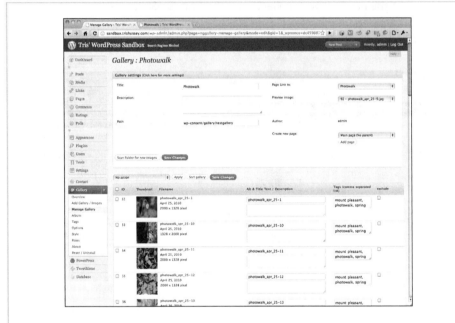

Figure 12.8 *Adding a gallery to a new Page*

    d. The page has now been created and you can go to your site, refresh the homepage if you need to, and navigate to the page (see Figure 12.9).

8. (Option 2) Click New Post in the top Menu bar to open the post editor.

    a. Enter your title, body text, categories, and tags as usual.

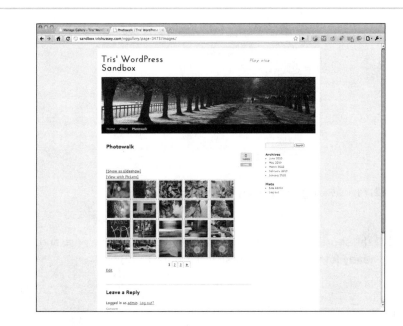

Figure 12.9   *Page created by NextGEN Gallery for the gallery I just made*

> **b.**   Place the insertion point where you'd like the gallery to appear in the post, and click the Add NextGEN Gallery button (see Figure 12.10).

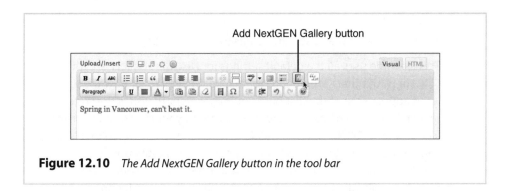

Figure 12.10   *The Add NextGEN Gallery button in the tool bar*

> **c.**   Choose your gallery from the list and choose whether you'd like a slideshow, image list, or Imagebrowser, and click Insert. I chose Image-browser for this example (see Figure 12.11).

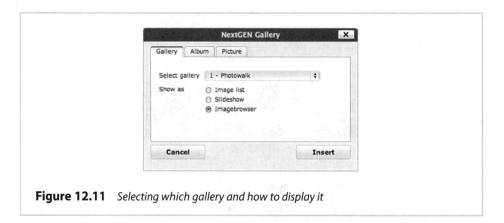

Figure 12.11   *Selecting which gallery and how to display it*

> **d.** The shortcode for the gallery has been added to the post, and it is ready for you to click Publish (see Figure 12.12).

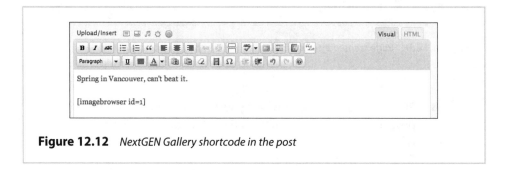

Figure 12.12   *NextGEN Gallery shortcode in the post*

> **e.** Click View Post and see the results (see Figure 12.13).

This example uses all the default settings for NextGEN Gallery and the Slideshow, but there are options for managing all parts of how the galleries appear. One of the first ones you might want to visit is the Watermark tab so that you can set a watermark for all your images and galleries (see Figure 12.14). Even using the default settings, you can see that NextGEN is more versatile than WordPress' native gallery function. Some of the handy features are being able to create a gallery (like we did in the example), then upload additional images into that gallery's folder on your server, and have NextGEN refresh the existing galleries to add the new images. If you are covering an event and uploading images several times throughout a day, that is a handy feature indeed! You don't even need to edit the posts or page the galleries are embedded in; those are just auto-updated the next time someone goes to the page.

Figure 12.13   *An Imagebrowser gallery version in a Post*

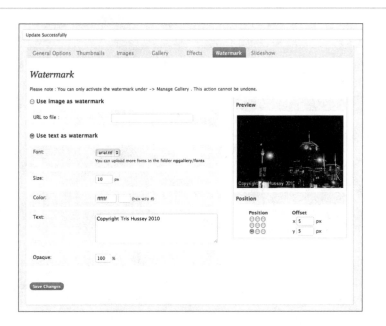

Figure 12.14   *Watermarking options within the NextGEN Gallery Options*

Adding images, video, podcasts, and files into your posts and pages isn't hard, as you've seen in this chapter, but you do need to have an idea and plan of how you're going to handle things. Lucky for us, many of the options for managing media are free or very affordable. So what are you waiting for? Add some media to your site!

WordPress.com Notes

For the most part, everything I've talked about in this chapter applies to WordPress.com, with the exception of uploading audio and video files. To upload those, you need to purchase the extra space option (for audio only) and VideoPress if you want to upload your own videos.

Remember that on WordPress.com, you're limited in the amount of space you're allocated, so this is one of those times when you want to think about using other alternatives to host large files, especially multimedia files.

In this chapter, learn how to maintain your WordPress installation, plugins, themes, and database.

13

Maintaining WordPress

You wouldn't drive your car and never change the oil, would you? What if you had a flat tire? Would you toss out your car or just change the tire (or buy a new one)? WordPress is no different; occasionally, you need to do a little maintenance. In this chapter, I talk about the three parts of WordPress that you have to keep in shape:

- WordPress itself
- Your plugins
- The database that powers WordPress

What about themes? They get updated sometimes, don't they? Yes, but not nearly as often as plugins or WordPress itself. Don't worry: I'll talk about themes when I'm covering plugins. (They use a similar system for letting you know that they have an update as plugins do.)

Keeping WordPress and your plugins up to date is *essential* to the security of your site. There aren't many times in this book when I lay it out more plainly than this: One of the most common reasons a WordPress-based site gets hacked is that it runs an outdated version of WordPress.

WordPress is a complex piece of software. Actually, it's a *very* complex set of *pieces* of software that all work together to make your site be bloggy. Because it is complex, and because there are so many different things going on, security holes are found from time to time in some part of WordPress or another. Some of the holes have been gaping, and others obscure, but because WordPress is open-source, the developers are in a *constant* battle with the "Forces of Darkness" to find, fix, and distribute a patch *before* blogs are hacked. Because it doesn't take a rocket scientist to look at version .1 versus .2 and see what has been fixed, as soon as a patch is released, the jig is up—hackers know *exactly* what the weakness was and (with a little work) how to exploit it. So, when the WordPress folks issue a "security update," you need to apply it, like yesterday.

As a whole, plugins are updated even more frequently than WordPress, and generally, it's the updates that improve the plugin's overall functionality. Sometimes there are security updates, too.

Finally, you need to do maintenance on your database, because that is the heart and soul of your blog (and the lungs, legs...everything but the brains, I'd say). From time to time, the database needs a touch to make sure there aren't bad entries in there that could slow it down or damage it. Because your database is so essential to your site, it's equally important, or maybe even more important, that you back up your database on a regular basis. (I back up mine every night.) Yes, I'm going to hit you with another "it's really important to back up your stuff" talk later in the chapter.

For WordPress.com users, this chapter might seem like one you could skip because all these tasks are done for you. However, I hope you do read it so that if you ever switch to hosting your own WordPress site, you will know how easy it is to maintain.

Before we talk databases, plugins, or themes, however, we have to take care of the big guy himself: WordPress.

Updating and Upgrading WordPress

As I said in the beginning of the chapter, keeping WordPress updated is *essential* to not only your blog getting new features, improved performance, and better stability, but also to keep it secure. Lucky for all of us, updating WordPress is just a one-click affair (if your host supports one-click, and most do; if you can install plugins just fine through the web-based administration area, you should be good to go) that handles deactivating, switching to maintenance mode (bet you didn't know WordPress even *had* a maintenance mode, did you!), bringing new files in, getting rid of old ones, and turning everything back on. It's nice, neat, and clean. Don't worry if things go sideways; there is always the manual install. If you want to make things easy, you can install WordPress straight from the source with Subversion. One thing to remember: If you mess up your WordPress install, all hope is not lost (and neither is your site) because all the "important" stuff is stored in the database, not the WordPress install directory. Yes, your themes, plugins, and uploaded files are in wp-content, but as far as making WordPress "work," those files aren't (generally) touched in the upgrade. Remember that backup thing I was talking about just a minute ago? Yeah, this is where that comes into play. You need to make sure you have regular backups of your database. Make sure before you update WordPress that you have a recent backup made.

Back Up Before You Update

Before I talk about how you actually do a WordPress update, let's talk about what to back up and how. You know already that wp-config.php holds a lot of the keys to the kingdom in your WordPress install, so if there is any one file you'll want to back up before you do an update, this is the one. Backing up this file is easy—just log into your server with your handy FTP client, navigate to the root of your WordPress install, and download that file to your local computer. Remember, this file has the username and password for getting into your WordPress database, so leaving it just lying around on your desktop isn't a good idea. After you successfully updated WordPress, you can safely delete that wp-config.php file that you downloaded for your backup.

Your wp-content directory is another kettle of fish entirely. Not only does this directory have all your plugins and themes, but it also has all the files you've uploaded through WordPress. (And through FTP, if you do as I do and upload large files there as well.) This makes wp-content a potentially large directory to download and back up. I'm not saying you can't or shouldn't download and back up wp-content, but it might take a while—a long while—to download. So, here is an alternative to doing that: Duplicate it on the server. Most FTP clients have this nifty feature that you can just "duplicate" a directory and have something like wp-content Copy in the larger WordPress root. Now, that *might* be a bit of overkill, but if I tell you, "Oh yeah, I've done it hundreds of times without duplicating wp-content and you'll be fine…," you won't be. It's just Murphy's Law, of course. If you want to save space on your server, you can focus on the uploads and themes directories within wp-content, because those are the ones where you're most likely to have things that can't just be redownloaded. Most plugins don't have you modify anything with them that stays there, so if that directory is lost, it might be annoying, but not more than that.

I'm going to talk all about database backups later in the chapter, so if you think I'm going to tell you to update WordPress without the critical step of backing up your database, you're wrong. I'm just going to get to that in just a minute.

If you're like me, you hope for the best and plan for the worst—and the "worst" part is that an automatic upgrade might not work. Even when I know that the automatic upgrade is going to go fine, I always have the latest version of WordPress downloaded and ready if I need it. Call it a good luck charm, paranoia, or just good planning, if I need to use it, I have it at the ready to upload.

With our core files ready and backed up and a copy of WordPress at the ready, let's get that WordPress install updated.

Automatically Updating WordPress

When there is an update available for WordPress, the Update To button displays in your Dashboard's Right Now box (see Figure 13.1). Click that button, and if automatic plugin installs usually work for you, in a moment or three, your WordPress install will be updated!

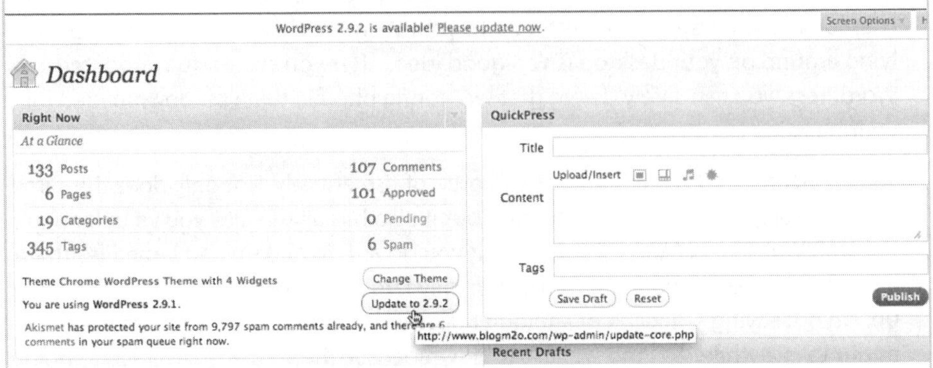

WordPress 2.9.2 is available! Please update now.

Screen Options

🏠 *Dashboard*

Right Now

At a Glance

133	Posts	107	Comments
6	Pages	101	Approved
19	Categories	0	Pending
345	Tags	6	Spam

Theme Chrome WordPress Theme with 4 Widgets — Change Theme

You are using WordPress 2.9.1. — Update to 2.9.2

Akismet has protected your site from 9,797 spam comments already, and there are 6 comments in your spam queue right now.

http://www.blogm2o.com/wp-admin/update-core.php

QuickPress

Title

Upload/Insert

Content

Tags

Save Draft   Reset   **Publish**

Recent Drafts

Figure 13.1   *How will you know if WordPress needs to be updated? Trust me—you'll know.*

It doesn't get much easier than "Automatic" does it? It's not really automatic, because you have to tell WordPress to do the upgrade, but the "hard parts" are done automatically. For the longest time, I was on a host that just didn't like doing the automatic updates smoothly. I would click "Update" and get a screen to enter my FTP/SFTP information (see Figure 13.2). This is because the way in which various web hosts set things up can vary (sometimes wildly). Some hosts have all the users and processes running in a nice, smooth, orderly fashion so that the right files can be updated at the right time—and others don't. On some hosts you have to only enter this information once and then never again. Other hosts require that you enter the information every time. As I said earlier, if you can install (and update) plugins automatically, you're probably going to be good to go. However if you tend to need to use FTP to install or update plugins, then WordPress will be the same. If you do get the Enter Your Login Information screen, for caution's sake, hold off on your update until you have time to do a quick FTP of the files. Don't feel compelled to proceed right then and there.

Obviously, there isn't much to say about an "automatic" update. If it works, you're done—even the database updates are done for you—but if it doesn't, then you switch into updating manually mode. This isn't terribly hard, so let's get to it.

Dashboard

⊺⊺ Connection Information

Posts

To perform the requested action, connection information is required.

Media

Hostname

Links

Username

Pages

Password

Comments

Connection Type   ⦿ FTP ○ FTPS (SSL)

Appearance

Plugins 22

(Proceed)

Users

Tools

Tools

Import

Export

Upgrade

Settings

Figure 13.2   *The Connection Information screen. Fill in your FTP information that your host gave you at the start.*

Manually Updating WordPress

Regardless of whether you're updating manually because you're old school, your automatic update failed, or automatic updates don't work on your server, the process is still the same. If you're trying to fix an automatic update, the process is a little more nerve-wracking than in the other scenarios. You should be ready by now for this, but let's just review what you're going to need:

- Copy of WordPress downloaded and zip file unzipped

- Your database backed up and ready, just in case

- Backup of wp-config.php

- Backup of your wp-content directory on the server

 LET ME TRY IT

Manual Update of WordPress Using FTP/SFTP

After you have everything all set as I described, you're ready to start the update process. Let's walk through the steps to update WordPress manually (there aren't many):

1. Start up your FTP client, connect to your server, and navigate to your WordPress install.

2. Delete your wp-admin and wp-includes directories. Yes, doing this the first time is a "yikes!" moment, but remember that these are just the files that power your site, not the content, and you're going to put new copies of the files up there in a moment.

3. Open the folder on your local machine where you unzipped the WordPress files. You're going to upload everything in that folder *except* wp-content. When your FTP client asks what to do (as it should), tell it to overwrite or replace. (The wording depends on the client.) This makes sure the *new files* are put into place and the old files are gotten rid of—in one fell swoop.

> My little WordPress secret is that I had an FTP client that worked just dandy for manual updates. I wouldn't bother deleting *anything* and would just upload *everything*. In that case—and note, *not all FTP clients work this way*—I had a setting where only newer files with the same name were replaced. If there were existing files (like all my additional plugins and themes), they were left alone. The secret here was how that FTP client worked. It didn't delete directories first; it drilled down into each directory, checked the files, and uploaded only new files. For a lot of FTP clients, when you click Overwrite, it deletes the original directory *first* and then copy files. What that does is to delete all your files that you want to keep (such as plugins and themes) and *then* start the uploading. That isn't what you want. If you want to experiment with this "drag, drop, and forget it" method, go ahead, but just make sure that you have that backup of wp-content already done.

There are *a lot* of files in wp-admin and wp-includes so be patient. What about wp-content? Don't worry about it for the moment; wait until all the files are uploaded and WordPress is updated to update wp-content. The reason for this is that although there might be files that need to be updated, they won't be critical to making your blog *run*.

4. When all the files are uploaded, you need to go to http://[your blog's domain]/wp-admin/upgrade.php to make sure that all the files are in place *and* to determine that your database is updated if it needs to be updated. (Don't worry about the Your Database Needs to Be Updated messages; that's what it should say.) If your database *doesn't* need to be updated, don't worry—it just says so, and you click Continue.

5. As for wp-content, all that you'd want to copy over and replace are the two default themes in the themes folder and akismet and hello.php from the plugins folder. My experience, though, is that Akismet might be updated once and a while, but that can be done through the plugins section of the updates.

SHOW ME   Media 13.1—Manually Updating WordPress with FTP/SFTP

Access this video file through your registered Web Edition at
my.safaribooksonline.com/9780132182836/media

If you have command-line, shell, or terminal access to your server, you can do some slick command-line tricks to do all this. This is somewhat advanced, however, and if you don't know how to use a UNIX/Linux command line, just skip this. This is one of those cases where one "oops" can have nasty consequences.

> Even if I've said this before, it's worth noting that *most* hosts don't offer command-line access to a basic shared hosting account. Why? Because it is very, very easy to cause a lot of damage to your websites in just the blink of an eye. There are commands like `rm -rf*.*`, which will delete *everything* without asking "Are You Sure?" a second time. So, if you have command-line access, like I do on my servers, you have to know what you're doing *and* know when you're in over your head.

 **LET ME TRY IT**

Updating WordPress from the Command Line

1. Log into your server.

2. After navigating to the root of your WordPress install (if you do an `ls` command), it should look like Figure 13.3.

Figure 13.3   *What a listing of a directory with WordPress install looks like*

3. Make a backup copy of your wp-content directory. You can do the backup of files with the handy copy command (`cp`), like this:

    ```
    cp -r wp-content wp-content_backup (Enter)
    ```

    Ta-da! Now your copy is complete.

4. Use the `cd ..` command to make sure your next steps don't interfere with your install (well, until you're ready). First, let's make a place for your install to go.

5. At the command prompt, type **mkdir new_wp** and press Enter.

6. Now type **cd new_wp** and press Enter.

7. To download WordPress, type **wget http://wordpress.org/latest.zip** and press Enter.

8. Then unzip them by typing **unzip latest.zip** and press Enter.

These steps create a new directory called "wordpress" in new_wp with all the files there and ready for you. The next part is where I hold my breath—copying the new files to overwrite the old. The whole sequence looks like Figure 13.4.

Figure 13.4 *The series of commands to do the preceding part of the sequence. I used unzip –q so that the whole list of files wouldn't fly across the screen.*

Personally, I like to do one more step to update my site's files from the new directory with the new files rather than changing to your WordPress install. I copy the new WordPress files and overwrite the old ones at the command prompt by typing **cp -avr wordpress/* [path to your wordpress install]** and pressing Enter. (For example, if your core site files are installed in /home/matt/wordpress/, use /home/matt/wordpress/.)

The "v" in the command stands for "verbose," so you'll see the files rush by. I like to do this to see a confirmation that things are going where I want them to go. If this is done right, you're not going to overwrite existing files that *aren't* in the source; it's a replace-only-what's-duplicated command. Again, if this short section is leaving you scratching your head, that's okay. This is a 9.5 on the geek-o-meter. You need to know how to double-check how you're doing through the process. I do this method on servers where I have command-line access, but not access to Subversion, which I'll talk about in a moment. If you have several sites to update, the process of FTPing up all the same WordPress files over and over takes *time*. There are *hundreds* of files to upload, so imagine doing this five or six times. It gets boring, and you can't interrupt the process after it starts or you'll have a mishmash of files there, and some missing entirely. By doing everything on the server, I download one copy of WordPress on the server, so copying and overwriting files is the same as copying files around on your local computer. It takes *moments* to make the copy instead of five to ten minutes via FTP, which makes a *huge* difference in workload when you're updating several sites.

If you think that even the *manual* update is pretty painless, yeah, you're right—it is. That's the point. WordPress is egalitarian in its philosophy. Nothing about using WordPress is hard or technically challenging. Between webhosts providing simple wizards to create databases and one-click installs to the one-click upgrades built into WordPress, anyone with a modicum of computer skills can use WordPress, and keep it updated, with ease. Of course, for us geeks, it's fun to do as much manually as possible, and now I'm going to crank the geek-o-meter to an 11 and talk about my new favorite way to install and update WordPress: Subversion.

Using SVN

Subversion is not what happens when undesirable elements get a hold of your blog. It's a free, open-source version control system that is popular among the geek-set. Version control systems are designed to help developers working together from overwriting each other's code when working on a project together. Subversion works with a repository of code maintained on a server and individual working copies on user systems. The development team involved with WordPress uses Subversion (or SVN) to manage the development of WordPress, but as just a mere user of WordPress, we can use SVN to both install *and* update WordPress with just a command.

Subversion is a tool that you run from the command line on your server, so if you don't have command-line/terminal access to your server, you can't use it to maintain your site on the Internet. If you do have terminal access, chances are that SVN is installed; just to be sure, at your command prompt, type **svn**. If SVN is installed, you should get a Type 'svn help' for Usage message, which lets you know that SVN is there and working.

Before you can use SVN to *maintain* WordPress, you need to have *installed* WordPress using SVN. Yes, you can switch from "regular" to SVN, but that's a little more complex for the moment. Let's just take things with the "easy" route first.

Log into your server and get to the command prompt. Remember that this is for a brand-new WordPress install, so we have to make a home for that install first.

Make sure you are in your public_html directory and create a directory for your install by typing **mkdir [site name]** (for example, **mkdir blog**) and then pressing Enter.

Then change to that directory with **cd blog**. (I'll use blog as the example here.)

Now the fun begins. SVN is a version control system, so the idea is to "check out" WordPress from the master repository. Most SVN repositories, and WordPress is no exception, have the repository organized with three top-level directories: trunk, branches, and tags. The *trunk* is the bleeding edge of development, so it is not recommended for anything but for developers or sandboxes (read: don't use it for your live, primary site—*ever*); *branches* are special versions and most people don't use them, and *tags* are where the final versions of WordPress from the current version all the way back to version 1.5 are stored. The tags are where we get our WordPress files. As I'm writing this book, the current released version of WordPress is 2.9.2, so that's what the following commands reflect. As WordPress versions are released, you can simply use increasing numbers in the commands. Enough chatter—let's get that install (at least the file copy part) going. All you need is one simple command (remember, you're in the "blog" directory):

```
svn co http://core.svn.wordpress.org/tags/2.9.2/ .
```

The space between the last "/" and the "." is deliberate. This puts all the files into the blog directory and not a WordPress directory *within* blog.

The "co" stands for "checkout" and tells the SVN server hosted on wordpress.org to send all the files down to you. Enjoy watching the files fly by because you have just put all the latest WordPress files on your server. To finish your install, you just have to create your MySQL database and edit the wp-config.php file, and you proceed as usual for installing WordPress manually. This chapter is about *updating* WordPress, so how do you do that? Of all the ways you can update WordPress, SVN is the hands-down easiest, fastest, and safest way to do it.

 LET ME TRY IT

Updating WordPress Using Subversion

It's a pity that only a few people can do it (there is a web-app in the making!). Here's how you do it.

1. Log into your server. (We're going command line here again, remember.)

2. Change directories to your SVN-installed blog. (From the preceding example, you would "cd blog".)

3. For this example, we pretend that we're updating to WordPress 3.0:

   ```
   svn sw http://core.svn.wordpress.org/tags/3.0/
   ```

4. Press Enter.

The "sw" stands for "switch," and like the "co" command, the SVN repository is told to bring down the WordPress files to your server. Here's the great thing about SVN: Only the *new, changed* files are downloaded and replaced. If it isn't new or isn't in the repository, it's left alone. One command and all the files are copied for you; all that's left for you is to use the update command (http://[your blog domain]/wp-admin/update.php), and you're done. This is why I like SVN so much. Not only are the commands simple, but also the process is almost foolproof. Like I said, I hope someone develops a way for people without command-line access. The only thing simpler than SVN is the WordPress automatic update, which does the same thing as SVN but is handled a little differently.

With WordPress updated now in three different ways (okay, four, if you count doing a command-line copy), we still need to work on updating plugins (which are updated more often than WordPress itself) and themes (which aren't updated often, as yet). The good thing is that after updating WordPress, updating plugins and themes are a piece of cake.

Updating Plugins and Themes

Updating plugins and themes work, essentially, the same way updating WordPress does. When you have a plugin that needs to be updated, you see a number on the Plugins button, and when you look at your plugins listing, you see a note below the plugin that an is update available (see Figure 13.5).

If your WordPress automatic upgrade works, click Upgrade Automatically and WordPress downloads, unpacks, and replaces the old plugin with the updated files. Now, if you have *several* plugins to update, go to Dashboard and click Updates. You'll be given a list of all the plugins that have updates available, and you can click check boxes to have some or all of them updated at once.

What if automatic updates don't work? Then it's the manual route for you—which, as you can imagine, isn't terribly hard. When I see a plugin that needs an update, I click the More Information link, which brings up a window from which I can click the link to the plugin's page on WordPress.org. That should open a new window or tab, where you can click to download the file. Then, it's just like installing the plugin in the first place, with a couple differences.

Figure 13.5   *Under Dashboard, Updates, you can see the plugins with updates available (and WordPress itself). Note the "22" next to the Plugins button; this is the number of plugins that have updates available.*

First, you should deactivate the plugin to be updated in your plugins list. Go to your plugins list and click Deactivate for the plugin that you're going to upload. Then, use your FTP client and drop it into place. When your FTP client asks what to do, have it Overwrite or Replace (whichever is the correct response for your client). When it's done, go back to your browser and click Activate. Simple as that.

Themes work in a similar fashion, but as yet not many theme developers take advantage that they can push theme update notifications to users. The one quirk of themes, of course, is that if you've modified the theme at all, updating to the "latest" version would eliminate those modifications. Updating themes is an annoying process to say the least, so the question is: Is it worth it? There isn't an easy answer, is it? If you've spent a lot of time customizing a theme, the new features or whatever will have to be pretty darn awesome to make you want to go through, file by file, to sync up your customizations with the upgrades. My advice is that if you have a "regular" theme, and not a framework, I'd hold off. My gut tells me, though, that more themes that opt for updating through just plugins and WordPress itself will become more like parent-framework themes, in which you have user-customizable sections and other sections that are "hands-off," so to speak.

SHOW ME   Media 13.2—Updating Plugins and Themes in WordPress

Access this video file through your registered Web Edition at
my.safaribooksonline.com/9780132182836/media

Database Maintenance for WordPress Users

Your database is the *most* important part of your WordPress site. It contains all your settings, all your posts—pretty much all your everything. With your database, you can transport your site anywhere, with the WordPress files being generic and readily available. The *only* crucial files that *aren't* in your database are the files you uploaded, so you can see why whenever you're updating WordPress or installing a plugin that potentially makes changes to your database structure, the advice you'll always read is to make sure you back up your database before proceeding. Like all databases, sometimes a little repair and optimization is needed to keep things in shape. For this reason, a database repair tool is included in WordPress 2.9.

Yes, if you are a whiz with MySQL, you can use PHPMyAdmin to make a backup of your database or use the command line. However, these are options that I don't think are ones that are all that practical for most people. What you want with a database backup is that it's just done for you automatically, everyday (that's my preference), so that you don't even *think* about it—it's just done. Rather than talk about the WordPress database repair and optimization tool first, I'm going to cover what I use for doing backup, repair, and optimization: Lester "GaMerZ" Chan's WP-DBManager.

WP-DBManager

If you haven't already installed WP-DBManager, click Plugins and the Add New button in your administration area and then search for WP-DBManager. Install and activate the plugin. After you activate the plugin, use your FTP client to move htaccess.txt from the wp-dbmanager directory in wp-content/plugins on your server to wp-content/backup-db/ and rename the file **.htaccess**. Until you do, you'll see a warning in a big red box that your database backups might not be secure from WP-DBManager.

WP-DBManager does everything that you need, including checking to make sure that all the right information is in place when you install and go to the settings. It confirms this check whenever you visit it as well. I think this is nice—a little comfort that things are all okay from the start. The first, and most important, setting is to have your database backed up nightly. I also chose to have the database compressed with gzip (that's the built-in UNIX compression tool) because my database has grown large with six years of posts within it! For the extra cautious, you can have a copy emailed to you as well. I suggest using a Gmail account to receive all these emails, because Google gives you 7GB of email storage; it's a nice way to have a redundant backup. Do you need to backup nightly? In most cases, no, but there is a default setting to keep only 10 backups, so you won't be continually taking up more and more server space—just getting more and more piece of mind. See Figure 13.6 for how I have configured WP-DBManager on my site.

The next step is the repair and optimization portion. Neither of these screens are hard; you have a list of all the major tables with the default set to optimize or repair (see Figure 13.7). It's actually easy to confuse one with the other! My personal preference is to run the repair first and then optimization. I want to make sure that if there are any problems with the DB, I don't carry them into the optimized version. Both these tasks take just a moment to complete. One of the additional settings that you can set is to have WP-DBManager optimize your DB automatically periodically. I have my blog set every seven days, but that is more than enough for most people. An average blog needs only to do this about once a month.

WP-DBManager also includes tools to run MySQL queries and to drop tables. These options and tools are for the advanced and knowledgeable user only. You can imagine that if you drop (which is database speak for "delete") the wrong table in the database (say, wp_posts, which holds *all* your Posts and Pages), you could be in a world of hurt (and pretty happy that you back up your DB every night!). Use these with caution and only if you're really, really—did I mention *really*—sure that you know what you're doing.

WordPress Built-In Database Repair Tool

As I said previously, WordPress now has database repair optimization tools built into it, so you can keep your database in shape without a plugin. Of course, before you do a repair or optimization, you should do a backup, but we'll skip that for the moment. Because of the potential damage a database repair-optimization can do if done at the wrong time or by the wrong person, you have to enable this capability in your wp-config.php file with the following line:

```
define('WP_ALLOW_REPAIR', true);
```

Then, to kick off the repair-optimization script, you go to the following:

```
http://[yourdomain]/wp-admin/maint/repair.php
```

It is also recommended that after you have made your repair run, you *remove* that line from your wp-config.php as soon as you're done.

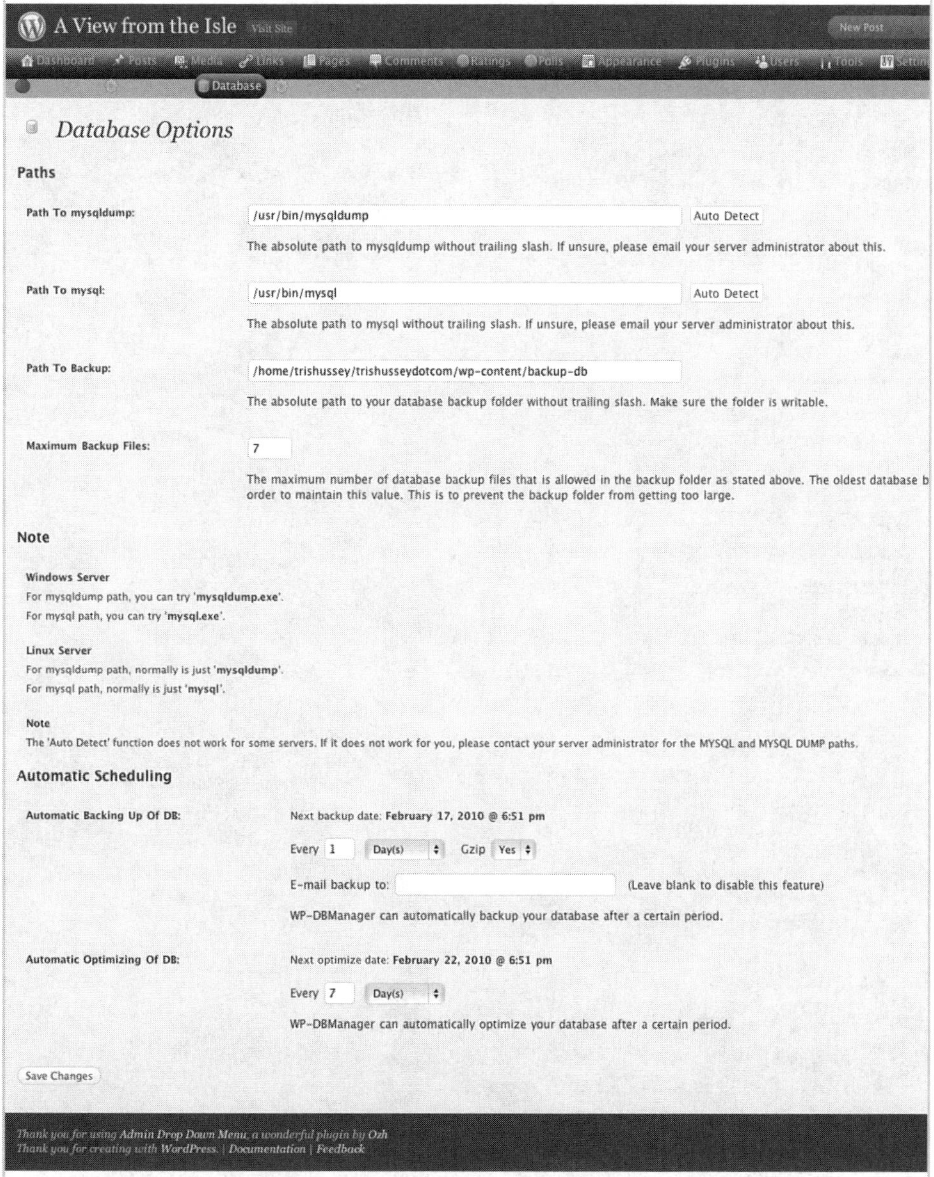

Figure 13.6 *WP-DBManager options and settings. I have it set to keep only seven backup files because my database is so large (over 30MB uncompressed and almost 7MB compressed).*

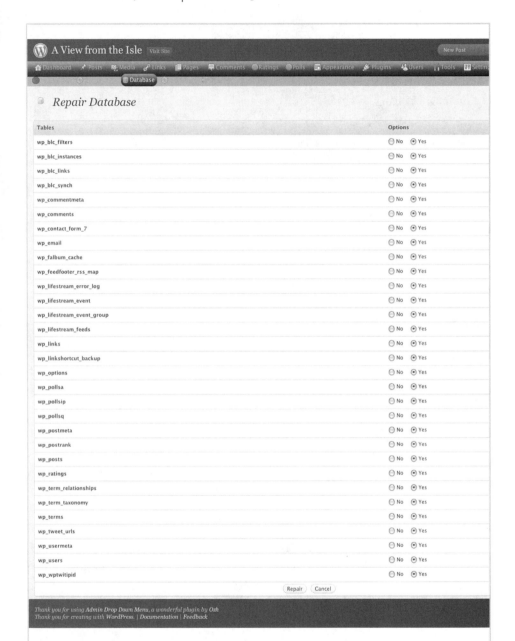

Figure 13.7   *The WP-DBManager Repair Database screen. The Optimize Database screen looks exactly the same, except it says Optimize at the top and on the button.*

Is the plugin route or the native WordPress setting better than the other? In my experience, they are the same from the repair-optimization routine. So, for my time, I'd go with the WP-DBManager plugin solution, so you can have your DB backed up automatically for you and the general maintenance that it occasionally needs.

SHOW ME   Media 13.3—Using WP-DBManager to Backup and Maintain Your Database

Access this video file through your registered Web Edition at
my.safaribooksonline.com/9780132182836/media

This chapter's goal is to help you keep your
website safe and secure from hackers.

14

Understanding WordPress Security

Throughout this book, I've been saying things like "WordPress makes great blogs and websites" or "A blog is just a website, albeit a cooler one," but there is one thing that you cannot forget—websites are on the Internet. I'm not going to kid you; people are on the Internet who like to mess with other people's websites. Hackers often aim for big targets, but no one is beneath a hacker to try to breach. Because your site is on the Internet, and bad people are out there, you need to be aware of security and things you need to do to keep from getting hacked. You should also know how to fix the damage done if a hacker strikes.

I will also not overdramatize that hackers are around every virtual corner, just waiting for you to slip up. Frankly, millions of websites are on the Internet, and lots of them are going to be far easier picking than your site. So, there is a balance between caution and paranoia when talking about security. If you run a high-profile website, you are a much bigger, and juicier, target than just any old website on the Net. The approach I take with you is pragmatic. I cover the low-hanging-fruit security techniques that everyone should employ and the next level that you can employ to harden the defenses.

Passwords Make a Difference

If there is one simple thing you can do to harden your defenses against hackers, it's to use strong passwords. I talked about passwords a bit in Chapter 4, "Configuring WordPress to Work Its Best," but it is worth restating here: Easy passwords are a hacker's best friends. Between that WordPress creates the first user with the username "admin" (although this is optional, and you can choose your own name as of WordPress 3.0), and that people want to pick passwords that they can remember, a lot of people leave the barn door wide open with a spotlight on their prize stallion.

Yes, when WordPress creates the first admin user, the password created is random, which is great, but even that isn't good enough. You need unique, random, and *long* to be safer. How long? Like 10–15 characters *minimum*. Granted, completely random, long passwords are hard to remember, which is why I employ two strate-gies in setting passwords. The first is that I use a password manager program to not only generate my passwords, but also to keep track of them. This enables me to keep almost all my passwords completely random (and long) but without requiring that I remember them. What I do *have* to remember is a master key password, which in my case is about 20 characters long and a mix of numbers, letters, and symbols (like $%#@). That password ranks on the strong gauge of passwords because of its length and complexity. I also have a few easy-to-remember, but also strong, passwords, for services that I often need on the go. Those I pay particular attention to so that they are long, secure, and memorable.

When you set up your WordPress site, you need to do two (simple) things:

1. Create a new administrator-level account for yourself and not have the username be admin or Administrator. Use an exceptionally strong pass-word for this account.

2. Log in with that account and disable the admin account by setting to the Subscriber role or delete the original admin account entirely.

These two things are simple and give you a leg up because hackers have to start guessing what the administrator login is in the first place. Some of my friends cre-ate an admin login but never use it unless they have to do "admin" tasks. Day to day, they use and post with an editor-level account, which lets them do almost everything except muck about with the important stuff. So if *that* account is com-promised, the amount of damage that can be done is *greatly* reduced.

I know that talk about passwords and such makes a lot of people, even some of my geek friends, roll their eyes. Here's the thing, though: Since late 2009 and early 2010, *several* incidents of security breaches occurred at major websites because of poor passwords. I'm not talking about users losing access; I'm talking about the people who *own* the sites—sites like Twitter.com. So, roll your eyes all you want, but using good, strong passwords and using different passwords for different sites is a great way to keep your sites and online information safe.

 SHOW ME   Media 14.1—Creating a Secure Password
Access this video file through your registered Web Edition at
my.safaribooksonline.com/9780132182836/media

Updates and Patches to Keep WordPress Secure

In Chapter 13, "Maintaining WordPress," I talked about how to update WordPress. I touched on why it's important to keep your install updated (and this includes plugins), but it's worth reinforcing here. Because WordPress is open source, both the good guys and the bad guys have the same access to the code to pore over it to find *potential* security holes. Lucky for the WordPress community, the good guys are *very* good at finding those holes and then relaying that information (securely) to the core WordPress team to investigate. Once a potential problem has been found and confirmed, the coders go to work to close the hole. Sometimes this is a quick process, and sometimes it takes awhile, but regardless of the time *needed* to fix the problem, once a patch is found and tested, it's released as an update.

This is where you come in. When you see the yellow bar at the top of the screen, this lets you know that there is an update to WordPress, and it behooves you to update right away. There is a small caveat to this, however. Most of the time, the smaller point releases (for example, 2.9.1 and 2.9.2) are the ones that have "out of the blue" security patches, and the announcement on the WordPress development blog will make that clear. When we move up from 2.8 to 2.9 or 2.9 to 3.0, those are bigger feature-focused releases, and although they *also* tend to have some security-related fixes, they tend to also be more heavy on larger changes. A lot of WordPress users wait until the first point release (for example, 3.0.1) to move to the new version, just to make sure all the major bugs have been found, worked out, and squashed. The decision as to when to jump up to a major release depends on you and your comfort level; however, if the major release includes an important (or critical) security update, just make the switch immediately.

The same thing goes for plugins that you have installed. Plugins, remember, hook into the guts of WordPress. Poorly written plugins, and lots of them are out there, can open a security hole that *had* been previously patched. So, when a plugin has an update, it's a good idea to take it. Most often, the update just improves functionality or performance, but sometimes there is a security component to the update. (Although it might not be explicitly stated as such.)

 SHOW ME   Media 14.2—Looking at a WordPress Update Change Log
Access this video file through your registered Web Edition at
my.safaribooksonline.com/9780132182836/media

Connecting Securely to Your Blog

One of the dirty, little secrets of the Internet is that a lot of the time when we send usernames and passwords to the sites we use, such as checking email or using FTP, that information is sent in plaintext or cleartext. Okay, so, what's the problem? The problem is that none of the information is protected or encrypted. A nefarious person, with the right software, can monitor a stream of data and pick up usernames and passwords with ease. The reality is that with the *huge* amount of data flowing through the Internet at any given time, the chances of your information being "sniffed" is pretty remote. That said, it is enough of a problem that Google announced in January 2010, that it would force connections to Gmail to use the secure https protocol, which encrypts the connection to Gmail just like when you connect to your bank or shop online.

In this section of the chapter, I cover how to securely connect to your blog, and believe it or not, it's not as hard as you might think.

SHOW ME   Media 14.3—See How Easy It Is to Get Your Password Using a "Regular" FTP Session

Access this video file through your registered Web Edition at
my.safaribooksonline.com/9780132182836/media

FTP/SFTP

Throughout this book, I talk about using your handy-dandy FTP client to transfer files to and from your WordPress install. Although I talk about using an FTP client, I'm not actually using the FTP protocol—I'm using SFTP instead. FTP, like a lot of Internet protocols, sends username and password information across the wires in cleartext; for that reason, it is considered insecure. Not only does your username-password combination travel out in the open, but so does the data itself. Not a big problem for most files, most of the time, but you know your wp-config.php file has some sensitive data in there. How do you eliminate this problem? Simple: Just use the SFTP setting instead of regular FTP.

All reputable hosts should enable an SFTP connection to transfer files; one host I use for some client sites now *requires* using SFTP. You can't connect via FTP no matter how much you might want to. Just like Google's decision to force https to use Gmail, this host's decision to force SFTP is in the name of better security for you and all the other people using that host. The reason that this host could force this change is that using SFTP is no different from using FTP, and for many FTP programs, you just have to select SFTP from a menu. There is no additional software needed. You don't have to manage encryption key pairs; you just use it. See Figure 14.1 for an example of what the selection looks like with FileZilla (a free and basic FTP client for Macs and PCs that I recommend to people).

Although FileZilla doesn't let me use my public-private key, other FTP clients do. I'll talk about using public-private keys when I talk about SSH in the next section.

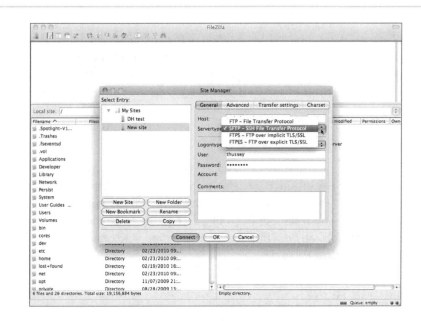

Figure 14.1   *In FileZilla, making your file transfers more secure with SFTP is as easy as choosing it from the menu.*

The same thing works for the Enter Connection Settings screen that you might get; just pick the SFTP radio button instead of FTP. What if your host doesn't support SFTP? Ask them to start supporting it. It isn't a terribly hard thing for them, and, frankly, it's just better for everyone. If you can't use anything but FTP, don't worry—the huns aren't waiting at the gate to pounce on your blog. If you connect from your home network, you should be safe from people easily sniffing out your passwords. Just be aware that your FTP session isn't secure if you decide to work on your site at the local coffee shop.

This isn't a book on network or wireless security, but if you have a wireless network set up at home, make sure you turn on your wireless security. Using WPA2 is best, but even WEP is better than nothing. This makes sure that unwanted guests don't connect to your network.

Just like when I talked about using FTP clients, I'm using the SFTP protocol to make the connection. When I connect to my server using the command line, I'm not using plain-old telnet—I use SSH to connect securely.

SSH

If your host lets you connect to your server to the command line (also called shell access), it will probably want you to use SSH to make the connection. Not long ago, when you wanted to connect to a remote server, you used telnet to do it. Telnet is one of the original protocols of the Internet and was the backbone of how we connected to do things "back in the day." But like FTP, telnet sends information out in cleartext, so it isn't secure. Usernames, passwords, commands, and other information can be intercepted.

The solution to this is using SSH, or *secure shell*, to connect to your server. If you use a Mac or Linux, SSH is included by default, and you use the Terminal application to start and SSH session with your host; PCs have to download a program to use SSH. Several clients are suggested for PCs, but the one I see recommended most often is PuTTY (available for free from http://www.chiark.greenend.org.uk/~sgtatham/putty/), so that is how I would go.

 LET ME TRY IT

Using SSH to Connect to Your Host to Use the Command Line

When starting an SSH connection to your server, both Mac and Linux Terminal clients work the same way, as follows:

1. Open Terminal. (On Macs, it's located in Applications/Utilities/; for Linux computers, it's generally found under Applications or Utilities.)

2. At the prompt, type **ssh username@server** and press Enter. For example, if my username on trishussey.ca is tris, I would type **ssh tris@trishussey.ca**.

3. You'll then be asked for your password. Press Enter.

4. If all is well, you'll see a command prompt. The prompt might look like ">" or "$".

For PCs, the process is similar:

1. Launch PuTTY.

2. Enter your server name in the field.

3. Click Open.

4. You see a green and black screen and are prompted for your username and password.

5. As previously, if all goes well, you'll now be at a command prompt.

Remember, using the command line on a server isn't for new or novice users. You need to know what you're doing. So, if you press that command prompt and *don't* know what to do next, you need to quit and leave it alone for now.

How to Login Without a Password, Securely

Thus far, I've been talking about using passwords to authenticate via SSH and SFTP, but there's another way that is even more secure; however, you have to make sure that you're going to be the only person using your computer. I'm talking about using a passwordless login by generating a public-private RSA encryption key pair.

This is a multistep process with generating the pair, securely copying your public key to the server, logging into the server via SSH, and copying the public key to a special directory. Your server will ask to match the public half with the private half of the key pair when you want to login via SSH.

The steps involved in doing this are rather complex and dependent on whether you use a PC or Mac and what SSH tool you use. Oddly enough, one of the best step-by-step explanations I've found is from the webhost DreamHost. Here is the URL where you can read it: http://wiki.dreamhost.com/SSH

Remember, when this is set up, if a hacker knows how, he can get into your server as you, and do anything he wants. So don't ever use this on a shared computer.

Keeping Tabs on Who Does What: User Management Made Simple

If there is one thing I wish WordPress did a little better, it's managing users. At a high level, the breakdown of user roles, and now being able to email a password to a new user, is great, but often the basic user roles, especially between administrator and editor, need some help. In this final section, I talk a little about managing users and also look at a plugin that lets you give a little more granularity to what users can do in each role.

In Chapter 4, I gave an overview of what each user role can do by default. Just as a refresher, here they are again:

- **Administrator:** Access to all functions of the blog. This is the master controller account, and you should only give admin privileges to users who can be trusted with them. A user with admin privs (there can be more than one user with the role of administrator) can take down a blog by accident or on purpose. In the wrong hands...well, you can guess. Giving the wrong users admin accounts is what gives guys like me ulcers and keeps us up at night.

- **Editor:** This role is an all-access pass to everything content-related, but no settings. The editor role can read, publish, and delete content, as well as edit pages, links, categories, and tags. Essentially, if it has to do with content, a user with editor privs can manage it. Many security experts recommend that you create an account for yourself with editor privs and use that account for your day-to-day writing and posting. The theory is if the editor account is compromised, the blog can't be completely wrecked, whereas a compromised admin-level account can be a bad thing indeed. You'll still need the admin account to manage the blog, but only log in with that account when you need that level of access. The editor is also a great role on a multi-author blog for a person who you not only trust to publish, but can also manage other peoples' work as well.

- **Author:** He can write and post their own material, but not anyone else's, or add new categories or links to the blog. This is the kind of person who you trust can write and publish on his own without you worrying about what he is writing about.

- **Contributor:** Contributors can write their own posts, but they can't publish the post to make it live on the blog. This is a good level for a guest author. Sure, you asked her to write a post or two, but you'd feel better if you can just give the post a once-over before it goes live.

- **Subscriber:** Subscribers can only read the blog and leave comments. The only time I've found this role to be handy is if I'm using a mailing list plugin (so new subscribers will receive the email) or use a plugin to restrict access to registered users only. A subscriber is a registered user, and that's about it.

One of the most important things about users and security is not to give users more privileges than they need to get the job done. Frankly, day-to-day, I don't need admin privileges most of the time; editor privileges are fine. I can create, edit, and manage my content as editor and wouldn't need to do much more. Practically, however, I'm often adjusting settings, checking settings (while writing this book especially), and updating plugins, so I need to be logged in as admin more often than not.

When you add new users to your blog or site, take a moment to think about who needs what kind of access. If everyone has admin privileges, well, that's a lot of people who can muck about with things. Even if there is someone who might occasionally need admin access—your backup, for example—maybe make *two* accounts for that person and be clear when to use an editor or author account on the blog. One final consideration regarding who to give what role to is that person's personality. You know the people who *think* they know what they are doing, but really don't. You probably know which folks are liable to decide to muck around with settings, add a plugin, or play with a widget, and those people are more than likely to do more harm than good. These people need to have locked-down access and privileges. This might be hard if that person is the boss, but you have to do what's in the best interest of the site. Maybe fake it with a clever setting as an admin, and then stealthily downgrade to editor later, or try a nifty plugin called Capabilities Manager (http://wordpress.org/extend/plugins/capsman/).

Because sometimes editors might need to do something with the users, such as reset a password or maybe editing or tweaking a widget, it would be great to give *trusted* people those additional abilities without making them an administrator. Through a series of check boxes, you can add, and remove, capabilities from existing roles or create a new role that has a mix and match of capabilities. You could create two levels of admins: one that can do everything and maybe one that can't mess with themes or plugins. You could have editors and super editors along the same lines. The question is, should you?

This is always a tough call for administrators. When it's your own site and there is no one else working on it, you know you're responsible for everything. When you're responsible for a site with several other users, and you're the person responsible for "keeping the lights on," trusting other people with access can be tough. Even when I've been a part of blogging networks, and already an experienced web developer, I had to prove to the sys admins that I wouldn't mess things up.

In the end, no matter how you mete out privileges, you need to keep tabs on what people are doing. If people abuse privileges, like deleting or editing another's content without permission, you need to clamp down on them and make adjustments. Remember: Only give out the privileges that people need to do their job.

Should I Use a Security Plugin?

As part of the research for this book, and my general interest in security, I have tested a few security plugins with mixed results. I tried plugins that fell into two classes: plugins for testing or hardening security and plugins for hardening defenses.

In the testing category, I tried plugins such as Exploit Scanner (http://ocaoimh.ie/exploit-scanner/) and Theme Authenticity Scanner (http://builtbackwards.com/projects/tac/), which double-check that your themes don't contain hidden nasties and also check if someone has breached your defenses. The good thing about both of these plugins is that neither of them try to change anything; they just make you aware of *potential* issues. This is also one of the drawbacks of these plugins. Both the good guys and bad guys use a lot of the same things in their code. This makes the decision of whether something is a problem a bit tricky. For themes, I think the good/evil distinction is easier to figure out, but with plugins, it's a different story. A quick run of Exploit Scanner on my sandbox came up with a slew of warnings— warnings of *potentially* malicious code in plugins that I know are safe. This isn't the plugin's fault; this is just how code is written. I had to go through the list and double-check what I saw there. For novice users, I know this will cause some confusion and panicked calls to geeky friends. Should you use these? Have them on hand. Activate them when you think you might have something wrong, but I'd have a geek on hand if you have any questions.

The next group of plugins I tried are the "hardening defenses" kind. These are easier to deal with, but I don't know if most users need them. Limit Login Attempts (http://devel.kostdoktorn.se/limit-login-attempts) works on a simple premise: to prevent people from hacking into your blog by trying password after password for "admin." After so many failed attempts, that user is locked out from trying again. I actually accidentally locked myself out of my own blog, so I know it works. The drawback to this is if you have several users on your blog, some of whom aren't great at remembering their passwords, you might get folks either picking bad passwords or using other tricks for not getting locked out. On the plus side, it would help prevent a brute-force password attack on your blog. I'm willing to take the risk for this bit of protection, so I have it on most of the blogs I run, including my own. The other plugin called Secure WordPress (http://wordpress.org/extend/plugins/secure-wordpress/) works to close things that aren't actually security holes, but rather little things that you can do to make it harder for hackers to find out more about your site than you might like them to. For example, knowing what version of WordPress you run lets hackers know what threats you might be susceptible to; or if all users can see when to upgrade and what to update to, those lines *could* be used to exploit a weakness or have something changed out from under you.

The question is, at the end, should you employ these tactics or just stick with the basics? That depends on how much of a target you are. Honestly, for 99% of bloggers, the basics of having good passwords and keeping WordPress up to date will be enough. For 1% of high-profile sites or companies, yes—you need to take extra precautions. You can take even more steps, such as adding lines to your .htaccess file and having special blocks on your wp-admin directory to prevent people from even getting to your dashboard if they aren't from the right IP, but these are for folks who know how to check, test, and fix problems when they occur.

If you'd like to read more about WordPress security, I recommend these posts: http://wpshout.com/10-practical-wordpress-security-tips/ and http://www. devlounge.net/code/protect-your-wordpress-wp-config-so-you-dont-get-hacked. Both of these give you some practical things you can do to keep the huns at bay. Remember, if you start editing the guts of WP, you need to back up core files such as wp-config.php and your database *first*. Let's just say I've learned this the hard way.

By the end of this chapter, you will know how to fix the most common, and some of the uncommon, problems that can crop up on a WordPress blog.

15

Troubleshooting Common Problems

Nothing always goes as planned. That's a maxim in life, and in WordPress, so it stands to reason that occasionally things will go wrong and you have to fix them to get back on track. In this chapter, I cover the most common gremlins that crop up and how to manage them, fix them, and prevent them from happening again. I've put the sections in order from most common to least common, which also turns out to be in order from easiest to hardest as well. It's at this moment you know that the usual lecture on backups comes. When things go wrong, knowing that you have a backup of your database is a *huge* comfort. So, don't skip over the section on automatically backing up your database from Chapter 13, "Maintaining WordPress." Yes, it's saved my tushie on more than one occasion. I'm just saying.

Before I get into the problems and fixes, you should also know that *most* fixes are simple, and although your blog might look strange for a little bit or at worst be offline, you'll be back up and running shortly. The most common problems are going to come from posts, sidebar widgets, and your theme (the latter usually after you've been customizing it), and it is *extremely* rare that any one of those problems will result in you losing all your posts or something that severe. Remember, the *most* important part of the whole system is your database. One post won't kill it. Your theme, plugins, and even the WordPress files themselves can all go to kablooey and your content will be fine. Repeat after me: Your content will be fine.

Fixing Posts and Pages When They Break

When we talk about Posts and Pages "breaking," it's not like a toddler knocked them off a shelf and they shattered on the floor. It's when the Post or Page doesn't look the way you intended. Sometimes it *never* looked as intended. Those are the "whoa, *that's* not what I was expecting at all" moments, and 90% of the time it's because you copied and pasted something into your post and, well, it didn't work out so well. Hey, don't sweat it—I've done it *hundreds* of times; thus, this is the first section I'm talking about. Sometimes you have a post break through no fault of your own, per se, but rather WordPress pulled a number on you. Thankfully, that doesn't happen often anymore. I'll talk about that in a second, but let's cover the copy-paste issue first.

The Easy Fix: Paste from Word Button

The number-one reason (by far) for Posts to look wrong is Microsoft Word. It usually goes like this. You have a post that either you or someone else has written in Word. So, you do what makes 100% sense (and isn't actually wrong) by selecting all the text, copying, and then pasting the text into WordPress. You hit Publish and...wait a second. That post looks different than all my other posts! What happened!?! What happened was that when you copy text from Word, and most other word processors, the text formatting is carried with it. This is, mostly, a good thing, but the other problem is that Word now writes (behind the scenes) the formatting codes *the same way websites do*. By the rules of HTML, what you put in that post window overrules all other formatting on the site. That includes what font, what font size, and even what color the text is. There is both an easy fix for this and a hard fix for this. If you still have the text in Word, the easy fix is as follows:

1. Reopen the post in WordPress.

2. Select all the text and delete it.

3. Go back to the Word version, select the text, and copy it.

4. Go back to WordPress and click the Paste from Word button on the editing toolbar (see Figure 15.1).

Figure 15.1 *Extended visual editor toolbar with the Paste from Word and Clear Formatting buttons circled*

5. Paste into the window that opens.

6. Click Insert.

Ta-da! There you have a nice, cleaned-up version of your text. What the Paste from Word button does (I like to call it the "magic" Paste from Word button) is to strip out almost all the formatting that is coming from Word but leave things like bold, italic, and underline in place. The declarations of font and font size are removed, as are the extraneous code that comes with that stuff.

In the newest versions of the component that runs the visual editor, TinyMCE, when you paste from Word into the editing window, some basic cleanup is done for you. What you lose is alignment and so forth. To be on the safe side, I still use the Paste from Word button, just to make sure nothing goes off the rails.

See, I told you that would be easy. From now on, if you're copying and pasting from Word, an email, or another website, you can use that button to keep *some* of the formatting, but lose the rest. If you don't want to keep *any* of the formatting, you can use the Paste as Plain Text button right next to the Paste from Word button, and you'll just get text.

The Hard Way: Manual Clean Up

Now, the "hard" way. If you don't have the Word document anymore, you're going to have to clean things up by hand. In older versions of TinyMCE (the open-source JavaScript visual editor that WordPress and many other systems use), you would wind up doing *a lot* of editing by hand to get rid of the extraneous code, but now you *should* be able to use the Clear Formatting button (right next to Paste from Word, interestingly enough). Of course, if that doesn't work, you will have to switch from the visual editor to the HTML editor and remove the extraneous code by hand. Unfortunately, this is a tedious process, and you might be better off selecting all the content in the visual editor, copying it, and pasting it into a plain text editor like NotePad (PC) or TextEdit (Mac). When you paste the text from the visual editor to a plain text editor, the formatting codes *should* be stripped out when you select, copy, and paste the text back. When my clients have done this, I show them how to do the cleanup and do it for them, once—after that, they're on their own.

Fixing Bad HTML: Close Tags

Now you know how to take care of a post that just looks *strange* but not "broken." Most of the time when the post is broken (or "borked," as we like to call it), it's because you pasted the embedded code into a post and something went wrong. Maybe you missed part of the code in the copy and paste (very common; I do this all the time). If you paste HTML code into the visual editor, then no matter how good TinyMCE is, that code isn't going to be read as code, but as text to publish as is (see Figure 15.2). You need to paste HTML code that you want to be read as code in the HTML view. Just click the HTML tab and paste the embedded code for video.

My rule of thumb is that when I paste code into the HTML editor, I don't flip back to the visual editor. In the past, doing that has been a surefire way to break whatever I've just pasted. The more recent versions of TinyMCE are a lot more forgiving (or tolerant, depending on your point of view), and it's less likely that what you've just pasted will break. The safest thing to do, though, is to paste into HTML mode, click Preview, see what it *should* look like, and then switch to visual mode if you're not done writing your post. In visual mode, click Preview again and see if the post still looks okay. If not, well, you know you need to stay in HTML mode.

Figure 15.2   *If you paste the embedded codes from any site into the visual editor, this is what you'll get.*

Geeks call something that is broken "borked." When it started, I don't remember, nor do I know who made the initial connection, but I do know where it comes from: The Muppets. Specifically, this is from The Swedish Chef, whose primary line (among his faux-Swedish) was "bork, bork, bork!" I guess because he was a rather hapless chef, we equated "bork" with being generally messed up or broken. Or geeks are just a little odd. Or both.

The last little trick—and I learned this from Mark Jaquith, who is one of the key WordPress developers and a WordPress security expert—is in HTML mode to click the Close Tags button before you post. This is a preventative measure to clean up errant HTML that you might have pasted in while editing. WordPress does have safety measures to prevent some kinds of bad code to be pasted into posts, but they aren't foolproof. WordPress will also try to close open HTML tags and fix bad HTML before posting.

The most common sign that you have a small HTML problem is that your sidebars are pushed down below your posts. When that happens, you know you have to just go in, edit the post, and try the Close Tags button (see Figure 15.3). This happens less and less now that WordPress and TinyMCE have much better code-cleanup functions (or maybe better described as human error correctors), but I still see it now and then. This is yet another reason to keep WordPress updated; the improvements in the editors make posting a lot more error-free.

Figure 15.3   *The HTML toolbar in the post editor. Note the Close Tags button, which is a handy tool.*

And, if nothing else, you can just delete the post and start over—although I know it's painful to do that.

SHOW ME   **Media 15.1—Reviewing How to Find and Fix Problems**

This video goes through all the preceding fixes so you can see them in action.

Access this video file through your registered Web Edition at
my.safaribooksonline.com/9780132182836/media

Widgets That Break Your Blog and How to Fix Them

Sometimes your posts are fine, but the site still looks, off. What is it? Oh, that new widget that you added. Sidebar widgets—which are moving beyond sidebars now—are a blessing and a curse. With widgets, you can easily add discrete chunks of code to the sidebar of your site, but you can also add discrete chunks of *bad* code to the sidebar of your blog. I don't mean bad as in nefarious, but as in poorly written, buggy, and so on.

There are a couple things that can go wrong with widgets. First, if the widget is loading something from another website, that website could be down or over-loaded, which causes the widget to break. Some widgets break gracefully with short time-outs that will allow the rest of the page to load in a timely manner; others, like YouTube widgets especially, seem bent on taking down the whole site with them. The next problem is the code. Either you didn't copy and paste it completely or correctly, or it was just plain bad to begin with. In my experience, when the code is bad or you haven't copied and pasted it correctly, the widget will just not load, and you'll have a blank spot in the sidebar. In both cases, the first thing to do is remove the widget from the sidebar, reload your page, and make sure that everything is working properly.

If the widget is something that you were loading from another site, say Facebook or Google, check other blogs that you know have the same widget and see if they are having issues as well. Visit the source site and see if the site loads and if they have any notices posted. If things are looking all clear, you might have either a temporary fluke (it does happen from time to time), or somehow something became messed up on its own (rare). If a widget that *was* working stops working out of the blue, chances are that it will start working again shortly. Usually, only *new* widgets that don't work are the ones where you have a code problem going on.

I think you know the recommendation that's coming next: Get a fresh copy of the code, delete what is in the widget, and try again. I know this seems like tired, old advice, but it's exactly what all of us do. When I have a widget or a movie I'm embedding and it doesn't work, the first thing I try to do is just get a fresh copy of it and start over. Given that I also tend to experiment a lot with my WordPress sites, and it's all for you as readers, I wind up getting fresh copies of things a lot. This is the real key to fixing a lot of these problems. Don't keep going, and don't try to "fix it." Just back it up, get a new copy, and try again.

When Your Blog Just Doesn't Look Right: Theme Issues

If you've decided to start editing/hacking your themes, it's only going to be a matter of time before you upload the new, edited file and get a blank page with a PHP error at the top. If you don't get a PHP error, you might load that new stylesheet and think, "Hmm, I didn't really think it should look like that...." Don't worry—it goes with the territory when you start editing themes.

By and large, if you don't touch your theme files, they aren't going to spontaneously come apart on you. It's only when you're trying to edit things do you run into trouble. Beyond code management practices and version control, the best thing to always do is to keep a "clean" copy of your theme stashed away before you start editing anything. This is your safety net; these are copies of the files that are original and untouched, so that if things get to a point where you can't reverse what you did, you just replace with a fresh, clean copy. If you have several versions of your modified theme—like the original, and then a version that you made some changes to (that worked)—and then you want to do more, well, make sure you have both those previous versions on hand.

Although this isn't a "fixing" thing, per se, just remember to only work on one piece of a theme at a time. When you have too many pieces of the puzzle moving at the same time, sometimes you won't know what is *actually* causing the problem and what is just collateral damage from an errant typo.

Fixing Problems with Plugins

Oh, plugins are fun. They can do so much to extend WordPress, to take it beyond what it was out-of-the-box and to make it just plain implode on itself. Yeah, good times.

There are several ways that plugins can come back to bite you. The first is that they are just incompatible with the version of WordPress you're running. This is common with older plugins and when WordPress makes major leaps ahead. The transition to WordPress 2.5 broke a lot of plugins, and many of us had to delay updating WordPress because several of our key plugins weren't compatible with the new version of WordPress. Although this isn't as much of an issue as it has been in the past, when you download and install an older plugin, it certainly could be. In the plugin repository, there are now indicators of what versions of WordPress the plugin is compatible with, so give that a double-check before you go ahead with the install (see Figure 15.4).

If you run into a plugin that is incompatible with your version of WordPress, and you can still get to your installed plugins page, just deactivate the incompatible plugin and call it done. If you have a complete failure, such as when your admin area or blog won't load, don't panic. WordPress has an easy way of dealing with this: Just delete the plugin from the server. Yep, fire up the FTP client, find the offending plugin in wp-content/plugins/, and delete the little bugger. You *should* be able to reload your admin area and your plugins page. When you get to the plugins page, you'll get an error that such-and-such plugin has been disabled because the files are missing or have been deleted (well, duh, I deleted them), but that's fine. It might be a good idea to run a little database repair and optimize, just to be on the safe side.

Now, if a plugin does more damage than can be fixed with just deleting it (note, I haven't seen this happen often at all), you might be looking at bringing your database back from a backup. That will certainly raise your blood pressure a few notches, and if you feel like you're in over your head, you might need to call in some help. Again, I haven't seen this happen often. Plugins that make large and irrevocable changes to your database give lots of warning ahead of time and recommend that you back up your database before proceeding. (Heed that warning, by the way.)

Figure 15.4   *The information panel from WP-SuperCache via the Plugin repository. Note the star ratings and the compatibility section. You get a similar view when you update a plugin from within WordPress and click More Details.*

Sometimes plugins just don't play nice with each other. You know, like two kids who can't sit next to each other without trouble starting. Luckily, when this happens, you know what the last plugin you installed was and you can just deactivate it. If the problem crops up when you update a plugin, you have a different problem on your hands. The first step is to deactivate the newly updated plugin. Next, go to the plugin repository and find the plugin that was just updated, and below the version number is a link to Other Versions, which keeps a historical record of previous versions of the plugin. (Refer to Figure 15.4 for the location of the Other Versions link. It's easy to miss.) Download the previous version of the plugin, and replace the newer version with the older one. If things are working again, visit the plugin developer's site and see if anyone else has had a problem with the new version. Often when there is a plugin that suddenly doesn't play nice with other plugins, users tell the authors, and it gets fixed pretty fast. Keep an eye on the updates, and if you see an updated update, try again.

The last way plugins sometimes fail is that your server's version of PHP is too low for the plugin to work. Although WordPress requires only PHP v4.3, some plugins need PHP v5 or higher to run. I've run into this problem before, and oddly enough, PHP 5 was available on the server but just not running by default. If your host doesn't have PHP 5 installed and available, installing it yourself is no small task, and frankly something that most hosts would probably rather you *not* do. Unfortunately, you'll have to forgo that plugin for now, but I would ask your host when it plans on updating to the latest version of PHP. (WordPress will require PHP 5 eventually.) If PHP 5 is available (just not the default version that is loaded for your site), the fix to this is easy:

1. Open your .htaccess file on your server through your FTP client, and at the top of the file, paste the following lines:

    ```
    AddType application/x-httpd-php5 .php
    AddHandler application/x-httpd-php5 .php
    ```

2. Save the file and close.

Those lines will tell the server to load PHP 5 instead of 4 for all .php files.

> Although the preceding declarations work for many hosts, it might not be how your host wants you to do it. Before you make this change, consult with your host's help files or support desk to double-check that this is its preferred way to activate PHP 5 versus 4.

Believe it or not, that's all there is to "when good plugins go bad," unless, of course, you decided to edit the plugin files themselves, and you knew what you were getting into, didn't you?

 SHOW ME   Media 15.2—How to Fix Problems with Widgets, Themes, and Plugins
Access this video file through your registered Web Edition at
my.safaribooksonline.com/9780132182836/media

When WordPress Goes Haywire

While I was researching this book, Chapter 13 especially, I did a bit of mucking about with the core WordPress files. Yeah, I took one for the team. Suffice to say, I started getting strange errors, and things didn't always work quite right all the time (especially when I was posting). I *thought* I had a major lead on a long-standing (and random) WordPress bug, but it turned out that I must have messed up something well and good. The solution? Delete and start over. Oh, I didn't delete everything—just most of the files. All the files that count, actually.

There are a couple ways to reinstall WordPress: automatically and manually (just like upgrading/updating). If automatic *updates* work for you, go to Dashboard, Update and you'll see something (see Figure 15.5).

Figure 15.5   *If you go to the Updates section under Dashboard, and you are at the current version, you'll see options to re-install WordPress automatically or download it.*

Click the Re-install Automatically button to give yourself a nice, fresh WP install. Just like the automatic upgrade, none of your unique files will be deleted. That said, I'd still back up your database first. If automatic installs don't work for you, just use the Download button to download the latest version and follow the steps for a manual update. Unless you're me, of course, because I don't seem to be able to keep things simple for myself, do I? My steps are essentially the same, just with a little twist.

Remember, I manage all my installs with Subversion, so I had a couple extra steps, which reminded me why most hosts don't give users shell access to their servers.

Essentially, if WordPress is just being wonky, often the easiest thing to do is to just delete wp-includes and wp-admin and drop fresh copies of those files, and all the php files at the root of the WordPress directory, onto your server. Most of the time, this will fix the problems that WordPress would be having. Because all the files unique to your site are in your database or wp-content, you won't be hurting any-thing—that is, unless after deleting wp-admin and wp-includes, you issue the fol-lowing command at the command line on your server:

```
rm *.php
```

For the non-UNIX initiated, rm stands for "remove" (or delete), and *.php says delete everything that ends in .php. When in the root of your WordPress directory, this would be all the files I wanted to delete, except for one. That command *also* deleted my wp-config.php file, which I *didn't* want to do. What this meant was that when I thought I would have my moment of triumph with a nice, fresh install of

WordPress, I actually had a moment of panic filled with expletives. Oh, everything turned out fine; I just had to re-create my wp-config.php file from the sample putting in the database info.

There is a lesson here—be careful. For most of you who *won't* be using Subversion (just doing the deleting and such), doing a manual update of WordPress will be just fine. Because you wouldn't delete all the .php files in the directory, just overwrite the existing ones (and wp-config.php isn't in the files in a clean WordPress install) and you'll be just fine.

Bottom line: If WordPress is acting a little wonky on you, just download a fresh copy from WordPress.org, pretend you're doing a manual update, and all should be better—or at least on its way to being better. Unless your database is corrupt.

Oh, and a word of advice: Watch out for geeks typing `rm *.` anything (especially `rm *.*`).

Identifying and Fixing Common Database Issues

This section comes with a caveat: If the basic repair and optimize doesn't fix database issues, and you're at all hesitant about doing things like deleting your entire database (which is required for switching to a backup version), this is the time to find a geek friend *who you trust*, buy a pizza, and invite them over. Trust me: This is the one area where I walk with more than a little trepidation myself. If there is a time when I'm double- and triple-checking instructions, and even doing a dry run on a test database, this is one of those times. No shame in saying that this is too much. If you even *have* a backup of your database that a geek friend can use to bring your blog back up from the dead, you get serious bonus points.

So, let's get to it.

Thankfully, having database problems in WordPress is something that doesn't happen often. When you're trying to fix a problem, you're usually faced with a WordPress error saying that there is a problem with the database, a plugin didn't play nice in the sandbox, or you were hacked and you have to clean up. Let's hope that after Chapter 14, "Understanding WordPress Security," you're feeling more secure, and getting hacked is unlikely.

The way most of us tinker with our databases is with the web-based tool phpMyAdmin, which looks more than a little daunting at first. Heck, it still looks daunting to me whenever I open it to do something. There are two kinds of things you're potentially doing when in the guts of your database: One is doing targeted queries that have a specific job (say deleting entries a plugin made), and the other is the wholesale deletion of the database and the re-importation of all the tables (hopefully from *before* the problems started).

Because the SQL queries to fix an issue with a plugin are specific, listing them here wouldn't be terribly helpful. However, there are some pretty great SQL queries on this site that are worth not only bookmarking, but also maybe printing out: http://www.catswhocode.com/blog/wordpress-10-life-saving-sql-queries.

 LET ME TRY IT

Resetting Your Password Through phpMyAdmin

It's not going to happen often, but if you somehow get locked out of your blog and you can't reset your password the usual way through email, but can still get access to your host control panel and with phpMyAdmin, you can *still* reset your password. These steps are based on instructions found in the WordPress Codex at http://codex.wordpress.org/Resetting_Your_Password#Through_phpMyAdmin:

1. Get to your host control panel and connect to your database through phpMyAdmin.

2. Select your WordPress database from the list.

3. Click wp_users from the list of tables in the sidebar (see Figure 15.6).

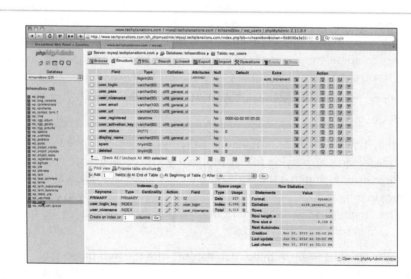

Figure 15.6   *Clicking into the wp_users table within phpMyAdmin*

4. Click the Browse tab.

5. Click the Edit icon (the pencil) in the row of the user whose password you need to change. (I'm going to use Silly User as my example; see Figure 15.7.)

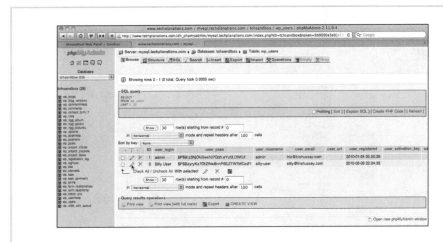

Figure 15.7   *Clicking to edit Silly User's password*

6. In the user_pass field, replace the string of characters (that is the old password, but encrypted) with a new password. I used newpassword for the example.

7. From the function pull-down menu, select MD5 (see Figure 15.8) and then click Go.

That's all it takes. Now Silly User can log in with the new password. It will be pretty rare that you'd have to do this at all, unless you have lost the admin password and can't receive the emails to reset it.

When you need to bring your database back from a backup, what you're actually going to be doing here is deleting your entire database and then bringing it back with a backup. The good news is that the deleting part takes just a moment. The bad part is that the importing part can take a while. You can see where this is going....

Wait, won't my blog be completely down while I'm doing this?

Oh, you betcha.

What should I do?

That depends....

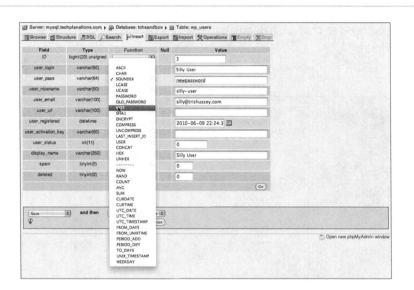

Figure 15.8   *Changing Silly User's password by editing the database record*

Here's the thing: When your database is kaput, there is nothing WordPress can do to help you. Maintenance mode plugins won't help, because WordPress won't be running to help you out of this jam. You can take this one of two ways:

1.   Don't worry about it right now. You have bigger fish to fry.

2.   Create a basic HTML page saying something to the effect of "Be back in 5."

I'm in the option-one group. There are enough blank index.php files in directories to protect your files while the site is down. Just worry about getting your site back up.

Now let's get to the "fun" stuff: deleting your existing database and getting the backup in place.

 **LET ME TRY IT**

Bringing Your Database Back from Backup with phpMyAdmin

This is another task that is cranking the geek-o-meter up into the 9 to 10 range. If you're not comfortable getting this far into your database, it's time to bring in your geeky friends to help.

1. Download your backup file from the server via FTP.

2. Check how big the file is. If it's bigger than 7MB, we're going to have to open the database in a text editor. (More on that in a moment.)

3. Through your browser, log into your host and get into phpMyAdmin so that you can view your database.

4. It isn't obvious, but the way to delete the tables is to first click Check All, and then select Drop from the pull-down menu (see Figure 15.9). (In the DB world, dropping a table means deleting it. Like if you drop your mom's antique vase, she might want to drop you from the will, or from a tall building.)

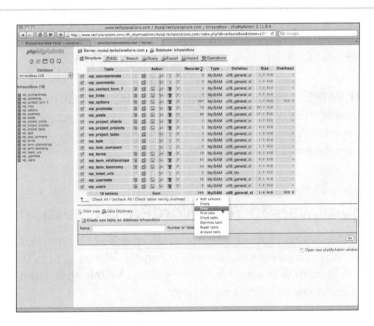

Figure 15.9 *Dropping the tables in your WordPress database*

Now that you have no database, it's time to import. This next step is going to assume that your database is less than 7MB.

If your database is greater than 7MB (or close to it), proceed to step 5b. Otherwise, follow step 5a.

5a. Click the Import tab. Pick the file to import and click Go.

5b. If your downloaded database file is compressed (gzipped), unzip it. If not, open the file in NotePad or TextEdit. This might take a while, so be patient. On Windows 7, Zip is an excellent, all around, tool that will handle gzip files nicely (http://www.7-zip.org/).

6. From the Edit menu, choose Select All, then Copy.

7. In phpMyAdmin, click the SQL tab and paste into that window (yes, "yikes" is a good response!), and click Go.

8. Wait.

If all goes well on the import, your blog should be back in shape, but....

Look, messing with MySQL and this amount of data (my *compressed* database is 7+ MB), stuff goes wrong. I strongly recommend that before you start dropping tables and importing, you have some help on hand.

If this section has you feeling a little scared about WordPress, don't be. How often do I mess around with my database? Almost never. Even when I'm researching and testing, it's pretty rare that mucking about in my database comes into play. The other, and more important, reason not to worry about any of this database stuff is the next section: finding help from the WordPress community.

 SHOW ME Media 15.3—phpMyAdmin and How You Use It for Managing Your WordPress Database
Access this video file through your registered Web Edition at
my.safaribooksonline.com/9780132182836/media

Finding Answers to Your WordPress Questions

All this troubleshooting info is great, but I know that I've only scratched the surface of all the things that you can do (or could go wrong). When I need to know something about WordPress, like double-checking things for this book, I turn to the best resource around: the WordPress community.

Between the Codex (the official documentation for WordPress), the various user forums, IRC channels, email lists, and websites, if you can't find an answer to your question or problem, there probably isn't an answer. All these resources are supported by the community, who are just regular people who love WordPress and helping out other WordPress users. Think about how amazing it is that volunteers put so much time and effort into WordPress and the larger community. Even the Codex is maintained (mostly) by volunteers. The only drawback to all this information is that it can be a little daunting to pore through all the info. Good thing there are some tricks to the trade to getting the right information and answers fast.

The Codex

The Codex is a massive, and growing, official documentation for how WordPress works now, worked in the past, and will hopefully work in the future. Through the Codex, you can find detailed information on every facet of WP, if you know how to find them. This is the challenge to the Codex. It's huge, it has a large volunteer contributor list, and it's mostly written by geeks. Geeks, I'm afraid, aren't the best folks to write documentation for anyone other than other geeks, and even then I have my reservations about that. The first trick to finding things in the Codex is not to search but to start with the Docs tab on the top of the navigation at WordPress.org (http://codex.wordpress.org/Main_Page) (see Figure 15.10). My usual inclination had been to just search straight off the bat, but I've found recently that starting at the main page of the Codex gets me where I'm going faster than a search.

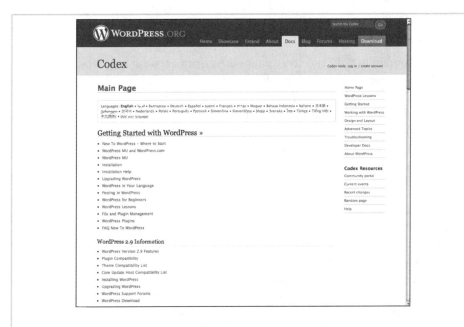

Figure 15.10   *The Codex home page, where all the documentation for WordPress starts*

I know it seems counterintuitive to browse instead of search, but what I've found is that the Codex is better organized than I suspected (given that a lot of it is written by volunteers, and it has evolved over time), so if I skim down to the section that I'm interested in, and then drill down from there, I usually get onto the right path. This isn't saying that you shouldn't search; just don't be surprised if you find what you're looking for with a quick browse. And here's the other secret of the Codex (that sounds like a bad adventure movie, doesn't it?): Because it's built on a wiki, a lot of the parts are connected to each other by links, so follow your nose when you're looking for an answer. The Codex is one of those references that if you're, for example, looking for information on how to edit your template with the `wp_list_pages()` template tag, following along with various links and examples, you will likely find the solution to your problem. If you want to contribute to the Codex, you are certainly welcome to. All you need to do is register for an account and get started. Don't expect your changes or additions to appear right away; not until you make a significant number of valid and helpful additions will your changes appear without moderation.

What if you don't find what you're looking for? Then your next stop should be the WordPress.org forums.

Forums

Like all community-built and community-driven projects, the heart and soul of the WordPress community are the user forums (http://wordpress.org/support/) (see Figure 15.11). This is where you can not only find the answers to simple questions, but also participate in discussions with the people who are writing plugins, creating the code, and making themes for WordPress. The WordPress user forums can seem daunting at first, because the scale of information is so huge, and it can be hard to find a specific answer to your question quickly. That's the nature of user forums; a thread is started to ask about category settings, and it might take a while for answers to come up.

Most of the time when I'm using the forums, I'm doing it passively. I search for the question or problem I'm having, find the answer, and move on. This is how most people use the forums, of course, and that's just fine. But if you want to *ask* a question or (better) contribute an answer, you need to register for the forums. This is an additional and separate registration from the Codex registration (don't worry; it confused me at first, too), and one where you can feel free to disclose as much or as little as you want about yourself (see Figure 15.12).

When you're asking a question in the forum, remember a few things:

- Most of the people who read the forums and answer questions are volunteers, not people paid to monitor the forums and answer questions.

- It might take a little while for someone to answer your question, so be patient (see the first bullet).

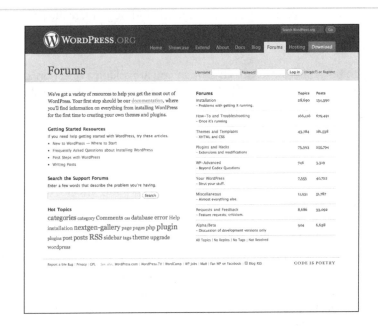

Figure 15.11 *The home page for the forums at WordPress.org. WordPress.com has its own set of user forums at http://en.forums.wordpress.com/.*

Figure 15.12 *My profile on the Wordpress.org forums*

- The *lingua franca* of the forums is English. Although there are people who speak other languages on the forums, almost all the questions and answers will be in English.

- Try to be as specific as possible when you are asking a question; giving a link to your site if possible will help people see what you're talking about.

- Don't *ever* put the username and password to your site in your forum post.

- Be cautious with people who offer help only if you'll give them your login information.

If you're answering a question, all the preceding certainly applies, but one thing is an absolute must:

Be respectful and helpful when you are answering people's questions.

Because many people *asking* the questions are new to WordPress and could be non-native English speakers, assume the best rather than the worst when reading questions and responses. Yes, like all parts of society, there are jerks and there are people who will be rude and condescending, but let's try to live up to the best of community-supported software and *help* people learn and improve their skills.

From a rough estimate looking at the forum as I'm writing this, there are millions of posts on hundreds of thousands of topics across the nine major forum sections. That, if nothing else, is a sign of a pretty vibrant user community.

For WordPress.com users, you have your own set of forums tied to your WP.com user ID. All the same rules apply there as on the WordPress.org forums. You will just get answers geared to WordPress.com (so no suggestions to install a plugin or edit your theme files).

Other Resources

If the Codex and forums aren't enough, there are several email lists (http://codex. wordpress.org/Mailing_Lists), as follows:

- **Announcements**: Low volume.

- **Development News**: Low volume.

- **Documentation**: For coordinating edits to the documentation.

- **Hackers**: Extending WP with plugins and changes to the code. Hard-core geeky here.

- **XML-RPC**: If you want geeky, this is geeky.

- **User Interface**: On improving the user interface of WordPress.

- **Testers**: When you're testing new versions of WordPress.

- **Support Forum Volunteers**: Just for the people who volunteer their time answering questions.

- **Community Support**: Like the forums, but through email.

- **Polyglots**: For translators.

- **Professional**: For posting professional opportunities and those looking for them.

- **SVN Updates**: Updates to the WordPress codebase.

- **Trac**: Bug tracking and reporting.

Like the forums, you need to follow the standard rules of online etiquette when participating in mailing lists. Some of these mailing lists can be high volume, so take a look at the archives and see if you can handle that kind of email flow in your Inbox. Don't be surprised if some lists have only a few messages for a long while and then suddenly explode with activity. That's just how these conversations go sometimes.

If you want to go old school, you can use Internet Relay Chat (IRC) to live chat with WordPress users around the world. There are two main chats that go almost all the time housed on irc.freenote.net. The first is #wordpress, which is for general users with questions. For developers and development questions only (this means writing plugins and core WordPress code), there is #wordpress-dev (see Figure 15.13).

If you aren't familiar with IRC, it's a text-only chat that preceded IM like MSN and AIM. It can be active at times. If you want a fast answer to a question, IRC is often the best place to ask.

If you are interested in the development of WordPress, you can tune into the weekly development chat Thursdays at 12:30 PM Pacific time (20:30 UTC) on the #wordpress-dev channel. As we approach the launch of new versions, the development channel does heat up with chatter about patching bugs and other improvements. It's geeky fun, for sure.

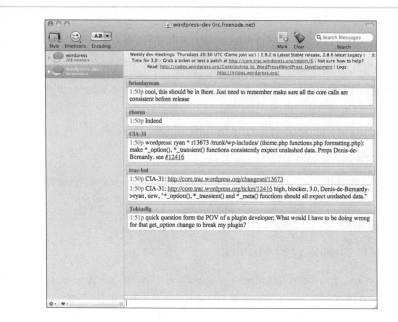

Figure 15.13 *The #wordpress-dev chat, discussing upcoming changes needed for WordPress 3.0*

Of course, beyond forums, the Codex, email lists, and IRC, there is the good old Web for information. Searching Google for your particular WordPress question or need will often get you a wealth of information. Like everything you read online, just be a little cautious with the information you read. Most of it is great and bang-on, but there is some bad (or just outdated) advice that is out there as well.

index

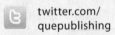
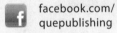
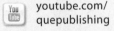
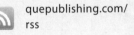